Observations On The Nature, Kinds, Causes, And Prevention Of Insanity V1

Thomas Arnold

OBSERVATIONS

ON THE

NATURE, KINDS, CAUSES, AND PREVENTION,

OF

INSANITY.

BY THOMAS ARNOLD, M. D.

FELLOW OF THE ROYAL COLLEGE OF PHYSICIANS, AND OF THE ROYAL
MEDICAL SOCIETY, OF EDINBURGH.

IN TWO VOLUMES.

VOL. I.

CONTAINING

OBSERVATIONS ON THE NATURE, AND VARIOUS KINDS OF
INSANITY; AND THE APPEARANCES ON DISSECTION.

SECOND EDITION,

CORRECTED AND IMPROVED.

Ταράσσει τυς ἀνθρώπυς, ὁ τὰ πράγματα, ἀλλὰ τὰ περὶ τῶν πραγ-
μάτων δόγματα.   EPICTETI ENCHIRID. CAP. X.

Men are not disturbed by things themselves; but by the opinions which
they form concerning them.

And moody madness laughing wild
Amid severest woe.   GRAY.

LONDON:

PRINTED FOR RICHARD PHILLIPS,
BRIDGE STREET, BLACKFRIARS.

1806.

Eumenidum veluti demens videt agmina PENTHEUS,
Et solem geminum, et duplices se ostendere Thebas:
Aut Agamemnonius scenis agitatus ORESTES,
Armatam facibus matrem et serpentibus atris
Cum fugit, ultricesque sedent in limine Diræ.

VIRGILII ÆNEIDOS, LIB. IV. v. 469.

Like PENTHEUS, when, distracted with his fear,
He saw two suns, and double Thebes appear,
Or mad ORESTES, when his mother's ghost
Full in his face infernal torches tost;
And shook her snaky locks: he shuns the sight,
Flies o'er the stage, surpris'd with mortal fright;
The furies guard the door, and intercept his flight.

DRYDEN'S VIRGIL.

Printed by B. M'Millan,
Bow Street, Covent Garden.

GENERAL PREFACE

———————

TO this *second edition* of my *Observations on Insanity*, which has been long called for, but by many important engagements unavoidably delayed, I shall prefix a few remarks, by way of illustration, or defence, or improvement, of the *first.* These remarks will be chiefly grounded upon such objections, or suggestions, as have occurred to me in books, or in private epistolary correspondence, or in the ordinary intercourse, and conversation, of society.

In one or other of these ways, it has been suggested, that some of the appellations which I have given to the species of insanity, are singular, and unscientific; that my arrangement appears to be complicated, and indistinct, the species not being sufficiently discriminated, or permanent, but liable to be confounded together, and to run into, and mix with, each other: that I have been guided by symptoms, or modes of derangement, in

distin-

distinguishing them, instead of having recourse to causes : that by confounding *medical* and *moral* insanity, I have too much enlarged the boundaries of the disorder, and
comprehended within the limits of mental derangement, the vices and follies common to
the whole human race : that my arrangement
is entirely founded upon a *gratuitous distinction* between ideas, and notions, and on the
apparent varieties of them which occur in insanity, rather than on the more immediate
nature of the diseases themselves : that I
have " described the disease which almost all
physicians have agreed to call *hypochondriasis*, not only as a species of *ideal insanity*,
which I choose to call *sensitive ;* but also as
a species of *notional insanity*, which I denominate *hypochondriacal ;*" and that of *sensitive insanity* I say, " that of the patients
who labour under it, some imagine themselves to be wolves, others dogs ; some lions,
cats, cows, cuckoos, nightingales, earthen-
vessels, pipkins, jars, tea-pots, or the like,"
which is in fact, it is observed, " the true
character of *hypochondriasis*, a disorder which
is not elucidated by the place in which I have
arranged it."

It

· It has been said, how philosophically, or *scientifically*, I leave to the scientical reader to judge, that some of the appellations which I have given to the species of insanity, are not only singular, but very *unscientific;* and that " one might as well pretend to distinguish water from all watery fluids, by the name of *aqueous* water, or wine from all other liquors, by calling it *vinous;* as to pretend to distinguish one species of insanity from another, by calling it *maniacal* insanity, and another by the name of *phrenitic insanity,* or a third by the name of *incoherent:* for, surely, every maniac is phrenitic, insane, and incoherent, if these terms are to be taken in the sense in which they are commonly, and properly received *."

·· The very *unscientific,* not to say *incorrect,* language of this paragraph, scarcely needs to be pointed out. If the writer would have given an exact parallel of my mode of arrangement, he should have considered FLUID as the *genus,* and should then have enumerated all those substances which agree in the

---

* See the Preface to " An Inquiry into the Nature, and Origin of Mental Derangement," &c. by ALEXANDER CRICHTON, M. D.

common

common generic character, as so many *species* of fluid, by the appellations of air, water, wine, spirit, oil, and the like, or of aerial, watery, vinous, spirituous, or oily fluids ; all of which would agree in possessing the character of fluidity, and in coming under the *genus* FLUID, of which they would constitute legitimate, and perfectly distinct, species : in like manner, as I have included all the species of permanent *alienation of mind*, under the common genus, which I, and most other, medical writers, have termed INSANITY; and have enumerated all those species of disorder which I suppose to agree in this one common character of permanent alienation of mind, under a variety of specific appellations, derived from the most striking, and peculiar characteristic of such alienation ; the propriety of which appellations, so derived, must be obvious to every man of a scientific mind, who has been conversant with the disease ; as my specific names, and my mode of arrangement, are, I believe, strictly logical, and scientific. Of the charge of the complication, and indistinctness of my arrangement, and of the instability of the species, I shall speak in another place.

The

The use of arrangement into species, in treating of a disorder like that which is the object of our present inquiry; of which, though much is known, much more remains to be discovered; is not so much to teach a system to the pupil, as to advance science, and to assist the philosopher, and practical physician, by such a disposition of what is known upon the subject, as may place the facts in as luminous a point of view as the state of present knowledge may admit, and may be some sort of clue in the farther investigation of a disorder, of which so much remains to be cleared up. It is but an orderly distribution of known facts; which may be a guide in our inquiry after unknown, and in a due research into what may be ultimately discovered of its entire nature.

Of causes we know too little to make them a foundation of the arrangement of diseases: and particularly of proximate causes; which alone can make us perfectly acquainted with their internal nature. When the science of causes shall be complete, we may then make them the basis of our classification: but till then we ought to content ourselves with an arrangement according to symptoms. And as

a 4   there

there is always a fixed relation between causes
and effects ; an exact arrangement according
to symptoms, which we see, may tend to
throw light upon their causes, which we do
not see ; and the analogy of the symptoms,
pointing out an analogy between the causes,
may lead to similar, and successful, methods
of cure in similar cases, how imperfect soever
may be our knowledge of the real, and immediate causes themselves. To this ground of
arrangement, which is as indispensable in medicine, as it is in natural history, I have
strictly confined myself : and if I have fallen
far short of perfection, it is but what I expected. Let others tread in the same path;
and they may have the prospect of advancing
farther than I have done. The road is right;
and must ultimately lead to no small success
in the discovery of truth, and the establishment of science.

To them who have objected to my arrangement, that, by confounding *medical* and *moral* insanity, it too much enlarges the boundaries of the disorder, and comprehends within the limits of derangement the vices and follies common to the whole human race; I
shall only observe, that, had they read what
I have

I have written upon *pathetic*, and the other species of *notional insanity*, with sufficient attention, they would have perceived that my definitions *exclude all but really insane persons;* that my descriptions, and specific characters, are taken from cases of actual insanity; that every species of notional insanity includes in its definition, or character, the definition of notional delirium, and is comprehended in the general definition of NO-TIONAL INSANITY, which is given in my first volume in these words*:

· " NOTIONAL INSANITY is that state of mind in which a person sees, hears, or otherwise perceives external objects as they really exist, as objects of sense; *yet conceives such notions* of the powers, properties, designs, state, destination, importance, manner of existence, or the like, of things and persons, of himself and others, *as appear obviously, and often grossly* erroneous, or unreasonable, to the sober and judicious part of mankind: it is of considerable duration; is never accompanied with any great degree of fever, and very often with no fever at all." · ·

---

* Page 56.

When,

When, therefore, I describe *fanciful in-sanity** as a species of delirium, displaying a very great activity, and vivacity, of imagination,—I do not suppose every person who discovers very great activity, and vivacity, of imagination, to be insane; but such persons only as are obviously under delirious delusion, strongly manifest insane activity, and plainly come under the definition of *notional insanity.* When I say that in WHIMSICAL INSA-NITY† *the patient is possessed with absurd, and* WHIMSICAL *fancies, aversions, fears, scruples, and suspicions,* I do not comprehend in this character every person who is more than ordinarily whimsical in his fancies, aversions, fears, scruples, and suspicions; but draw from cases of actual derangement, which I have seen, or read of, those extraordinary instances of absurd, and whimsical fancies, of which no one can dispute the insanity. The same may be said of my definition of IMPUL-SIVE INSANITY‡, which is followed by an account of various instances of those *insane impulses* which constitute the species, and of the insanity of which none can doubt, who

---

* Page 161. † Page 154. ‡ Page 163.

have

have witnessed their absurdity, and extravagance. So in describing SCHEMING INSA-
NITY*, I do not include every extravagant
schemer among the insane; but such only
whose wild schemes obviously arise from
insane notions, and are seen by all but the
infatuated madman, to originate in the delusive dreams of notional delirium. In like
manner, in defining VAIN, or SELF-IMPOR-
TANT INSANITY†, I do not consider vanity, and self-importance, in themselves, as
indicative of insanity; I only comprehend
those persons in this definition who are undoubtedly insane, and the character of whose
insanity is marked by striking symptoms of
obviously insane vanity, and *self-importance*.
The same observation is applicable to my definition of PATHETIC INSANITY‡, and of
its numerous *varieties*. I do not esteem persons insane, merely because they are under
the influence of strong, or even habitual passion; merely because they are characteristi-
cally amorous, or jealous, or avaricious, or
misanthropic, or the like: I reckon such
persons *vicious*, but *not insane*. I include

---

* Page 170.　　† Page 171.　　‡ Page 185.

under the character of pathetic insanity only
those cases of actual, and acknowledged, derangement, in which some one passion pre-
dominates, and of which it forms the prominent and peculiar character.

All this must be plainly perceived by such
readers as consider what I have said upon
each of the species of notional insanity, with
that attention which the difficulty, and importance, of the subject demands.

My species, whether of *ideal*, or *notional
insanity*, are not hypothetical, but real; they
are drawn from Nature, and from actual observation of insane persons. A few individual
instances may be derived from books; but
the species are founded upon the authority of
Nature.

Indeed all the species, to be real, must be
drawn from Nature, and must occasionally
exist separately, and distinctly; though they
may be liable to be combined, and complicated; and do not, like plants, preserve uni-
formly, and universally, their unmixed and
invariable specific characters: and being thus
drawn, as those in my book for the most part
are, from actual observation, they must ever
be valuable, as facts, to the philosophical, and
practical,

practical, physician: and must at least form so many interesting articles in our knowledge of insanity, disposed in a methodical, if not perfect, arrangement; which farther inquiry, and accumulated experience, may enable us to fix in the stations already allotted to them, or to remove to others, where they may be placed with more propriety, and associated with other facts more congenial with their nature.

And even in our present state of imperfect knowledge, and defective arrangement, the several species, as they now stand, in *these Observations*, point out such differences in the state of the mind and body, as have more or less use in practice: and whether they be honoured with the appellation of species, or be degraded into varieties, the knowledge of them will be useful, as of so many forms which insanity may, and does assume; and which may indicate something of its nature, when they appear, which an experienced and skilful physician may know how to appreciate, and how to turn to advantage.

A general knowledge of the different states of the brain, in the different species of insanity,

nity, either when they exist separately, or when they are variously complicated, is of much importance; and so much does a just conception of its different states in notional, and ideal, insanity, contribute to this knowledge, as to render the use of that division of no inconsiderable value: since the method of cure must be more or less varied, according to the degrees of derangement under the several species, which point out the varying degrees of affection of the brain; in the *notional*, as they differ from each other, are more or less simple, or as they approach to ideal; in *ideal*, as the delirious ideas are more or less active, unceasing, and intense; and in all, as they approach to, or partake more or less of, the highest, and most violent species, phrenitic insanity.

How much disposed the several species of insanity are to run into, and mix, and blend, with each other, I have expressly, and fully, noted in my book; and if that circumstance be considered as incompatible with the discrimination of species, all distinction of species in this disorder must be annihilated; and as I have allowed but of one genus, so I fear we must admit that there is but one species, of
insanity;

insanity; since whatever distinction of species we adopt, I suspect that we shall find it difficult to keep clear of this propensity to intermix, and combine. I know of no arrangement which is not objectionable on this account. I am sure that *mania furibunda*, *mania mitis*, and *melancholia*, or raging mania, mild mania, and melancholy, the three species into which Dr. CRICHTON divides insanity, are all commonly seen to run into each other; and I have observed in the same individual patient, the symptoms of each of them in the course of a few days.

It has been asserted that I have founded my general division of insanity upon a gratuitous distinction between ideas and notions: and that while LOCKE had observed " that all our ideas are either obtained by means of our external senses, or by reflexion;" I have chosen to confine the name of *ideas* to the first of these, and to the second to give the name of *notions.* Now I must confess that I think that the use of the term *idea* in the extensive sense in which it is used by the great Mr. LOCKE, is unphilosophical, though sanctioned by some eminent names, both among the ancients and moderns; is of too great a latitude;

tude·; and is not consistent with his usual accuracy of discrimination : since idea seems,
strictly speaking, to mean the internal representation, or mental perception, of an object
of sense only * : and that he ought to have
distinguished the stores of the human mind
into *ideas* images or phantasms, and mere
notions; and to have given some common appellation to the aggregate of both.; for though
notions are derived from sensations, they certainly are not sensations, nor the direct re-
presentatives of sensations, and therefore not
ideas. But however this may be, I had a
just, a philosophical right, to make this distinction, in treating of a disorder to which it
was so naturally applicable ; and to limit the
sense of the terms I made use of, by a definition of each. The term *idea* has been used
in various senses, not only by different metaphysicians, but even by the same : and I had

---

* Les sensations, considérées comme représentant les
objets sensibles, se nomment *idées;* expression figurée,
qui, au propre, signifie la même chose qu' *image.*—*La
Logique,* par M. C. l'Abbé DE CONDILLAC, 12mo. p. 26.

Sensations, considered as representing objects of sense,
are called *ideas* a figurative expression, which, properly,
signifies the same thing as *images.*

as

as fair a title as others, to define and fix the sense, in such a manner as seemed to me to be most philosophical; or as best served to explain my views. They who have seen the various, and discordant, opinions about ideas, which have been advanced by PLATO, ARIS-TOTLE, CUDWORTH*, LOCKE, BOLIN-BROKE†, HARTLEY, CONDILLAC, REID, and others, will not be disposed to abridge me of a privilege which those philosophers have freely enjoyed; nor confine me to the one sense which they may have espoused, amidst the variety which occurs in the writ-

---

* CUDWORTH calls what I term ideas, *passive ideas,* and *phantasms;* and what I term notions, he calls *noematical or intelligible ideas.* The distinction is the same as mine; only he retains the term ideas, which I discard. —See his Treatise concerning eternal and immutable morality, 8vo. 1731, p. 196, and other places. He often calls the latter simply *notions,* or *intelligible notions,* or conceptions of the mind. Treatise, &c. p. 138, 139, et passim.—He opposes *noemata* and *phantasmata,* p. 139, notes.

† BOLINBROKE uses the distinction of *ideas* and *notions.* He says, I distinguish between *ideas* and *notions;* for it seems to me, that as we compound simple into complex ideas, so the compositions we make of simple and complex ideas may be called more properly, and with less confusion and ambiguity, NOTIONS, &c. &c. &c.—BOLIN-BROKE's *Works,* 5 vols. 4to. Lond. 1754, vol. iii. p. 875.

ings

ings of metaphysicians, in opposition to all others, or to any new sense which may appear to me to be more consistent with truth.

The opinion which I have formed on this subject has not been lately, or lightly taken up; and in favour of it much might be said, were it proper to swell this preface by such a discussion. I think it enough in this place to assert, that the distinction is not founded on a gratuitous assumption; but appears to me to be drawn from the nature of things, to be perfectly philosophical, and not unsupported by respectable authority.

But not only is my *distinction* between *ideas* and *notions* not gratuitous, and my GENERAL DIVISION *just* and *proper;* but my use of terms, as it appears to me, perfectly scientific. It has been asserted, in proof of the impropriety of terming one of my species of IDEAL INSANITY phrenitic, another maniacal, and another incoherent, that " every maniac is phrenitic, insane, and incoherent." But that every *maniac* is not *phrenitic,* is as certain as it is that no maniac, as such, labours under an *inflammation of the brain:* and though it must be acknowledged that every *maniac* is *insane,* as every species

must

must be comprehended in its genus, there is
no hazard in asserting, that every *insane* person is not a *maniac*, since, to give no other
proof, not only is mania very generally allowed to be a species of insanity, but the writer
who makes this objection divides insanity, or
delirium as he very *unscientifically* terms it,
there being a delirium of fever, as well as of
insanity, into " *mania furibunda, mania mitis,*
and *melancholia"*—furious and mild mania,
and melancholy :—and to prove that every
maniac is *incoherent*, we must either have a
new definition of mania, or of incoherency,
or of both : since it is certain that every maniac, as described by authors, is either not at
all, or not at all times, incoherent, however
absurd he may be : for as some maniacs have
lucid intervals of rationality in a great degree;
and others, though insane on particular subjects, can reason well, allowing them certain
premises, on the very subjects of their insanity, and on other subjects can discourse,
and reason, as *connectedly* as other men;
none of them can be said to be characteristi-
cally incoherent, if the term be taken in the
sense in which it is commonly, and properly,
received. No person, indeed, can be more

b 2   cunning,

cunning, more consistent, more acute, or more connected, than maniacs, not only according to my definition, but according to the definitions, and acknowledgments of others, are not only sometimes, but often, found to be.

Phrenitic insanity is by me so called, because its delirium is of a more violent, and acute kind, and much resembles that of the fever termed *phrenitis,* or frenzy, which arises from an inflammation of the brain. Though there is much incoherency in this, yet not incoherency, but almost incessant raving forms its character, with frequent violence, sometimes fixed to one object, sometimes occupied about many, with occasional intervals of calmness, and coherency, and usually little or no sleep. Raving, and violence, form its characteristics: and it is usually attended with some degree of fever, and often with a good deal of other bodily disorder.

Incoherent insanity is that species of *ideal insanity* in which the incoherence is so very great, that the power of rationally connecting the ideas seems to be almost entirely lost, at the same time that, though there is ideal delirium, there is no appearance of, and only

in

in a few cases an approach to, the phrenitic. This species is rarely attended with violence, or with any degree of fever, or of obvious bodily disorder.

In giving the appellation of *maniacal* to the third species of *ideal insanity*, I only used the privilege of fixing down to one sense, a term which others, and especially HIPPO-CRATES himself, had used in a variety. The term *mania*, and its derivatives, as employed by the ancients, as I have shown in the body of the work, are of great latitude, and some-times mean raving madness, sometimes mad-ness in general, sometimes melancholy, and sometimes that kind of madness to which I have confined it by denominating it *maniacal insanity*. Not to add, that, so loose were the ancients in the application of terms, that in their writings melancholia is sometimes the appellation of actual, and violent, mania, in the sense in which mania is most commonly understood by the moderns, and sometimes by the ancients. In this species of insanity there is often coherency, and even much ra-tionality, on most, or all, but the delirious subjects; as is well illustrated by HORACE :

At

At Argos liv'd a citizen well known,
Who long imagin'd, that he heard the tone
Of deep tragedians on an empty stage,
And sat applauding in ecstatic rage;
In other points a person who maintain'd
A due decorum and a life unstain'd,
A worthy neighbour, and a friend sincere,
Kind to his wife, nor to his slaves severe,
Nor prone to madness, tho' the felon's fork
Defac'd the signet of a bottle-cork;
And wise to shun (well knowing which was which)
The rock high pendent, and the yawning ditch,
He when his friends, at much expence and pains,
Had amply purg'd with ellebore his brains,
Come to himself—" Ah! cruel friends!" he cried,
" Is this to save me?   Better far have died
" Than thus be robb'd of pleasure so refin'd,
" The dear delusion of a raptur'd mind."

FRANCIS'S HORACE.

SENSITIVE INSANITY is exactly discriminated, and properly placed. The absence
of phrenitic symptoms distinguishes it from
phrenitic insanity: a degree, and often a
great degree, of rationality, on every other
subject but that of the peculiar ideal delirium
in which it consists, distinguishes it from incoherent insanity: from maniacal insanity it
is readily discriminated by the nature of the
delirium: and as the perceptions of sense are

in

in so disordered a state, that false perceptions, which have no cause out of the body,
but arise from disease within it, are mistaken
for real perceptions of sense from actually
existing external causes; it is properly arranged under the general division of ideal insanity; and the application of the term *sensitive* to this species is correct, appropriate,
and philosophical. Ideal delirium distinguishes this, as well as every other species of
ideal, from every species of notional insanity.
It is always attended with symptoms of a
disordered state of the brain, and nervous
system; and frequently with disorder in the
stomach, and hypochondriacal region.

Of the several SPECIES of NOTIONAL IN-
SANITY, *each* is founded upon some characteristic difference, which is exactly expressed by its *specific appellation;* and each
is drawn from actual observation of the disorder, under its peculiar, and specific, form,
as seen by myself, in the course of practice.
Whether they ought all to be ranked as distinct species, or might not some of them have
been arranged as varieties, I will not con-
tend. But of this I am certain, that they
exist in nature; and that a knowledge of

them

them is necessary to a complete illustration of the nature, and valuable as a useful guide in the cure, of insanity.

The different species of notional insanity are, in general, no less marked than those of ideal; and so distinct from each other, that they could not well be reduced to a smaller number. Were I to attempt to reduce them, I think it would be by making fanciful, and impulsive, insanity, varieties of the same species, under the appellation of *impulsive insanity;* and, in like manner, by uniting scheming, and self-important insanity, as varieties, under the species, and name, of SELF-IM-PORTANT INSANITY: by which means the number of species would be reduced from THIRTEEN to ELEVEN: certainly much fewer than the species enumerated by SAU-VAGES, who makes *thirteen species* of melancholy only; *eight species* of dæmonomania, and *three species* of mania; in all TWENTY-FOUR *species:* or than the number of *twenty-five* species of insanity since enumerated by my ingenious, and learned friend, the late Dr. DARWIN of Derby. But I do not see that any advantage would be gained by this change: rather perhaps the contrary: and therefore

therefore have chosen to let the species in this edition retain the number, and names, which they possessed in the former.

It has been thought to be a peculiar singularity, that I should " describe the disease which almost all physicians have," it is said, " agreed to call HYPOCHONDRIASIS,. not only as a species of *ideal insanity,* which I chose to call *sensitive insanity;* but also as a species of *notional insanity,* which I denominate *hypochondriacal insanity:"* and that in my description of sensitive insanity, I say that the patients who labour under it imagine themselves to be wolves, dogs, lions, cats, cuckoos, nightingales, earthen vessels, pipkins, jars, tea-pots, and the like, which, it is said, are symptoms of illusion, and not of insanity, and are the true character of that species of illusion termed HYPOCHONDRIASIS.

But that I have properly arranged what some have called *hypochondriasis,* in certain states of it, at least, among the species of insanity; and not arbitrarily, and altogether without authority, or good ground, adopted the specific term *hypochondriacal;* my own experience is to me satisfactory evidence; to which

which I can add the example of many excellent medical writers, of established reputation, both ancient and modern, who consider
it as a species of melancholia, under the denomination of *melancholia hypochondriaca,*
from the supposed seat of its causes, and of
some of its frequently accompanying symptoms, about the hypochondriacal region. The
lower degrees of hypochondriasis, before erroneous notions are become singularly absurd,
invariable, and intense, I do not consider as
coming under the character, and denomination, of insanity; but merely as being afflictive bodily disorders, which powerfully affect,
and are peculiarly apt to discompose, and de-
range, the mind. To these I leave their ancient, and very general name, of *morbus hypochondriacus,* or *malum hypochondriacum,*
or, as it has been termed by modern writers,
hypochondriasis. And for this I have the
authority of DIOCLES CARYSTIUS, if not
of HIPPOCRATES; and of SENNERTUS,
HOFFMAN, FRACASSINI, SAUVAGES, and
DARWIN. But when the symptoms of obviously insane wandering, and fixed mental
derangement, commence, I am as perfectly
justified, by the symptoms, and consequences ;

quences; and especially by its frequent deviation into other, and even the worst, species of acknowledged insanity; in receiving
this also within the pale of that disorder; as
I am in calling the same kind of derangement
insanity, when it succeeds a fever, whether
with or without delirium, or any other disorder
whatever. Let *hypochondriasis* retain its appropriate station, and let indigestion, wind,
pain and noise in the bowels, acid eructation,
and a variety of distressful feelings, acute
pains, debility, and even low spirits and dejection of mind, be its afflictive symptoms:
but do not let it detain with it, and out of its
proper place, the *hypochondriacal insanity**,

---

* Vide Melancholia argantis, SAUVAGES, Nosolog.
tom. iv. p. 383. Also Hypochondriasis of SAUVAGES,
tom. iv. p. 296. The former he distinguishes from the
latter, in this manner: " Differt ab hypochondriasi hæc
melancholia, quod nullo morbo corporeo laborent melancholici illi, ast multiplici laborant hypochondriaci, ut fla-
tulentiâ, ructibus acidis, spasmis, qui simul hanc melancholiam sibi subjectam habent, unde vulgò, sed immerito,
confunduntur," p. 384.—Hypochondriasis differs from
this species of melancholy in this, that the melancholic
labour under no bodily complaint, but hypochondriacs
under many, as flatulency, acid eructations, spasms, which
often have this species of melancholy united with them,
whence they are commonly, but very improperly, confounded.

of

of which it forms no other part than that of
an attendant symptom, and occasional cause.
As to the patient's imagining himself to be
transformed into a wolf, or a dog, or to be
made of earthen-ware, or glass, or a thousand
other absurd, and, on a less serious occasion,
ridiculous things, which constitute the symptoms of my *sensitive insanity*, GALEN reckons them among the symptoms of *melancholia hypochondriaca;* CÆLIUS AURELIANUS,
and ARETÆUS CAPPADOX, among those of
mania; and SAUVAGES distributes them between *melancholia vulgaris*, and melancholia
zoantropia.

That HIPPOCRATES described the simple
morbus hypochondriacus under the title of
ἑτέρη νοῦσος ἡ λεγομένη ἀναυτὴ*, appears to me
highly probable, as it did to MARTIANUS†,
SENNERTUS‡, and others; and that he described *hypochondriacal melancholy* under
that of φροντὶς νοῦσος χαλεπή§, seems not less
likely.

---

* HIPPOCRAT. Oper. tom. i. p. 484, l. 20, &c.
† Magnus HIPPOCRATES Cous Prosperi Martiani Me-
dici Romani Notationibus explicatus, p. 128, I. E.
‡ Prax. Med. Operum. tom. iii. p. 494.
§ HIPPOCRAT. Oper. tom. i. p. 486, l. 32, &c.

Also

Also Diocles Carystius, as quoted by
Galen*, describes the same disorder in its
simple state, and unaccompanied with delirium. Nor, says Fracassini†, was Diocles Carystius, physician to Antigo-
nus, king of Asia, the first name in physic
next to Hippocrates, unacquainted with
this disease. In a book which he wrote upon
the nature, cause, and cure, of the hypochondriacal affection, as we read in Galen's
third book *De Locis affectis*, he has this passage: " Moreover another disorder arises
from the stomach, not dissimilar from those
already mentioned, which is by some termed
the *morbus melancholicus*, by others *morbus
flatuosus*, the paroxysms of which come on
after eating, especially of food of difficult digestion, or of an acrid nature, which is accompanied with a copious flow of saliva, with
acid eructation, wind, heartburn, and distention of the stomach, which does not come on
immediately after eating, but when the food

---

* Lacunæ Epitome Operum Galeni, p. 743. 30, &c.
et p. 744. 15.

† Naturæ Morbi Hippochondriaci, ejusque Curationis,
Mechanica Investigatio: Auctore Antonio Fracassini
Medico Veronensi, 4to, Veronæ 1756, p. 4.

has

has been retained awhile. Sometimes there are violent pains in the stomach, which in some cases shoot through to the back. All these disturbances subside when the food is digested. On taking food again they are again renewed. Sometimes they afflict the patient when fasting, as well as after eating; when he vomits up crude, and indigested aliment, and phlegm, which is either bitter, or hot, or so acid as to edge the teeth *."

GALEN blames DIOCLES for not men-

---

* Nec latuit quoque [Affectio Hypochondriaca] DIOCLEM CARYSTIUM Antigoni Asiæ Regis Medicum, cui post Hippocratem primas deferunt. Iste ut apud GALENUM legitur [lib. iii. de Locis affectis] in libro, cujus titulus: *Affectio, Causa, Curatio*, de Hypochondriaca Affectione hæc habet: " Porro alius oritur a ventriculo morbus, qui supra propositis non dissimilis est, nominaturque ab aliis melancholicus, ab aliis flatuosus, quem sumpto cibo maxime coctu difficili, et caustico, sputum humidum idemque multum comitatur, item ructus acidus, flatus, æstus in præcordiis, fluctuatio non illico, sed cum retinuerint : interdum ventriculi quoque vehementes dolores, qui nonnullis ad dorsum usque procedunt : concoctis deinde cibis quiescunt, mox aliis ingestis eadem rursus revertuntur accidentia, quæ interdum jejunos, interdum etiam a cæna molestant, atque evomunt crudos cibos, et pituitam, vel subamaram, vel calidam, vel acidam adeo, ut torpedine dentes afficiantur."

tioning

tioning the symptoms of FEAR, and dejection*, which he considers as characteristic of
hypochondriacal melancholy †, of which he
was treating; whereas .DIOCLES, as SEN-
NERTUS‡ remarks, was only treating of the
simple morbus hypochondriacus, the *hypochondriacal* or *flatulent disease*, without considering it as a cause of those frequent delirious consequences, which GALEN § tells us are
so apt to arise from a consent, or sympathy
between the stomach and the brain‖, and with
which when it is accompanied, he calls it a
third sort of melancholy¶, under the title of
melancholia hypochondriaca. Indeed, why
GALEN should blame him for this, does not
appear: since GALEN himself must be viewed
as treating of the flatulent disease simply,
when he considered it as the cause of fainting
away, convulsions, lethargy, and epilepsy, as
well as of melancholy**; and says that the

---

* Vide SANNERTI Opera Pract. lib. iii. Part v. § 1,
cap. i.
† LACUNÆ Epit. GALENI, p. 741, l. 60.
‡ SENNERTI Oper. loco citato.
§ LACUNÆ Epit. GALENI, p. 741, l. 50.
‖ Id. p. 764, l. 28.
¶ LACUNÆ Epitome GALENI, p. 743, l. 27.
** Id. p. 764, l 1. 36.

flatulent

flatulent disease of the hypochondriacal region produces no other* of the symptoms of melancholy but gloominess, despondency, and dejection. He calls it *morbus flatulentus hypochondriorum*, or the flatulent disease of the hypochondriacal region, when it is without insane symptoms; and considers it as only then producing a *third species of insanity*, or *hypochondriacal melancholy*, when the fumes of the corrupted aliment, and of thick blood resembling black bile, rise up to the brain. Those symptoms which I have attributed to *sensitive insanity*, he does not consider as symptoms of simple illusion, or of hypochondriacal melancholy, but of melancholy in general†.

CÆLIUS AURELIANUS, in enumerating the antecedent, or predisposing and occasional causes, of melancholy, enumerates the precise causes, and symptoms, of the *morbus hypochondriacus*: such as " *indigestion, continual vomiting*, the taking of purging medi-

---

* Jam vero flatulentum illum hypochondriorum morbum, omnes professi sunt, tristitiam, desperationem, atque mœstitiam inducere, nihilque ad melancholiæ accidentia reliqui facere.—LACUNÆ *Epit*. GAL. p. 764, l. 30.

† LACUNÆ Epitome GALENI, p. 743, l. 60.

tines after a meal, *acrid food*, *dejection*, and *fear*, and such other causes as are capable of bringing on this disease*." These are the acknowledged causes, or symptoms, of the simple hypochondriasis, unaccompanied with insanity.

The signs of *approaching melancholy*, he adds, are the same as those of approaching *insanity*, or fury†.

When melancholy is *actually come on*‡, the patient, he says, is filled with *anxiety*, and distress of mind, as is manifested by *great lowness of spirits*, *silence*, and *aversion to society*. These symptoms are succeeded by a solicitous desire of *life*, and sometimes by an equal desire of *death*, with *suspicions* of plots contrived against him: also with *weeping* and *lamentation* without cause, with the occasional intervention of causeless *hilarity*, especially after a meal, with *distention* of the stomach, coldness of the *extremities*, slight *perspiration*, gnawing at the *stomach*, especially

---

* CÆL. AURELIAN. de Morbis Chronicis, lib. í. c. vi. p. 340, l. 3.

† CÆL. AURELIAN. de Morbis Chronicis, lib. i. c. vi. Melancholia, p. 340, l. 4.

‡ Id. ib. p. 340, l. 5.

VOL. I. c at

at the upper orifice, extending to the shoulder
blades: also heaviness and stupor in the head,
a *complexion* more or less dark and livid,
emaciation, loss of *strength*, corruption of
the food taken into the stomach, with fetid,
or fishy, or otherwise nauseous *eructations*,
also *griping in the bowels*, vomiting, sometimes ineffectual, sometimes of bilious, sometimes of ferrugineous, and sometimes of black
matter; and evacuations of similar matters
by stool. This disorder, he adds, by THE-
MISON* and his followers, and others, is
termed a species of *fury*; but in this it differs,
that in *melancholy* the *stomach* chiefly suffers,
but in *fury* the *head*†; that it is to be cured,
however, by the same means as *fury*‡. In
all this we have a description of the melancholy of the ancients, in which is included
hypochondriacal melancholy.

Under the article *mania*, or *fury*, he enu-

---

* Id. lib. i. cap. v. Mania, p. 328, l. 10, and cap. vi.
Melancholia, p. 340, l. 24.

† Id. ib. p. 340, l. 23. In another place he observes—
"Patitur autem omnis *nervositas*, ut ex iis quæ sequuntur,
vel accidunt conjicere poterimus: magis tamen *caput.—Id.*
lib. i. cap. v. Mania, p. 328, l. 26.

‡ Id. lib. i. cap. vi. Melancholia, p. 340, l. 29.

merates

merates symptoms which I consider as characteristic of *sensitive insanity*. He mentions
one *maniac* who thought himself a *sparrow;*
another who imagined himself a *domestic
cock;* another who believed himself to be an
earthen vessel; another who supposed himself
a *brick;* and, lastly, one who fancied that he
was a helpless *infant*, and cried to be led by
the hand *.

Thus he plainly points out three distinct
states of disorder ; *one* connected with, and
preceding, and the *other two* constituting insanity : the *first* being merely an antecedent,
or predisposing, cause, of insanity, in which
are comprehended the characteristic symptoms of the simple MORBUS HYPOCHON-
DRIACUS only : the *second*, MELANCHOLY,
which he allows to be a species of insanity,
and in which he includes the *melancholia hypochondriaca* of the ancients, as well as what
I, in a more restricted sense, have called
HYPOCHONDRIACAL INSANITY : and the
third, MANIA, to a certain species of which
he expressly ascribes the symptoms which I

---

* CŒL. AUREL. de Morbis Chronicis, lib. i. c. v.
Mania, p. 328, l. 18.

have

have given as characteristic of SENSITIVE
INSANITY.

Indeed the ancient medical writers in general, either in express words, or tacitly, and
in effect, agree in this, that they consider the
morbus hypochondriacus either as a peculiar,
and distinct disease, not necessarily connected
with *delirium melancholicum*, or as joined
with melancholia, when they generally make
it a distinct species, and term it *melancholia
hypochondriaca*: and as to the symptoms
which I have given to *sensitive insanity*, they
are so far from considering them as characteristic of the *morbus hypochondriacus*, or *hypochondriasis*, that some, as GALEN and
PAUL of Ægina, give them to melancholy;
and others, as CÆLIUS AURELIANUS, and
ARETÆUS CAPPADOX, to *mania*; and all
of them consider them as symptoms of *insanity*.

ARETÆUS CAPPADOX, than whom perhaps no ancient physician has written upon
insanity with more judgment, or more from
his own observation, gives nearly the same
account. He says that if *atrabilis* rises up
to the stomach, or to the diaphragm, it produces melancholy; for it causes wind, and
fetid

fetid and fishy eructations ; and expels wind downward ; and also overturns the under-standing. For which reason, he observes, the ancients termed the disease both flatulent, and melancholic: but that there are some insane persons who neither suffer from wind, nor atrabilis: but from immoderate anger, or grief, or dreadful dejection of mind. And he adds, that *melancholy* appears to him to be both a beginning, and a part of mania *. He does not treat those symptoms which I have considered as characteristic of *sensitive insanity*, as belonging to *melancholy ;* but enumerates them among the symptoms of *mania*. Thus he reckons him a maniac who thought himself a brick †, and dared not drink, lest he should be dissolved ‡.

Aetius follows Galen in terming the hypochondriacal affection, when accompanied with *delirium*, a *third species of melancholy §*.

Paul of *Ægina* treats melancholy as an

---

* Aretæus Cappadox, de Causis et Signis Morbor, p. 29, C. D. E.

† Id. ib. p. 32. A.

‡ Meaning a brick dried in the sun.

§ Aetii Tetrabib. 2. Serm. 2, cap. ix.

insanity,

insanity, or alienation of mind, proceeding chiefly from the *humor melancholicus,* and being of *three sorts : one* in which the *humor melancholicus* affects the brain only ; *another* in which it affects the whole body, as well as the brain ; a *third* which, arising from a disordered state of the stomach, and other parts about the hypochondriacal region, is called *flatulent,* or *hypochondriacal melancholy,* and is accompanied with flatulency, acid eructations, and heat and load at the stomach, from whence a vapour, and humour, is sent up to the brain. The common symptoms of melancholy, he says, are 'fear, dejection, and aversion to society ; besides various other symptoms, differing in different cases; among which he reckons those which I have ascribed to *sensitive insanity.*

To these three species of insanity, he adds a fourth, *mania,* or raging madness, which he says has its origin from *yellow bile,* become adust, and converted into *black bile*.*

Of the many *modern writers* who have considered the MALUM HYPOCHONDRIACUM

---

* PAUL. ÆGINET. de re Medica, lib. iii. cap. xiv. p. 19.

as

as a disease of the stomach, and bowels, un-accompanied with delirium, and only con-nected with insanity as a predisposing cause; and when connected with delirium as consti-tuting a peculiar species of insanity; I shall quote only a few.

SENNERTUS distinguishes the HYPO-CHONDRIACAL AFFECTION from *hypo-chondriacal melancholy*; and asserts not only that DIOCLES wrote upon the former, con-sidered as distinct from the latter; but that even HIPPOCRATES appears to have de-scribed it under the appellation of νουσος αναντη'. And adds, that " it ought to be noticed, that the hypochondriacal affection is by no means confined to hypochondriacal melan-choly: and that it is obvious from experience, that many labour under the former, who are not at all affected by the latter; and that not a few are afflicted with melancholy, who ex-perience nothing of the hypochondriacal dis-order *."

HOFFMAN calls the disorder *affectus spas-modico-flatulentus, seu hypochondriacus*: and says, in defining it, " It is, if we attend to

---

* SENNERTI, Pract. lib. iii. p. 5, sect. i. cap. i.

its true idea, a spasmodico-flatulent affection
of the first passages, that is, of the stomach
and intestines, deriving its origin from their
inverted and perverted peristaltic motion;
and throwing, by sympathy, the whole nervous system, and the whole economy of the
functions, into irregular action*."

He then gives a history of its symptoms,
as affecting the bowels and nerves, which
when at their greatest height, he says, disorder the animal functions;—and then, he
adds, the mind irritated by no apparent, or
by the slightest cause, is hurried into per-
verse commotions, inquietudes, agonies, terror, distress, anger, fear, and irresolution,
and gives credence to vain images, and a
perverted imagination; the memory fails,
reason is enfeebled, and sleep becomes

---

* Est illa, si realem spectemus ideam, affectus prima-
rum viarum, nominatim ventriculi, ac intestinorum spas-
modico-flatulentus, ab inverso ac perverso illorum motu
peristaltico natales suas mutuans; per consensum vero
totum nervosarum partium systema, in irregulares motus
conjiciens, et totam œconomiam functionum.—HOFF-
MANNI, *Med. Rat. System.* tom. iv. part. iv. sect. i.
cap. iv. § i. *Operum,* tom. iii. p. 64.

turbulent,

turbulent, interrupted, and full of terrors *."

'In the fourth section he notes the agreement of the ancient physicians with him in
this view of the disease; and particularly
quotes the description of it by Diocles†;
who, he says, places the seat of the disorder
in the stomach, and intestines.

He then proceeds, in the fifteenth section,
to show how this disordered state of the stomach, and intestines, may gradually impair
the functions of the brain, and at length bring
on vain images, and visionary ideas, and in the
end introduce hypochondriacal melancholy‡.

He frequently mentions melancholy, and
mania, as rising out of the morbus hypochondriacus; but treats them as distinct diseases
from it, under the title of *melancholia hypochondriaca*, or *mania hypochondriaca*§:
reckons the malum hypochondriacum and

---

* Animus vel nulla, vel saltem levissima causa incita-
tus, ad perversas commotiones, inquietudines, angores,
terrorem, tristitiam, iram, metum, diffidentiam abripi-
tur, ad vanas inclinat imagines, perversamque phantasiam;
perit vis memoriæ, ratio labascit, somnus est turbulentus,
difficilis, terriculamentis plenus.—*Id. ib.* p. 64.

† Id. § iv. p 65.
‡ Id. § xv. p. 67.
§ Id. p. 81, Obs. xiii.

                                    hystericum

hystericum among the causes of the delirium
melancholicum, and maniacum ; and relates
a case in which melancholy, mania, and the
hypochondriacal disease were united ; and
another in which melancholia hypochondriaca
alternated periodically with mania; and another in which mania and melancholy were
combined *.

He begins the chapter upon *melancholic*
and *maniacal delirium*, in this manner :—
" I am well aware that not a few will wonder,
that I should treat disorders which in their
nature, and symptoms, appear so different,
under one head, and refer them to one species. But we learn by attentive experience,
and exact observation, that both arise from
one and the same cause, and origin, to wit,
from too great an afflux of blood to a weak
brain, and differ only in degree, and the
time of invasion; so that we may justly consider melancholy as the primary disease, and
mania as its exacerbation, and accidental
consequence. A fact which the ancient physicians have excellently observed. Hence
TRALLIAN, in the sixteenth chapter of his
first book, has told us that *mania is nothing*

---

* Med. Rat. Syst. tom. iv. cap. iv. Obs. ii. iii. vi. vii.
Op. tom. iii. p. 264.

else

else but a higher degree of melancholy, and that it is by this close connexion between the two disorders that they *so readily pass into each other.* ARETÆUS asserts, in the fifth chapter of his third book, that *melancholy is the beginning and origin of mania,* into whieh it makes its transition by an increase of dis-order, more than by any other cause. This agreement between them is daily confirmed by attentive observation, in the common course of which we see the melancholic, espe-cially if their disorder be of long standing, readily falling into mania, and, that ceasing, the melancholy again manifesting itself, to be afterwardss again periodically interrupted by mania*."

Thus

---

* Haud paucos fore arbitror, qui mirabuntur, me af-fectus, qui natura et symptomatibus plane dissimiles vi-dentur, in uno capite tractandos sumsisse et ad unam re-tulisse speciem. Attentiori vero usu et observatione disci-mus, utrumque morbum ex una eademque origine et causa continente, videlicet, nimio sanguinis ad imbecille cere-brum appulsu, suboriri, et nisi gradu ac invasionis tem-pore variare, adeo ut melancholia pro morbo primario, mania vero pro ejus exacerbatione et effectu accidentali habeatur rectissime. Id quod etiam quam optime medi-corum agnoverunt veteres. Hinc TRALLIANUS, lib. i. cap. xvi. nihil aliud esse maniam prodidit, quam melan-choliam ad majorem gradum redactam, ut propter tam
arctam

Thus we see that Hoffman considers the *affectio hypochondriaca*, or *morbus hypochon-driacus*, or *malum hypochondriacum*, or HY-POCHONDRIASIS, as it is variously called, when simple, as a disease of the nerves and abdominal viscera only; and as not necessa-rily accompanied with *delirium* or *illusion;* which, however, when it rises to a great height, it is apt to produce, and thus to give rise to vain images, and unreal ideas; and that these, when they are become intense, fixed, and permanent, constitute, and take the name, as the symptoms vary, of melan-cholia hypochondriaca, or mania hypochon-driaca, or affectus melancholico-maniaco-hypochondriacus, or melancholia hypochon-driaca cum mania periodice alternans. That, in plain terms, he views melancholia, and

arctam connexionem facillime ex uno morbo in alterum fiat transitus. ARETÆUS, lib. iii. cap. v. melancholiam maniæ initium et originem esse, illamque incremento ma-gis quam alia causa in furorem prolabi perhibet. Quam conspirationem etiam quotidiana et attentior confirmat observatio, cum melancholici, præsertim si morbus inve-teratus fuerit, perfacile in maniam incidunt; qua cessante, melancholia rursus sese prodit, licet postea per certas periodos furor revertatur.—HOFFMANNI, *Med. Rat. Syst.* tom. iv. part. iv. cap. viii. p. 251.

mania,

mania, with ARETÆUS, ALEXANDER
TRALLIANUS, and others, as *the same disease, in different states; as capable of existing separately, of being united together, or
of alternating with each other.*

FRACASSINI, one of the latest, and
fullest, and perhaps best, writers upon
the MORBUS HYPOCHONDRIACUS, differs
from SENNERTUS, and HOFFMAN, in that
he considers it as " an universal affection ;
not confined to any one viscus, but occupy-
ing the whole nervous, and membranous,
system*." He says that it affects not only
the cavity of the abdomen, but also of the
breast, and head ; but that it especially rages
in the stomach, which, whatever other part
of the body may suffer with it, rarely es-
capes.: and after enumerating the various
distressing feelings of the several cavities, and
of the whole body†; he adds that " the
temper of the mind is discomposed and
altered ; that hypochondriacs are irritated

---

* Affectionem hypochondriacam non esse morbum
alicui visceri peculiarem, sed universalem, nervosum ac
membranosum systema præsertim corripientem.—*Naturæ
Morbi Hypochondriaci Investigatio,* p. 7, col. 1,

† Id. p. 7, 8, 9.

by

by the slightest causes, or are thrown into
extreme dejection, inquietude, agony and
terror, conceive of their own complaint as
most grievous, and deadly, have no confidence in their friends, who endeavour to con-
sole them, and to free them from this false
opinion of their malady, and study by better
omens to raise them from their deep despondency : hence the imagination often becomes
diseased, the memory impaired, the reason
deviates, and at length they fall into the *delirium of melancholy*.*"

Thus we see that he considers the visceral,
and nervous symptoms, and painful and distressing feelings of the whole body, as cha-
racterizing the malum hypochondriacum ;
which may act as a cause of, but does not
constitute, hypochondriacal melancholy : that

---

* Animi quoque mores perturbuntur, commutanturque,
ex levi siquidem causa irascuntur, aut valde mœrent, in-
quietudine, angore, et terrore præhenduntur, proprium
morbum, ut gravissimum ac lethale mente concipiunt,
amicis adstantibusque, qui eosdem solari conantur, et
a falso morbi conceptu liberare, nec non a profunda mœstitia bonis ominibus eruere student, fidem minime pre-
bent, hinc sæpe imaginatio læditur, memoriæ vis deficit,
ratio deflectit, proinde in melancholicum delirium incidunt.—*Id. ib.* p. 10.

he

he allows that in the MALUM HYPOCHONDRI-
ACUM, to a certain degree fear, and anxiety,
may exist relative to the *health* of the sufferer, that the imagination may on *this* subject be disturbed, and reason may somewhat
deviate from the course of perfect firmness;
but that till a fixed derangement takes place,
of which these symptoms are often the fore-
runners, the disorder can only be reckoned a
high degree of hypochondriacal affection:
that when actual derangement begins, which
may easily be distinguished by the obstinacy
of error, in opposition to the most cogent
reasoning, and even to absolute demonstration, then, and not till then, the disorder
drops the name of hypochondriasis, and assumes that of MELANCHOLIA HYPOCHON-
DRIACA, in the common and established
language of medicine: and, let me add, if
it answers to my definition of that disorder,
in the language of my arrangement it takes
the name of HYPOCHONDRIACAL INSA-
NITY; or if it be accompanied with certain
errors of sensation, it changes its character
from *notional* to *ideal,* and takes the appellation of SENSITIVE INSANITY.

The late Dr. DARWIN, in his *Zoonomia,*
says

says that "'The *hypochondriac disease*. consists in indigestion and consequent flatulency,·
with anxiety or want of pleasurable sensation.
When the action of the stomach and bowels
is impaired, much gas becomes generated by
the fermenting or putrescent aliment, and to
this indigestion is catenated languor, coldness
of the skin, and fear. For when the extremities are cold for too long a time in some
weak constitutions, indigestion is produced
by direct sympathy of the skin and the stomach, with consequent heartburn, and flatu-
lence. The same occurs if the skin be made
cold by fear, as in riding over dangerous
roads in winter, and hence conversely fear is
produced by indigestion or torpor of the stomach by association."

" This disease is confounded with the fear
of death, which is an insanity, and therefore
of a totally different nature*."

And under the fourteenth species of insanity, which he denominates *lethi timor*, and
which corresponds with my *hypochondriacal
insanity*, he says that " The fear of death
perpetually employs the thoughts of these pa-

* DARWIN's Zoonomia, vol. ii. p. 131.

tients;

tients; hence they are devising new medicines, and applying to physicians and quacks without number. *It is confounded with hypochondriasis*, in popular conversation, *but is in reality an insanity* *."

Having now taken due notice of all such objections to my " Observations on Insanity," as, to the best of my knowledge, or recollection, have in any way been made to them; and given such elucidation, and defence, as they appear to me to require; and having made considerable improvements, and corrections, in the work itself; I leave, with confidence, what I have written, to the candour of the well-informed, and intelligent; not doubting that, whatever may be its imperfections, the many interesting truths which it contains, the exact method in which they are arranged, and the great importance of which they may be to mankind; by contributing something valuable towards the successful investigation of the various derangements of the human intellect, and towards their more certain restoration to the healthful order of sound understanding; will conti-

---

* DARWIN's Zoonomia, vol. ii. p. 377.

nue to me that estimation in the eye of the public, which I have endeavoured to merit, and which I have just reason to believe I have not altogether failed to obtain*.

I shall here take my leave for the present. My next business will be to turn my thoughts more immediately to the second, and most important part of my undertaking, the CURE OF INSANITY: to which what I have hitherto written on this disorder is preparatory; and without which it can be of but little value. And having drawn from long experience, and observation, no inconsiderable funds of practical knowledge on this interest-

---

* My " Observations on Insanity" have not only been well approved by some of the most eminent physicians of this country; but have been translated, and commended, abroad. To mention no other instance, they were translated into the *German* language by ACKERMAN, and published at Leipsic, very soon after their first appearance in England; and were reviewed with unreserved approbation in the " *Commentarii de Rebus in Scientia Naturali, et Medicina, gestis :*"— commonly called the Leipsic Commentaries, or the Leipsic Review :—the *first volume* in the 25th volume of that work, part iv. p. 699, published at Leipsic in 1784; and the *second* in vol. xxx. part iv. p. 642, published in 1788.

ing

ing subject; I shall henceforth fix my attention on the not very easy task of putting my observations on the cure of this deplorable malady, into such a form as shall appear to me most likely to convey them to the public with perspicuity and usefulness.

Belle Grove, Leicester,
March 8, 1806.

PREFACE

TO THE

FIRST EDITION OF THE FIRST VOLUME.

———

IT is with much diffidence that I offer to the Public the following observations. They were written at intervals, in the midst of many interruptions from professional, and other necessary engagements; and contain but a short, and imperfect inquiry, on a subject, which is of too much consequence to mankind not to merit a full, and accurate investigation. But whatever may be their defects, they have at least the merit of being founded on observation, and experience : and though they offer but merely the outlines of an important object, it is not the chimerical delineation of an imaginary form which they exhibit; it is not a fancy-piece; but a real copy, how little soever it may discover the hand of a master, drawn with some care and exactness immediately from nature.

As it is not every painter who can give a just, and striking representation of his original; so I am sensible that it is not every one who pretends to be an observer of nature, who can discern her genuine and characteristic features; or make a true copy of them for the use, and information of others. How far I have succeeded, in this respect, must be left to the decision of the few who have had the opportunity, and possess the abilities, of being well informed in this matter.

The

The definitions, and the arrangement, of the several species, and varieties, of Insanity, have at least a claim to novelty : and I flatter myself that, while they convey to the reader clear, and distinct, ideas, relative to a disorder which has hitherto been very imperfectly understood, and of course very inaccurately defined, they will be found to possess a kind of merit, which ought ever to hold the first place in all our medical researches, that of leading to greater certainty, and precision, in our knowledge of the disorder, and to greater efficacy in our methods of cure.

This part of the work I have endeavoured to execute according to the ideas of Sydenham; to whose recommendation "that every disease should be reduced to certain, and determinate species, with the same care, and accuracy, with which we see botanists define, and arrange, the species of vegetables *,"—we are indebted for the valuable performances, in this way, of Sauvages, Linnæus, Vogel, and Cullen, writers of the first character in the medical world, who have taken an extensive range through the whole field of diseases; and whose successful labours in this, and other branches of medicine, in chemistry, and in natural history, will carry down their names with honour to the latest posterity.—My inquiries of this kind take a less ambitious scope, and are content to be confined within the narrow boundaries of one disease : and I shall esteem myself happy, if a more limited attention, joined to careful observation, and diligent assiduity, shall enable me, like the inferior statuary of Horace †, to express with accuracy the hairs, and the nails, though less fitted

---

* Opera Universa, Præfatio. p. 13.   † De Arte Poetica, v. 32.

to design and execute a greater work; and if while *they* acquire immortal reputation by defining, and reducing to order, the whole catalogue of diseases, I may have the good fortune to labour with success, and approbation, in my lesser department, and to advance, if but a few steps, farther than my illustrious predecessors, in the knowledge of a disorder, which I have made it my peculiar province to cultivate, and improve.

I am sensible, indeed, that my enumeration, and definitions, of the several species, and varieties, of Insanity, are still very incomplete; and that in some instances they may possibly be erroneous. Farther experience, and observation, may enable me to correct errors, and to supply deficiencies: and as truth, and the advancement of useful knowledge, are the chief objects of my inquiries, I shall always have improvement in view; and shall never scruple to add, or to retrench,—to correct, or to retract, —as longer experience, and more exact observation, shall suggest.

Though this kind of arrangement of diseases, recommended by SYDENHAM, and attempted by the above-mentioned eminent writers, is an imitation of the botanical arrangement invented by modern naturalists, and now so greatly improved by the wonderful industry, and comprehensive genius, of the late illustrious LINNÆUS; yet it ought to be remembered that *diseases* are incapable of that permanent uniformity of character, and of that exactness of discrimination, which so much facilitates the distinction, and arrangement, of *plants* and *animals:* and that while the *two latter* can only be mixed, and confounded, to a certain degree, by the production of *hybrid,* or mule species, which are far from being common, or numerous, and are incapable of propagating their kind;

diseases

diseases may be combined in an infinite variety of degrees, and proportions, and varied without end *.

This necessary inconvenience no care, or attention, can obviate: but there is another, and accidental one, into which SAUVAGES has frequently run, which might readily be avoided; and that is, the not adhering strictly to the Linnæan method, of distinguishing the species by proper specific definitions. Instead of thus distinguishing them, he has sometimes taken the name, and the distinction, solely from an *internal cause*, which could seldom be discovered early in the disorder, and which in many cases could not be certainly known till after the death of the patient. But as some uniform, and permanent, differences, in the number, position, and form, of certain parts, constitute the only proper generic, and specific, distinctions, of plants ; so some obvious, and essential differences in symptoms, are the only ready, and infallible means, of distinguishing disorders : the *distinction from causes being exceedingly vague, and uncertain :* and though the knowledge of causes be of the greatest importance in the cure of diseases, the introduction of them into the specific definitions, or otherwise employing them to distinguish the species,—to the neglect of definitions drawn from the obvious and essential symptoms,—serves rather to confuse than to inform ; and unnecessarily multiplies species to an amazing degree. Causes ought to be enumerated, as far as they are known; but let them be enumerated in their proper places; and never

---

* Nonnunqnam etiam morbi mire complicantur, &c. HOFFMAN. *Med. Rat. System.* tom. iii. sect. i. cap. 2. *Oper.* tom. i. p. 389.

" Sometimes diseases are wonderfully complicated," &c.

enter

enter into the definition either of genus, or species, unless where they are perfectly obvious, and no obvious, permanent, and essential symptoms, can be discovered. An arrangement of diseases formed upon a plan of exact adherence to such a method, might be attended with much difficulty, and trouble, in the execution; but would, I apprehend, abundantly repay the labour bestowed upon it, by its simplicity, accuracy, and practical utility.

With a view to illustrate the species, I have subjoined a considerable number of particular histories of Insanity, transcribed from practical writers. It was often difficult, and sometimes impossible, to find such as exactly corresponded with my definitions; owing to the frequent combination of symptoms, already mentioned. For this reason, some of my species will be found, perhaps, but imperfectly illustrated by the histories adduced; and others will be unaccompanied with any history, because I could meet with none that would in any tolerable way answer my purpose.

For the convenience of such of my readers as may be not at all, or but imperfectly acquainted, with any other language besides their own, I have given translations of the passages quoted from Greek, Latin, or French writers. Why I have left a few untranslated, will be obvious to the learned reader.

As, in the course of my reading, I have frequently experienced much inconvenience; often a great waste, and sometimes a total loss, both of time, and labour; by a loose, and negligent mode of reference from one author to another; an imperfection from which the references even in the inestimable writings of the accurate MORGAGNI, and the no less accurate HALLER, are not entirely

free;

free; I have not only been, in general, so full in my references, as to render them as extensively applicable as may be to the various editions; but have also drawn up, for the emolument of the learned reader, a catalogue of the principal books quoted, or referred to, with an account of the editions made use of, in these observations.

Leicester,
Feb. 23, 1782.

A CATALOGUE OF THE PRINCIPAL BOOKS

QUOTED, OR REFERRED TO, IN THE FOLLOWING WORK,
WITH AN ACCOUNT OF THE EDITIONS MADE USE OF.

ACTA Eruditorum, 4to. Lipsiæ, ab anno, 1682—1727.

Adami (Melchioris) Vitæ Germanorum Theologorum, 8vo. Haidelbergæ, 1620.

Alberti (D. Michaelis) Introductio in Universam Medicinam, 4to. Halæ Magdeburgicæ, 1718.

Alpini (Prosperi) de Medicina Methodica, Libri xiii. Edit. 2da. 4to. Lugduni Batavorum, 1719.

————— ————— De Medicina Ægyptiorum, Libri iv. Et Jacobi Bontii Medicina Indorum, 4to. Parisiis, 1645.

Andry de la Generation des Vers, dans le Corps de l'Homme. 12mo. A Amsterdam, 1701.

Arbuthnot's Essay concerning the Effects of Air on Human Bodies, 8vo. London, 1751.

Artis Medicæ Principes, Hippocrates, Aretæus, Alexander, Aurelianus, Celsus, Razis. Recensuit, præfatus est Albertus Haller, tomi xi. 8vo. Lausaunæ, 1769, 1770, 1771, 1772, 1774.

Aretæi Cappadocis de Causis et Signis acutorum, et diuturnorum Morborum Libri quatuor. De Curatione acutorum et diuturnorum Morborum Libri quatuor. Editionem curavit Hermannus Boerhaave, fol. Lugduni Batavorum, 1735.

Baglivi (Georgii) Opera Omnia Medico, Practica et Anatomica. Editio 8va. &c. 4to. Lugduni, 1714.

Burneti (Thomæ) Thesaurus Medicinæ Practicæ, 4to. Londini, 1673.

Bartholini (Thomæ) Historiarum Anatomicarum rariarum Centuriæ, I. et II. 12mo. Hagæ-Comitum.

————— ————— Acta Medica & Philosophica Hafniensia. Volumina V. ab Anno 1671—1679. 4to. Hafniæ.

————— ————— de Morbis Biblicis Miscellanea Medica. 12mo. Francofurti, 1672.

Battie's Treatise on Madness, 4to. London, 1758.

Bayle's

Bayle's Dictionary, Historical and Critical, By Mr. Des
Maizeaux, fol. 5 vols. 2d edition, London, 1734, 5, 6, &c.

Bellini (Laurentii) De Urinis et Pulsibus, de Missione Sanguinis, et Febribus, de Morbis Capitis, et Pectoris, Opus dica-
tum Francisco Redi, Ed. quinta, 4to. Lugduni Batavorum,
1717.

Boerhaave (Abrahami Kaau) Impetum Faciens dictum Hip-
pocrati per Corpus consentiens, Philologice et Physiologice il-
lustratum, &c. 12mo. L. Bat. 1745.

Boerhaave (Hermanni) Prælectiones Academicæ de Morbis
Nervorum. Edit. a Jacobo Van Eems, 12mo. 2 tom. L.
Bat. 1761.

————————————— Institutiones Medicinæ, 8vo. L. Batavorum, 1727.

————————————— Prælectiones Academicæ in Pro-
prias Institutiones Rei Medicæ. Edidit et Notas addidit Albertus Haller, tom. vii. 12mo. Lugd. Batav. 1753.

Boileau.—Oeuvres de Nicolas Boileau Despreaux. En deux
tomes, 12mo. A Amsterdam, 1715.

Boneti (Theophili) Sepulchretum, sive Anatomia Practica,
ex Cadaveribus Morbo denatis, in 3 tomos distributata, fol.
Editio Altera, Genevæ, 1700.

————————————— Polyalthos, sive Thesaurus Medico-
Practicus, &c. in qua viri excellentissimi Johannis Jonstoni,
Syntagma explicatur, 2 tom. fol. Genevæ, tom. i. 1691.
tom. ii. 1694.

————————————— Medicina Septentrionalis Collatitia : sive
Rei Medicæ, nuperis Annis a Medicis Anglis, Germanis, et
Danis emissæ, Sylloge et Syntaxis, tom. ii. fol. Genevæ,
1685 et 1686.

Broen (Johannis) Animadversiones Medicæ, Theoretico-
Practicæ, in Henrici Regii Praxin Medicam, &c. 4to. Lugd.
Bat. 1695.

Bishop Butler's Fifteen Sermons preached at the Rolls
Chapel, 8vo. London, 1736.

Cælii Aureliani, Siccensis Medici Vetusti, Secta Methodici,
de Morbis Acutis & Chronicis, Libri viii. Jo. Conradus Am-
man, M. D. recensuit, emaculavit, notulasque adjecit. Accedunt seorsim Theod. Janss. et Almeloveen, Notæ et Animadversiones, 4to. Amstelod. 1722.

Celsi (Aur. Cornel.) de Medicina, Libri viii. &c. Cura et
Studio, Th. J. ab Almeloveen, 8vo. Rotterdami, 1750.

Cheyne (George).—The English Malady, or a Treatise on
                                            Nervous

Nervous Diseases of all Kinds, &c. By George Cheyne, M. D. 8vo. 2d Edit. London, 1734.

Ciceronis (M. Tullii) Opera cum Delectu Commentariorum, ex Editione Josephi Oliveti, tomi ix. 4to. Amstelædami, 1745, 1746, et 1747.

———————— Opera quæ extant omnia, ex MSS. Codicibus emendata, Studio atque Industria Jani Gulielmii et Jani Gruteri, &c. et nunc denuo recognita ab Jacobo Gronovio, tom. xi. 12mo. Lugd. Batav. 1692.

———————— Tusculanaraum Disputationum Libri quinque. Accedunt Lectiones variantes, et Doctorum præcipue Cl. Bouherii Conjecturæ, 12mo. Glasguæ, 1744.

Clerici (Johannis) Logica, Ontologia, et Pneumatologia, 12mo. Cantab. 1704.

Dionis,—Cours d'Operations de Chirurgie, demontrees au Jardin Royal. Par M. Dionis, 8vo. A Bruxelles, 1708.

Diogenis Laertii de Vitis Dogmat. et Apophth. Clarorum Philosophorum, Libri x. &c. Græce et Latine. Is. Casauboni Notæ, &c. 8vo. Genevæ, 1615.

Dolæi (Johannis) Encyclopædia Medicinæ Theoretico-Practicæ, 4to. Amstelodami, 1686.

Flemyng (Milcolumbus).—Neuropathia : sive de Morbis Hypocondriacis, et Hystericis, Libri tres, Poema Medicum. Cui præmittitur Dissertatio Epistolaris Prosaica ejusdem Argumenti. Auctore Milcolumbo Flemyng, M. D. Eboraci, 8vo. 1740.

Grainger's Biographical History of England, from Egbert the Great to the Revolution, 8vo. 2d edition, 4 vols. London, 1775.

Galenus.—Epitome Galeni Operum in quatuor partes digesta pulchrerrima methodo universam, illius viri doctrinam complectens, per And. Lacunam, Secobiensem, fol. Basileæ, 1551.

Gaubii (H. D.) Institutiones Pathologiæ Medicinalis, 12mo. Edinburgi, 1762.

Gerard (Alexander) An Essay on Genius by, 8vo. London, 1774.

Gorter (Johannes de).—Medicina Dogmatica, tres Morbos particulares, Delirium, Vertiginem, et Tussim, &c. Pro Specimine exhibens. Auctore Johanne de Gorter, 4to. Harderovici, 1741.

Haen (Antonius de) de Magia Liber, 12mo. Venetiis, 1776.

Harris

Harris (Gualterus) de Morbis Acutis Infantum, 8vo. Lond. 1705.

Haller (Alberti V.) Elementa Physiologiæ Corporis Humani, tom. viii. 4to. Tom. 1, 2, 3, 4, 5, Lausannæ, 1757, 1760, 1761, 1762, 1763. Tom. 6, 7, 8, Lugduni Batavorum, 1764, 1765, 1766.

Helmont (Joan. Babtist. Van.) Ortus Medicinæ, id est Initia Physicæ inaudita, progressus Medicinæ novus, in Morborum ultionem ad vitam longam, fol. Lugduni, 1655. [*Opera* scilicet *Omnia*].

Hartley's (David) Observations on Man, his Frame, his Duty, and his Expectations. In Two Parts. 2 vols. 8vo. London, 1749.

Hippocratis Opera Omnia. Ab Anutio Foesio Mediomatrico, fol. Genevæ, 1662.

———— Coaca Præsagia. Cum Interpretatione & Commentariis Jacobi Hollerii Stempani: Desiderii Jacotii Vandoperani Opera in lucem Editis, &c. fol. Lugduni, 1576.

Hippocrates.—Anutii Foesii Oeconomia Hippocratis, fol. Genevæ, 1662.

Heisteri (Laurentii) Compendium Medicinæ Practicæ, 8vo. Amstelædami, 1748.

Histoire et Memoirs de l'Academie Royale des Sciences, et Histoire, du Renouvellement de l'Academie en 1699, 12mo. A Amsterdam, ann. 1699—1717.

Home (Franciscus).—Principia Medicinæ. Auctore Francisco Home, Medico Regio, &c. 8vo. Edinburgi, 1762.

History of the Royal Society of London, for the improving of Natural Knowledge. By Thomas Sprat, D. D. Lord Bishop of Rochester, 2d edition, 4to. London, 1702.

Horstii (Georgii), Senioris, Opera Medica, tom. iii. 4to. Goudæ, 1661.

Hoffman's Works, with all the Supplements, the last Edition, divided into six volumes, as follow, viz.

Hoffmanni (Frederici) Opera Omnia Physico-Medica denuo revisa, correcta et aucta, in 6 tomos distributa, &c. Cum Vita Auctoris. In vol. iii. divisa, fol. Genevæ, 1761.

———— Supplementum Operum Omnium, &c. in duos partes distributum, fol. Genevæ, 1754.—Operum sc. Omnium cum Supplementis, volumen iv^m.

———— Supplementum Secundum, in Partes tres distributum. Pars prima, fol. Genevæ, 1753.—Operum sc. Omnium cum Supplementis, volum. v^m.

Hoffmanni

Hoffmanni (Frederici) Supplementum Secundum. Pars secunda, et pars tertia, fol. Genevæ, 1760.—Operum &c. Omnium cum Supplementis, volumen vi^n.

Jonstoni (Joh.) M. D. Idea Universæ Medicinæ Practicæ, Libris xii. absoluta, 12mo. Amst. 1654.

Junckeri (Johannis) Conspectus Physiologiæ Medicæ et Hygieines, &c. 4to. Halæ Magdeburgiæ, 1735.

Locke (John, Esq.) 's Essay concerning the Human Understanding. In four books, 3 vols. 8vo. Glasgow, 1759.

Linnæi Materia Medica, per Regna tria Naturæ, &c. Edit. à Schrebero, 8vo. Lipsiæ, 1772.

———— Amœnitates Academicæ, 7 vols. 8vo. Lugd. et Holmiæ, 1749—1769.

Lorry (Annæus Carolus).—De Melancholia et Morbis Melancholicis. Ab Annæa Carolo Lorry, D. M. P. 2 tom. 8vo. Lutetiæ Parisiorum, 1765.

Luther (Dr. Martin) His Life and Death, by Thomas Hayne, 4to. London, 1541.

Massariæ (Alexandri), Vicentini, Opera Medica, fol. Lugduni, 1634.

Mercurialis (Hieronimi), Foroliviensis, Opusucula Aurea et Selectiora, fol. Venetiis, 1644.

———————————— in Lib. Epidem. Hippocratis, Prælectiones Bononienses, fol. Forol. 1626.

Mead (Richard) M. D. his Medical Works. In 3 vols. 12mo. Edinburgh, 1763.

Montesquieu's Spirit of Laws, 12mo. Edinb. 1772.

Morgagni (Jo. Babtist.) De Sedibus et Causis Morborum per Anatomen indagatis. Inter Opera Omnia in 5 tomos divisa, fol. Venetiis, 1763, 4, 5.

Newton's (Sir Isaac) Opticks, 8vo. London, 1730.

Pauli Æginetæ Opus de Re Medica Latinitate donatum per per Johannem Guinterium Andernacum, fol. Parisiis, 1632.

Philosophical Enquiry into the Origin of our Ideas of the Sublime and Beautiful, 8vo. London, 1757.

Passiones Animæ. Inter Cartesii Opera Philosophica, 4to. Amstelodami, 1685.

Pisonis (Nicolai), Medici Lotharingi de cognoscendis et curandis præcipue internis, Humani Corporis Morbis, Libri iii. Et ejusdem de Febribus Liber unus. Accessit Præfatio, Hermanni Boerhaave. Volum. duo. 4to. Lugduni Batavorum, 1736.

Pitcarnii

. Pitcarnii (Archibaldi) Opera Omnia Medica, 4to. Lugduni
Batavorum, 1737.

Platonis de Rebus Divinis Dialogi selecti Græce et Latine,
8vo. Cantabrigiæ, 1683.

Plateri (Felicis) Praxeos Medicæ, tomi iii. Cum Centuria
Posthuma, 4to. Basileæ, 1656.

C. Plinii Secundi Historiæ Mundi Libri, xxxvii. fol. Basileæ,
1539.

Priestley's (Dr.) two Discourses; 1. On Habitual Devotion.
2. On the Duty of not living to ourselves, 8vo. Birmingham,
1782.

Raii (Joannis) Historia Plantarum, fol. tom. iii. Londini,
1686.

Review.—The Foreign Medical Review, 8vo. 4 Numbers,
making one Volume, London, 1779—80.

Riverii (Lazari), Opera Medica Universa, fol. Genevæ, 1728.

Riedessel's (Baron) Travels through Sicily, and that part of
Italy formerly called Magna Græcia. Translated by J. R.
Forster, F. R. S. 8vo. London, 1773.

Rousseau Juge de Jean Jaques. Dialogues d'apres le manuscript de Mr. Rousseau, laissé entre les mains de Mr. Brooke
Boothby, 8vo. A. Litchfield, 1780.

Robinson (Bryan's) Observations on the Virtues and Operations of Medicines, 8vo. Dublin, 1752.

————————— Dissertation on the Food and Discharges
of Human Bodies, 8vo. London, 1748.

Sauvages.—Nosologia Methodica sistens Morborum Classes,
Genera et Species, Juxta Sydenhami Mentem et Botanicorum
Ordinem. Auctore Francisco Boissier de Sauvages, Regis Con-
siliario ac Medico, tom. iii. in vol. v. divis. 8vo. Amstel.
1763.

Schenckii (Johannis) Observationum Medicarum rariarum,
Libri vii. fol. Lugduni, 1644.

Sennerti (Danielis) Opera Omnia, in sex tomos divisa. fol.
Lugduni, 1676.

Senecæ (L. Annæi) Opera, quæ extant, integris Justi Lipsii
et Fred. Gronovii, et selectis variorum Commentariis illustrata,
tomi iii. 8vo. Amstelodami, 1672.

Simpson's (Thomas) M. D. Inquiry how far the Vital and
Animal Actions of the more perfect Animals can be accounted
for independent of the Brain. In 5 Essays, 8vo. Edinburgh,
1752.

                                                    Simpson

Simpsoni (Thomæ) De Re Medica Dissertationes quatuor, 8vo. Edinburgh, 1726.

Storčk (Antonii) Libellus quo Demonstratur Stramonium, Hyoscyamum, Aconitum non solum tuto posse exhiberi usu interno Hominibus, verum ea esse remedia in Multis Morbis maxime salutifera, 8vo. Vindobonæ, 1762.

Swieten (Gerardi Van), M. D. Commentaria in Hermanni Boerhaavii Aphorismos de cognoscendis et curandis Morbis, tom. v. 4to. Lugduni Bat. 1742, 1745, 1753, &c.

Stuart (Alexandri) Dissertatio de Structura et Motu Musculari, 4to. Londini, 1738.

Sydenhami (Thomæ) M. D. Opera Universa, 8vo. Lugduni Batavorum, 1726.

Turner (Daniel) M. D. A Treatise on the Diseases incident to the Skin, by. 8vo. London, 1726.

Tissot (S. A. D.) M. D. et Prof. Sermo Inauguralis de Valetudine Literatorum, 8vo. Lausannæ, 1766.

————————————— Letter to Zimmerman, on the Morbus Niger. Translated from the French, by John Burke, M. D. 8vo. London, 1776.

Tozzi (Lucæ) Opera Omnia. Tom. v. 4to. Venetiis, 1728.

Tulpii (Nicolai) Observationes Medicæ, Ed. 5. 12mo. Lugd. Batav. 1716.

Wall (John) M. D. Medical Tracts by, collected and republished by Martin Wall, M. D. Oxford, 1780.

Whytt (Robert) M. D. the Works of, 4to. Edinburgh, 1768.

Wieri (Johannis) Opera Omnia, 4to. Amst. 1660.

Willis (Thomæ) M. D. Opera Omnia, Ed. à Blasio, 4to. Amstelodami, 1682.

————————————— De Anima Brutorum, quæ Hominis vitalis et sensitiva est, Exercitationes Duæ, 12mo. Londini, 1672.

Xenophontis de Cyri Institutione, Libri octo. à Thomæ Hutchinson, A. M. 8vo. Londini, 1730.

Zacuti Lusitani Opera Omnia in duos tomos divisa. Priore continentur de Historia Principum Medicorum, Libri vi. Introitus ad Praxin. Pharmacopœia. Praxis Medica Admiranda, multis, &c. fol. Lugduni, 1649.

CONTENTS.

OBSERVATIONS

ON

INSANITY.

SECT. I.

INTRODUCTION.

AMIDST the many useful discoveries and improvements which the several branches of medical, as well as every other species of knowledge, have for the three last centuries been continually receiving, as the natural consequence of that facility with which science has been diffused since the happy invention of the art of printing: —but more especially, amidst the rapid and almost daily accumulation of medical science for the last hundred and ten or twenty years, since the establishment of philosophical societies*, and

. the

---

* The English Royal Society may date its commencement from the meetings of some learned men at Dr. WILKINS's lodgings in Wadham College in Oxford, about the year 1645 ; which they continued without intermission till the year 1658, when being dispersed, they afterwards renewed their meetings in London, and from that time usually assembled at Gresham

the publication of literary journals*, have not
only much increased that facility of diffusion, but
have greatly contributed to the advancement of
sound philosophy, by promoting a free and liberal
spirit of inquiry; in consequence of which, the
whimsical inventions of a childish and undisci-
plined fancy have been taught to give way to the
severest inductions of correct and manly reasoning from facts and experiments :—admidst such
large and splendid acquisitions of knowledge, it is

College; and were incorporated under the title of the Royal
Society by *letters patent* from King Charles the Second in the
year 1660.—SPRATT's *Hist. of the Royal Society.* See *Biogr.
Britan.* art. BOYLE (Robt.), vol. ii. p. 449. See also art. BA-
THURST, vol. i. p. 693, n. (G), which says July 15th, 1662.—
The Society began to publish its Transactions in 1665.—
HALLER.

The Royal Academy of Sciences at Paris was first established
by order of Lewis XIVth, in 1666; but not incorporated till
1699.—See *Histoire du Renouvellement de l'Academie Royale
des Sciences en* 1699, *et les Eloges Historiques,* &c. par M. de
FONTENELLE, tom. i. p. 27.

The *Academia dell' Cimento* at Florence was instituted in
1657 by Leopold, Grand Duke of Tuscany; and began to publish in 1667.

The *Ephemerides Naturæ Curiosorum* were first presented to
the world in 1670.

* The *Journal des Scavans* commenced in 1655, and has
with little interruption, continued for above a hundred years.

The *Acta Eruditorum* of Leipsic, first made their appearance
in 1682, and are now continued under the new title of *Commentarii de rebus in scientia naturali et re medica gestis.*

matter

matter of surprise, that the most important branches of the *Healing Art*,—the *History of Diseases*,—and the *Method of curing them*,—should have hitherto received so little proportional improvement.

Of this very small accession to practical improvement, we have no where, perhaps, a more remarkable instance, than in that class of disorders which is the object of my present consideration. Little, very little, has been communicated to the world on this important subject, by modern writers. They who have been obliged to treat of it, as a matter of course, in delivering a regular system of medical practice, have for the most part given little else but mere compilation,—and have almost wholly borrowed, either directly or indirectly, from the truly practical writings of the ancient Greek and Roman physicians. And if at any time a man of science and observation, quitting the trite and illiberal practice of transcribing, and retailing, what is already to be found in almost every author who has gone before him, and of writing a *new treatise* which shall contain not a single article of *new matter*, has ventured to throw out some original facts, or to hazard some new and ingenious reflections, tending to open our views, and spread a clearer light over the nature of these obstinate and obscure disorders of our best and noblest faculties, they have usually been few and solitary, and amidst the more

plentiful

plentiful remains of antiquity, as Virgil speaks on another occasion,

" Apparent rari nantes in gurgite vasto."

And, to add to our mortification, we have not been so happy as to retain all that the ancients knew on this important subject; having lost their most general, and, if we may believe them, scarcely ever failing method of cure*.

Extra-

---

* It will be obvious to every one who is but slightly acquainted with medical matters, or has the smallest familiarity with the Greek and Latin classics, that I here allude to the noted method of curing these disorders by the use of hellebore; a lost art, to which the moderns, who have written much to little purpose about the thing, have at least the merit of giving a name,—and which is now pretty generally known by the title of *helleborism*. Of the great deal that has been said upon the subject, I shall content myself at present with a few extracts; —one from the learned and elegant Dr. LORRY's epistle to his friend Dr. LE MONNIER, prefixed to his treatise *De Melancholia*,—a book which contains much excellent matter, both old and new, but which is obscured, and rendered of less value, by an indulgence in too minute a theory, and too servile an attachment to the doctrines and hypotheses of the ancients;— my other extracts shall consist of a few passages, out of the many that might be brought together, alluding to this practice, from several of the classical writers of antiquity.

" Meministi porro," says Dr. LORRY, " in felicibus illis colloquiis, quibus jam frui vix datur, actum sæpius inter nos fuisse de melancholia; non unam esse ejus naturam sæpius diximus; alteram scilicet legibus regi atque administrari mechanicis advertebamus; alterius mirebamur effectus, non solum om-

nem

Extraordinary as this stationary, if not indeed
retrograde state of medical knowledge in these disorders

---

nem judicii captum superantes, sed et vulgarem ordinem phy-
sicarum legum eludentes. Unde sæpe incerta medendi metho-
dus et titubantis artis tacitus timor. Actum etiam inter nos de
veterum *helleborismo, miserrimaque hodiernorum Insanorum
sorte*, quos nimium ars dedignatur, dum mavult impotens dici,
quam anxiæ atque delicatæ curationis fastidia tolerare. Nec
minus tamen stupebamus antiquiores medicos passim de eorum
sanatione, tanquam de *arte vulgatissima* loquentes."—Tom. i.
p. x.

You remember too, that in those delightful conversations,
which we have now but little opportunity of enjoying, we frequently considered the subject of Melancholy ; we agreed that
it was of more than one kind ; and observed that while one
was governed and regulated by mechanical laws ; another appeared wonderful in its effects, and not only beyond our com-
prehension, but out of the reach of the common order of phy-
sical laws. Whence often arose an uncertain method of cure,
and a secret distrust of an art so little secure of the success of
its proceedings. We considered, likewise, the *hellelorism* of the
ancients, and the unhappy lot of the modern *Insane*, on whom
art bestows too little of its regard, while it chooses rather to ac-
quiesce in the charge of impotency, than to undertake the disagreeable office of attempting a cure which must be accompanied with the most anxious feelings, and require the minutest
attention. Nor did it appear less wonderful, that the ancient
physicians should on all occasions speak of their cure as of an
art universally known.—Vide etiam Mercurialis variar. Lection.
lib. ii. cap. 25. *Opusc. Aureor.* p. 411.

The Latin poets frequently allude to this noted method of
curing insanity ; and of such specific virtue was hellebore
esteemed for clearing and invigorating the intellectual faculties,

that

orders may seem ; it will, perhaps, appear less
wonderful, if we consider, that their peculiar nature

---

that it was not unfrequently used by men who were engaged in
literary and philosophical pursuits, as will presently be seen
from PLINY and AULUS GELLIUS, with a view to strengthen
the understanding, and to prepare it for the nicer parts of composition, the more difficult researches of critical inquiry, or
the more accurate investigation of moral or metaphysical truth.
HORACE alludes to it, on several occasions, as a well known
practice. Speaking of a happy madman, he says :

> Hic ubi cognatorum opibus curisque refectus,
> Expulit *elleboro* morbum bilemque meraco,
> Et redit ad sese: pol me occidistis, amici,
> Non servastis, ait ;————
>
> *Epist.* ii. lib. ii. v. 136.

> He, when his friends, at much expence and pains,
> Had amply purg'd with *hellebore* his brains,
> Come to himself—" Ah ! cruel friends ! he cried,
> " Is this to save me?   Better far have died,
> " Than thus be robb'd of pleasure so refin'd,
> " The dear delusion of a raptur'd mind."—FRANCIS.

In another place, to express a great degree of madness, he
says :

> ————Tribus Anticyris caput insanabile————
>
> *De Arte Poetic.* v. 300.

> ————A head so disordered as not to be curable even by
> three Anticyras————

—the islands of Anticyra, of which there were only two,
being famous for producing great plenty of *hellebore*, and for
the cure of this disorder by a judicious and safe exhibition of so
herculean a remedy.

In one of his Satires, in which he copiously illustrates the
stoical

ture has necessarily confined the treatment of them, and consequently the information which experience

---

stoical doctrine,—" that all are mad who are not wise and vir-
tuous,"—are the following passages :

" Danda est *ellebori* multo pars maxima avaris :
Nescio an Anticyram ratio illis destinet omnem."
Sat. iii. lib. ii. v. 82.

Misers make whole Anticyra their own :
Its *hellebore's* reserv'd for them alone.—FRANCIS.

——Verum ambitiosus et audax.
Naviget Anticyram.—*Ib.* v. 165.

But if your breast with bold ambition glows,
Set sail where *hellebore* abundant grows.—FRANCIS.

OVID, in the fourth book of his " *Epistolæ ex Ponto*," in
the conclusion of the third Epistle, has the following lines :

" Littus ad Euxinum, si quis mihi diceret, ibis,
Et metues arcu ne feriare Getæ ;
I, bibe, dixissem, purgantes pectora succos :
Quicquid et in toto nascitur Anticyra."

To Pontus thou shalt go, whoe'er had said,
And dread the wound from Getan bow that flies ;
Go purge, I had replied, and clear thy head,
Go drink whate'er Anticyra supplies.

PERSEUS alludes to this celebrated medicine for purging the
brain, and curing madness, in the sixteenth verse of his fourth
Satire, where he tells NERO, that, instead of taking upon himself the great and weighty task of government, which demands
much experience, and sound judgment, he ought rather to
take the most powerful medicines to clear his understanding.

B 4 " Anti-

rience alone is capable of affording to a few individuals; and that of those few, by far the greatest number,

———" Anticyras melior sorbere meracas."

Thou hast not strength such labours to sustain :

Drink *hellebore*, my boy, drink deep and purge thy brain.

DRYDEN.

PLINY, in his natural history, gives a pretty long account of both kinds of *hellebore*; from which a short extract will serve to illustrate what has been already quoted above.—" *Nigrum* (hellebori genus) purgat per inferna. *Candidum* autem vomitione, causasque morborum extrahit, quondam terribile, postea tam promiscuum, ut plerique studiorum gratia ad pervidenda acrius quæ commentabantur, sæpius sumptitaverint. CARNEADEM responsurum ZEONIS libris : DRUSUM quoque apud·nos—constat hoc medicamento liberatum comitiali morbo in Anticyra insula. Ibi enim tutissime sumitur, quoniam (ut diximus) *sesamoides* admiscent."—*Lib.* xxv. c. v. p. 457.

" *Black hellebore* purges by stool. But *white hellebore* acts by vomiting, and expels the causes of diseases ;⸱it was formerly dreaded as a violent medicine; but its use in time became so familiar, that it was common for men of study to take it frequently, in order to sharpen the faculties, and enable them more clearly to comprehend the whole extent of·their subject. CARNEADES took hellebore when preparing to answer the writings of ZENO; and we are assured that our countryman DRUSUS—was freed from the epilepsy, by the use of this medicine in the island of Anticyra ; where it is taken with most safety, in consequence of their mixing with it, as I have formerly observed, the herb *sesamoides*."

I shall conclude this long note with the following passage on the same subject from AULUS GELLIUS —" CARNEADES academicus scripturus adversum stoici ZENONIS libros superiora corporis *helleboro candido* purgavit, ne quid ex corruptis in

stomacho

number, have unfortunately been almost totally ignorant of medical matters; For as Insanity of every
species, besides the exhibition of proper medicines,
and an exact attention to regimen, generally requires a particular management, which cannot
easily be accomplished without an appropriate ap-
paratus, a house adapted to the purpose, and servants who have been properly instructed, and
much conversant with such kinds of patients; it
has always been found convenient, and frequently
absolutely necessary, to put unhappy sufferers of
this sort, under the care of those persons, who,
however ill qualified as to the knowledge of medicine, are furnished with the requisite conveni-
ences for their government and safety, and have
made it their particular province to undertake the
confinement of the *Insane*, whatever may be their
pretensions, or abilities, to effect a *cure*.

Medical people, therefore, being in a great

---

stomacho humoribus ad domicilia usque animi redundaret, et
constantiam vigoremque mentis labefaceret : tanta cura tanto-
que apparatu vir ingenio præstanti ad refellenda, quæ scrip-
serat ZENO aggressus est."

CARNEADES the academic, when preparing to answer the
writings of the stoic ZENO, purged himself upwards by means
of *white hellebore*; that there might be no foul humours in his
stomach to overflow the habitation, and injure the *firmness* and
vigour of his mind. With so much care and preparation did a
man of excellent parts enter upon the refutation of ZENO's
writings.—*Vide etiam* HOFFMAN, *Oper.* tom. iii. p. 259, § 11,
12, 13, 14, 15, 16.

measure

measure excluded from this branch of practice,
can have little or no valuable experience in these
disorders ; and of the few whose situations have
afforded ample room for observation in this way,
how small a number have seen it proper to throw
what is so conducive to their private emolument
into the public stock!

I cannot hope, I do not pretend, in the small
compass of this essay, to supply these defects.
To give a true and complete history of *Insanity* in
all its variety of appearances,—to enter minutely
and specifically into the investigation of its causes,
—to lay down clear, exact, and sufficient rules of
prevention,—to invent, and to delineate with accuracy and precision, experienced and efficacious
methods of cure in every species of this disorder,—
would require more than the labour of one man,
or of one age; and whenever it shall be accomplished, must be the object of a much larger treatise than I have any thought of laying before the
public at present. Hereafter I may endeavour
to do something towards the completing of such a
plan ; and I am not without hope that the diligent
observation even of one man, conducted with
a steady attention to so great and important an object, may do more than could be expected when
we take a retrospective view of the small advances
that have hitherto been made, in a series of ages,
by the numbers who have had no such plan in
prospect: at least it is my intention, at some future

ture period, if I have life and health, to offer to
the world as full, and exact a description of the
nature, causes, and *cure* of the *various kinds
of Insanity,* as my small abilities, aided by no
small experience in these deplorable maladies, will
enable me to execute.—This essay will, in the
mean time, sufficiently attain its end, if, by ac-
quainting such of the less informed part of the
public, whom it may most concern, with the great
variety of those disorders which are called by the
general appellation of *Madness, Insanity,* or *Lunacy;* many of which, contrary to what seems
commonly to be imagined, require very different,
and some very opposite methods of cure; it shall
in any degree contribute to put a stop to the
usual practice of imprudently trusting their unhappy friends, who have the misfortune to be
afflicted with so various, terrible, and obstinate a
disease, to the common empirical practice of indiscriminate evacuation, not to mention harsh and
cruel treatment, in the hands of any illiterate pre-
tender:—and if, by more clearly explaining some
points relative to the nature and symptoms of
Madness, by enumerating its several causes, by
cautioning against some which are in a great measure in our own power, and by pointing out probable methods of preventing so humiliating a de-
gradation of our reasoning faculties, it shall not
only tend to eradicate some errors and prejudices
relative to these matters, which have been deeply
rooted,

rooted, and almost universally approved and propagated; and consequently to point out some improvements both in our knowledge, and practice, relative to this disorder; but shall be successful in persuading many of my fellow creatures to that temperance and moderation in the whole of their thoughts and conduct, which will in every respect be conducive to their ease and happiness, and will almost infallibly secure to them those greatest of earthly blessings—a *healthful body,* and a *sound mind.*

It not being the object of my plan to take a complete view of my subject, but only to go through an inspection of some parts of it, and to throw out a few hints and observations which I imagine may not be altogether void of utility; I shall depend much on the candid indulgence of the intelligent reader,—who will not expect a full and elaborate treatise, where but a short essay was intended; which it is presumed, may have its value, though much will necessarily, and from the very nature of the design, be left imperfect;—as a rough sketch, containing only the outlines, and those but rudely marked, and faintly traced, of a future painting, may not be destitute either of use or beauty, though greatly deficient in almost every part, and falling infinitely short of a finished piece.—Such readers, therefore, may find much room for cavilling, who are not disposed to judge with candour; and to whom the triumph of literary

rary ostentation, or the gratification of literary malevolence, can afford more satisfaction than the discovery of truth, or the advancement of the public good.

It may here be proper to observe, that throughout this essay, unless where otherwise expressed, I shall use the words *Madness, Insanity,* and *Lunacy,* as *synonymous terms ;* and as conveying the complex idea of all those disorders, excepting such as shall hereafter be excepted, in which the faculties of the mind are very considerably, if not, principally, or solely affected ;—in which its *imagination is disturbed,* its *affections are perverted,* and its *judgment is depraved.*

SECT.

SECT. II.

INSANITY, especially of the melancholy kind, has been commonly supposed, to prevail so much more in this island than in any other part of Europe, that it has acquired among foreigners the denomination of the *English disease**. How justly,

---

* This opinion of *foreigners*, that the English are peculiarly liable to what he terms *nervous distempers, spleen, vapours*, and *lowness of spirits*, furnished the late Dr. CHEYNE with the title of his book, called, The *English Malady*; the publication of which he had been induced, as he tells us, to hasten, by " the late frequency and daily increase of wanton, and uncommon self-murderers, produced mostly by this *distemper*; and their blasphemous and frantic apologies grafted on the principles of infidels;—to try what a little more just and solid philosophy, joined to a method of cure, and proper medicines could do, to put a stop to so universal a *Lunacy* and *Madness*."—CHEYNE's *English Malady, Preface*, p. 3.

SAUVAGES among the *species* of *Melancholy*, has one under the title of *Melancholia Anglica*, or *English Melancholy*; by which he means that disposition to *suicide* so frequent among the English; and though he allows that the same disposition to *suicide* is not uncommon among what he calls *Melancholy Maniacs*, yet *English Melancholy*, he tells us, differs from all others in being unaccompanied with fury, or any very grievous affliction, and owing its existence merely to *lowness of spirits* and *weariness of life*. This horrid act is chiefly, he says, committed

justly, might be difficult to determine. There is, I believe, some foundation for the supposition; though, perhaps, much less than is generally imagined. This is certain, that it is not uncommon among the French, as their medical writings abundantly testify. I am inclined however to allow that they have less of it, so far as the passions are concerned, than any *other nation* in *Europe;* —I should not, perhaps, greatly err were I to add, than any other *civilized nation* in the *world.*

Some of the most powerful causes of this kind of Insanity are—*religion,—love,—commerce,* and the various passions which attend the desire, pursuit, and acquisition of riches,—every species of *luxury,*—and all violent and permanent attachments whatever.—These causes less affect the French than most other nations.—As to *religion,*

---

mitted by such as have thrown aside *all religion*, and have so little fortitude of mind, as to be incapable of bearing the common afflictions of human life.

" Apud Anglos—frequens est suicidium ob tædium vitæ, quo capti languidi, mœsti, omnium remediorum pertæsi, res suas componunt, testamenta scribunt, amicis per epistolas dein transmittendas valedicunt, et deinde laqueo, veneno, vel alio modo vitæ suæ finem imponunt; quod criminis genus admittunt illi qui religionem omnem exuerunt, et ita debili sunt animo, ut ærumnas vitæ humanæ sustinere nequeant.—Pluribus *maniacis melancholicis* suicidium familiare est; ast *Melancholia Anglica* in hoc discrepat ab aliis, quod sine ullo furore, aut gravi ærumna, ex solo vitæ tædio tranquille mori decernant."—*Nosolog. Method.* tom. iii. Par. i. vol. iv. p. 390.

they

they are much in the same situation with all other true catholics. Pardon for sins of all sorts and sizes, is so easily obtained in every popish country, that very few true believers, as all good catholics undoubtedly are, in the comfortable doctrine of the absolving power of the priesthood, can be supposed to be much troubled with *religious melancholy*. Not to mention that a religion whose chief characteristic is superstition, must be much less apt to produce Melancholy, than one that has less superstition, and more enthusiasm in its composition*. In one the heart and affections

tions

---

* See an excellent paper of Mr. ADDISON's on these two opposite deviations from true religion, in the *Spectator*, vol. iii. No. 201. See also some good observations on the same subject in HUME's Essays, p. 105.—"The Roman Catholic church seems, indeed," says Mr. ADDISON, in the above-mentioned paper, "irrecoverably lost in this particular. If an absurd dress or behaviour be introduced into the world, it will soon be found out and discarded; on the contrary, a habit or ceremony, though never so ridiculous, which has taken sanctuary in the church, sticks in it for ever. A Gothic bishop perhaps, thought it proper to repeat such a form in such particular shoes or slippers; another fancied it would be very decent if such a part of public devotions were performed with a mitre on his head, and a crosier in his hand : to this a brother Vandal, as wise as the others, adds an antic dress, which he conceived would allude very aptly to such and such mysteries, until by degrees the whole office has degenerated into an empty show."

That this superstitious character of modern *christian*, was derived from the idolatrous superstition of ancient *heathen* Rome,

tions are but little concerned ;—in the other they are the first and principal agents. The one is ever furnished with some ready ceremony—some convenient penance—to atone for every transgression,—while the other, though it often elevates its adherents with raptures of assurance, yet, at other times, it depresses and overwhelms them with the deepest despair :—and in both ways, but most frequently in the latter, produces religious Madness.

Even invincible *love*, that has made more madmen in every age and nation than any other passion beside,—perhaps more than all of them together,—can boast, I believe, few such triumphs over the hearts of modern Frenchmen. For, however rapturously they may affect to speak of the *belle passion*, the universal taste for gallantry has almost entirely banished the *tender passion* from among them. *Love*, with them, is almost wholly

Rome, has been displayed at large, with his usual sagacity and elegance, by the late learned Dr. MIDDLETON, in his *Letter from Rome*; where he saw " popery exercised in the full pomp and display of its pageantry; and practising all its arts and powers without caution or reserve."—*See his Works*, vol. v.

How humorously the absurd and childish *vows to their saints*, and other *contemptible superstitions* of the *Roman Catholics* are ridiculed by ERASMUS in his *Naufragium*, and in his *Peregrinatio religionis ergo*, is well known to every schoolboy; and that the ridicule is as just as it is humorous, none can doubt who are acquainted with the character of that elegant writer.

an affair of *art*;—it has more of fancy than passion; and is rather an amusement of the imagination, than a serious business of the heart*.—
                                             This

---

* That this is their true character, might be proved by a
thousand testimonies; and even from the internal evidence of
the very love scenes of their plays, and of their other compositions which relate to love. A few witnesses on this head may
be sufficient for my present purpose.

STERNE alludes to this peculiarity of the French on several
occasions. In one of his letters, written from some part of
France, he has these words : " I make myself believe that I
am in love—but I carry on my affairs quite in the French way,
sentimentally. *L'amour*, say they, *n'est rien sans sentiment*—
Love is nothing without sentiment. Now notwithstanding
they make such a pother about the word, they have no precise idea annexed to it."—STERNE's *Letters*, vol. ii. letter 56,
p. 120.

One of their own countrymen, Mons. DE PINTO, in a letter
to the celebrated Mons. DIDEROT, gives much the same account of the almost total annihilation of real affection among
the French; which he humorously attributes to the universal
passion for card-playing : " The men in those days," says he
(*i. e.* before card-playing was so much in fashion), " not having by means of the talisman of the cards, the opportunity of
satiating their eyes with the charms of women in full counter-
view to them, over the green carpet, friendship and love were
passions; but, at present, thanks to those same cards, there is
little more left than gallantry : there may be found plenty of
acquaintance, and not a single friend; a number of mistresses,
and not one beloved."—*Vide Annual Register for* 1774, p. 188.

These may be considered as sufficient authorities, without
troubling the reader with long extracts from their plays, odes,
songs, and other compositions, in which they exhibit what they
experience when under the influence of what passes with them
                                                            for

This source, therefore, of Insanity, must of course much less affect the inhabitants of France, than of this island, or of any other European country; all of whom seem less disposed to trifle with so serious a passion, than our agreeable, volatile neighbours.

Nor can so many suffer among them, as with us, from the next mentioned cause of Insanity,— *the desire, and prospect, of acquiring riches, or the actual acquisition of them.* Since there can be but little desire, where there is but little hope: and there can be but little hope of attaining riches in a land of slaves, where the bulk and strength of a nation is depressed and impoverished, and commerce and agriculture, the two great sources both

---

for love. If point, conceit, and wit, may be considered as the genuine effusions of passion, it must be acknowledged that they possess it in an eminent degree: but if the tenderness of affection, in a heart of sensibility, so possesses and fills it, as to exclude every idea that is not immediately and closely connected with its object; and is not at leisure to adorn with the tinsel of imagination, the warm, but simple language of the heart; then can they have but small pretensions to the serious passion of love. In the Appendix to the sixty-second volume of the *Monthly Review*, at p. 579, is a very just observation to this purpose. In giving an account of an "*Essai sur la Musique ancienne et moderne,*" by M. De Laborde, it is remarked by the Reviewers, that—" songs are among the characteristical marks, from which an observer will learn much of the genius, spirit, and character of a people, and it will appear from the historico-poetico-musical details, into which our au-

thor

both of national and private wealth, are of course greatly checked, and much obstructed in their operation. This is well known to be the case in France; as it must be, more or less, in every country whose inhabitants, being subject to the will of an absolute monarch, cannot feel that encouraging confidence of the security of property, or that animating boldness of a conscious freedom of project and exertion, which are experienced in a very high degree in this *happy* land of liberty;— *happy* as to the externals of opulence and freedom, had they but enough of sound philosophy, and genuine christianity, to teach them the proper use and intrinsic value of the blessings they enjoy.

It was an observation of the *great* Lord LYT-TELTON, in the year 1735, when residing in France, that " *the mercantile interest had at no time been much considered by the French court* *." It is now, indeed, more attended to; but still the occupation of a merchant is too much held in contempt; and commerce can never flourish there, as it does in this country, while the character of a trader and a gentleman are supposed to be incom-

---

thor here enters, that the French excel other nations in their amorous, satirical, and bacchanalian songs." They add, in a note—" By the word *amorous,* we do not mean *love,* nor any thing out of the sphere of gallantry. It is almost only among the Italian and British bards that love is sung with genuine sensibility."

* See his works, 4to. p. 662.

patible,

patible, and their *noblesse* would rather see their sons idle priests, or needy soldiers of fortune, than industrious and opulent merchants.

And though it is true, that the French nation has of late years, more than formerly, attended to these only eligible means of acquiring opulence,— agriculture, and commerce ; and, while it has improved the former in many respects, has so far pushed the latter, that it is now become very considerable and extensive ; both of which must consequently have some effect in producing this disease, by giving birth to the desires, fears, anxieties, disappointments, and other affections which accompany the pursuit, or possession, of riches ; yet as agriculture is still in a very imperfect state, and flourishes but little among them ; and as their commerce is confined to a much less number of individuals, in proportion to the great extent of country, than in England ; and as they who are concerned in either of them, must be less ardent in their desires, less sanguine in their hopes, and less liable to be elevated by success, or dejected by disappointment, in consequence of the enervating effects of the nature of their government,—which by its perpetual checks and restraints, produces a habit of tame moderation, and patient acquiescence ;—not to mention the easy versatile temper so peculiar to Frenchmen ;—much fewer, in proportion, will suffer from this cause of Insanity in France than among us.

I think

I think I may safely add, that even *luxury*, which is so fruitful a parent of Insanity in this island, has much less influence, because it is much less general, in France. In high life, it is true, they are not less infected with it there, than we are in England ;—but it is by no means so universally diffused among all ranks of people, as it is in this rich, free, and commercial nation. Their lower orders of people know, I believe, but little of it,—and their wretched peasantry nothing at all; thankful if they earn their daily homely morsel, they eat it with cheerfulness,—and know no other luxury than good humour and a good appetite.

But, above all, they are shielded from the attacks of this disorder by that national *lightness of heart*, that *vivacity and volatility of temper*, which will seldom suffer them to fix their attention too long, or their affections too violently, and seriously, upon any particular object. In short, they are too lax in their attachments, and have too much gaiety and versatility, ever to be much troubled with *religious*, *amorous*, or *commercial Melancholy**.

All

---

* STERNE calls them a laughter-loving nation. Lord LYT-TELTON gives a very lively description of this native temper of the French in a letter to his father, from Paris, dated September the 28th, 1729: " Sunday, by four o'clock," says he, " we had the good news of a dauphin, and since that time I have

All these circumstances being taken into the account, it seems not improbable that this disorder is not only much more prevalent in England than in France, but more peculiar to this than to any other country. For even waving the other considerations just enumerated, an *excess of wealth and luxury*, in which perhaps no nation upon earth can vie with this, seems to entitle us to an abundant share of the curse which appears too plainly to be entailed upon their possessors. Whatever may be the cause, we hear of few or no instances of Insanity among barbarous nations, whether ancient or modern: and even among the

---

have thought myself in Bedlam. The natural gaiety of the nation is so improved on this occasion, that they are all stark mad with joy, and do nothing but dance about the streets by hundreds and by thousands. The expressions of their joy are admirable : one fellow gives notice to the public, that he designs to draw teeth for a week together upon the Pont Neuf, gratis."

A late traveller draws the following character of them : " During this and several former expeditions to the Continent, I have studied the manners of the French nation, and have found them volatile, even to a degree of childishness.—It is more uncommon to see the lower sort out of spirits than out at elbows ; for in this country (strange to relate!) the song and the dance are the companions to slavery and poverty. All ranks of men, almost all ages, seek after pleasure, or rather amusement, with a wonderful avidity ; and there are many who debar themselves of necessaries, in order to lavish their *sols* on the *spectacle*, or the *comedie !*"—*Letters from an Officer in the Guards to his friends in England.*—See a similar character of them in the *Guardian*, No. 101, vol. ii. p. 92.

C 4   poorer

poorer and less civilized inhabitants of modern Europe, we hear but little of this disorder; and the little which we do hear of, arises chiefly from a partial attachment to their native soil. This extraordinary disorder, which is termed by the French the *maladie du pays,* and by medical writers *nostalgia,* exists, we are told, in the dismal wilds of Lapland, in the less frequented parts of Germany, and on the bleak mountains of Switzerland.

Even in this island we find Insanity an uncommon disorder, in proportion as wealth and luxury are but little known. In *Scotland,* where the inhabitants in general are neither opulent nor luxurious, Insanity, as I am informed, is very rare: nor is it more frequent in the poorer, and less cultivated parts of Wales. Indeed there can scarcely be a doubt that, where other circumstances are similar, this disorder must be more or less common among any people, as wealth and luxury more or less abound.—This, at least, is certain—that instances of Insanity are, at this day, amazingly numerous in this kingdom;—probably more so than they ever were in any former period:—and I see no other way of accounting for this vast increase of the disorder, than by attributing it to the present universal diffusion of wealth and luxury through almost every part of the island.

This consideration makes the object of our
present

present inquiry a very interesting one to Englishmen. If I shall be so happy as to let in more light upon any part of it; and especially if any thing which I shall advance shall point to a real improvement in the method of cure; towards which all our medical investigations ought, either directly or indirectly, to lead us;—I shall not think my time and labour bestowed in vain.

With this view, I shall now proceed to make some observations on the *nature, kinds, causes,* and *prevention* of Madness; which I shall do under the following heads, and in the following order.— I shall first consider the *definition;* then propose a new method of *arrangement;* and add such descriptions and remarks as may appear necessary for illustrating the meaning, and confirming the propriety of both:—after that I shall give a concise view of the *appearances on dissection, as they are exhibited by* BONETUS and MORGAGNI:—I shall then proceed to examine into the *causes of Madness;* in doing which, I shall have occasion to delineate the most considerable of the *passions,* and to demonstrate their very great influence in producing this disorder;—this will naturally lead me to lay down some *rules for its prevention,* which will chiefly turn on the *due regulation of the passions.*

OF THE DEFINITION AND ARRANGEMENT OF
INSANITY.

INSANITY, or *Madness*, or *Lunacy*, has
usually been considered by medical writers, with
some few exceptions, from the earliest ages down
to the present time, as consisting of two kinds;—
to one of which, they have almost unanimously
given the name of *Melancholy ;* and to the other
that of *Mania,* *Phrensy*, or *Fury*. Of these various names of the latter kind, the most common
is that of *mania ;* the term *phrensy* being more
frequently appropriated to the delirium of a violent fever; and *fury* being used, for the most part,
rather as descriptive of a striking symptom of the
disease, than as a name, or generic term. This
kind answers to the idea which is vulgarly affixed
to our English word *madness ;* and is sometimes
popularly distinguished by the epithets *raving,*
or *raging*, prefixed to the common appellation of
madness.

These two kinds of Insanity have generally
been defined in words to this effect :—

" *Melancholy* is a permanent delirium, without
fury, or fever, in which the mind is dejected,
and timorous, and usually employed about one
object."

" *Mania*

" *Mania* is a permanent delirium, with fury and audacity, but without fever."

In the various *definitions* of Insanity which are to be found in medical writings, some of which I shall presently transcribe, the term *delirium*, or something synonymous, is commonly used. It is however very differently defined by different writers;—by many it is not defined at all ;—and by some it is used, in defining madness, in a sense not very consistent either with the usual definition, or with that which themselves have given, of this variable, and unsettled term.

But notwithstanding this uncertainty in the use of the term delirium, it were easy to transcribe a long list of definitions of melancholy and mania; from the most noted practical writers, both of ancient and modern times, in which it would be seen that they universally borrow from the same source; and that almost every successor of GA-LEN treads with little variation in the footsteps of his master, who himself did not materially deviate from the track which had already been marked out for him by his predecessors, at the head of whom was the great Father of Physic, with those other ancient medical authors whose works are confounded with his.

These early writers, who were not accustomed to deal much in definitions, have, it must be acknowledged, given us no express ones of these disorders; but that their notions concerning them
have

have served as a foundation for the definitions of
their successors, might easily be proved by collecting and comparing such detached passages, relative
to the several kinds of delirium and insanity, as are
to be found in that invaluable body of practical trea-
tises written by various authors, of various merit,
which have come down to us as the works of
HIPPOCRATES ; of which the greatest part are
undoubtedly very ancient, and all of which, whatever may be their deficiencies in point of real
medical science, serve at least to make us acquainted with the opinions of physicians who flourished
long before the time of GALEN.

A very minute inquiry of this kind, with a critical examination of every passage adduced, would
take up more room than would be consistent with
my present plan ; and, after all, might be thought,
perhaps, rather curious than useful. I shall only,
therefore, make a few extracts from the works of
HIPPOCRATES in confirmation of this assertion ;
and content myself with merely referring to some
others which tend to the same purpose.

That permanent fear, and distress, are there
considered as characteristic of melancholy, is
obvious from the twenty-third Aphorism of section the sixth, where he says,—

" If fear or distress continue for a long time,
this is a symptom of melancholy*."

---

* Ἢν φόβος ἢ δυσθυμίη πολὺν χρόνον διατελίῃ, μελαγχολικὸν τὸ τοιοῦ-
τον.—Oper. Omn. p. 1257.

And

And that such fear and distress* are esteemed symptoms of delirium, may justly be inferred from a passage to be quoted at length on another occasion†, in which it is said that—" There is a great simlarity, as to the disorder of mind (παρά-νοια‡), in those who are ill of a phrensy, and those who are affected with melancholy."

Nor is it less obviously deducible from the same passage, if compared with what precedes it‖, and with other passages below referred to, in some of which fever is expressly mentioned as essential to phrenitis §; as well as from many others, in various parts of his works; that he

---

* I make use of the word *distress* in a general and comprehensive sense, as implying grief, dejection, despondency, anxiety, and in short every depressing affection with which the mind may be permanently afflicted: an extent of meaning which seems not unaptly to correspond with δυσθυμίη, which I take to signify a state of mind in which its " healthful tone is impaired, and it with difficulty exerts a due degree of fortitude and constancy." And it may be observed that Aretæus, who is a close imitator of Hippocrates, uses, in his definition of melancholy, a similar, but stronger expression, in the word ἀθυμίη, which seems to imply " a total defect of mental vigour."

† Foesii Hippocr. de Morbis, lib. i. Oper. Omn. p. 460. 50.

‡ Vide Foesii Œconom. Hippocr.

‖ Hippocr. de Morbis, lib. i. Oper. Omn. p. 460. 30—44.

§ Hippocr. de Morbo Sacro. Oper. Omn. p. 309. 1—20. —De Morbis, lib. i. Op. p. 461. 30. lib. ij. p. 486. 30.—De Affectionibus. Oper. Omn. p. 518. 20.

supposes

supposes the delirium of melancholy to be without fever.

That he reckoned mania a kind of delirium, is
clearly expressed in the above passage, to mention
no others :—and that in the idea of maniacal delirium, he comprehended that of violence, is evident from the same passage, and from many more
which might be referred to,—whether he uses the
term *mania*, or its derivatives, as he not unfrequently does, to denote a violent degree of delirium
in a phrenitis, or in any other fever, in opposition
to the slighter degrees with which these disorders
are sometimes accompanied, and which are simply termed παράνοια, παραφροσύνη, παραφρόνησις, or
the like ;—or to indicate that kind of madness
which has since acquired the exclusive title to
that appellation ; which it is plain he understands
to be without fever, and to be distinguished from
melancholy only by the violence or ferocity of
the delirium, by which it is rendered as specifically different from that kind of Insanity, as it is
from phrenitis by the absence of fever*.

GALEN affords us no definition, so far as I
know, which comprehends every characteristic circumstance of delirium, melancholy, or mania ;
but they may all be collected from the following
extracts from LACUNA's epitome of his works:

" The faculty of imagination is sometimes vi-

* Vide Loc. supra citat:—Item HIPPOCR. Aphor. § 3.
Aph. 20, 22. Oper. p. 1246, et § 6. Aph. 56. 1256.

tiated,

tiated, as in delirium. And the reasoning faculty is sometimes injured and depraved; a symptom which is likewise called delirium. For the
most part delirium consists in the union of both
these symptoms, the imagination presenting erroneous images, and reason at the same time
judging amiss. But sometimes it consists in
one of them only. For there are cases in which
reason is injured, while the imagination and memory remain unhurt: and on the other hand, in
which the imagination and memory are vitiated,
and yet reason is unimpaired.

" Sometimes a disordered action of the principal faculties is accompained with fever ; as in
phrensy and lethargy. Sometimes it is without
fever ; as in mania and melancholy.

" Every delirium is a depraved action of a
principal faculty, arising from vitiated humours,
and a disordered temperament of the brain. It is
called *phrensy* if it be accompanied with fever;
but if there be no fever, it is called *mania*. But
alienations of a melancholy kind only, are produced by a cold humour.

" In every alienation of mind, if fear and distress continue for a long time, it is a sign that the
disorder is caused by black bile.

" Whenever that kind of atrabilious humour,
which when thrown up from the stomach by
vomiting has an acid state and smell, abounds in
the substance of the brain, it brings on that species

cies of Insanity which the Greeks call *melancholia*.
As when that other atrabilious humour which
owes its origin to adust yellow bile, is a kind of
feculent part of the blood, is very thick, and not
unlike the lees of wine, abounds in the substance
of the brain; it produces furious Delirium, sometimes with and sometimes without fever*."

CÆLIUS

---

* "Hæc (imaginatrix functio)—interdum—vitiatur, ut in
delirio :—sic ratiocinatio—nunc læditur ac depravatur, quod
symptoma vocant delirium.   Plerunque—in utrisque simul
consistit delirium, tum parum probe imaginando, tum parum
apte ratiocinando.   Est quando duntaxat in altero.   Interdum
quippe ratio vitiatur, imaginatione simul atque memoria illæsa.
Quemadmodum etiam ratione integra, contigit tum imaginationem, tum memoriam vitiari."—*De Symptomatum Differentiis*,
p. 666. 16.

" Interdum vero ubi principales actiones sunt læsæ, febris
quoque accedit : ut in phrenitide et lethargo.   Interdum sine
febre adest vitium : ut in mania et melancholia."—*De Locis
affect.* lib. iii. cap. iii. p. 739. 44.

" Delirium omne, depravatus est principis facultatis motus,
a pravis succis aut cerebri intemperie ortum habens.   Cæte-
rum phrenitis dicitur, si febris adsit ; ut mania si absque febre accidat.   Solæ autem melancholicæ alienationes, a fri-
gidiori succo produci solent."—*De Causis Symptomat.* lib. ii.
p. 683. 13.

" In omnibus autem animi alienationibus, si timor atque
tristilia diu perseverent, atram bilem in causa esse est indi-
cium."—*De Causis Symptomat.* lib. ii. p. 683. 24.

" Ubi vero in ipso cerebri corpore abundat (atra bilis, quæ
vomentibus ipsam et olfacientibus videtur acida) eum Insaniæ
speciem, quem Græci vocant melancholiam, inducit.   Quemadmodum

CÆLIUS AURELIANUS*, and ARETÆUS CAPPA-
DOX†, who probably both lived a little before the
time of GALEN, define melancholy and mania
nearly in the same manner; but the latter adds to
the definition of melancholy—that " the distress
is confined to one object,"—ἔςι δὲ ἀθυμὶη ἐπὶ μιῆ
φανίασίη :—a circumstance in which the example
of ARETÆUS has been followed by JONSTON and
the illustrious BOERHAAVE,—and which, though
far from universal, must be acknowledged to be
neither rare, nor unworthy of attention; and,
therefore GALEN‡ at the same time that he distinctly pointed it out as frequently existing, very
judiciously excludes it from a place in the definition.

Modern writers have, for the most part, strictly
adhered to their masters of antiquity. Of their
scrupulous exactness in copying from these ancient models I shall exhibit a few specimens, and
refer to more which the reader may consult, if he
pleases, at his leisure.

___

madmodum alter atræ bilis succus, qui præassata flava bile
nascitur, [et est veluti fæx sanguinis quæ admodum spissa ex-
istit, fæcibus vini haud absimilis], ferina gignit deliramenta,
modo cum febre, modo absque illa, in cerebri corpore abun-
dans."—*De Locis affect.* lib. iii. cap. iii. p. 741. 16—26.—
Vide etiam Foesi Œconom. HIPPOCR. sub Μανία et Μιλαίχολία.

* Morb. Chronic. lib. i. cap. v. p. 326, et cap. vi. p. 340.
† De Causis et Sign. Morb. Diuturn. lib. i. cap. v. p. 29, E.
et cap. vi. p. 31, A.
‡ De Locis affect. lib. iii. cap. iv. p. 743. 60.

The

The following are modern definitions of delirium:

" Delirium may in general be defined to be a depraved action of the faculties of imagination and reasoning, arising from an impurity of the animal spirits, which gives occasion to the internal representation of some absurd and unreal image to the mind*."

" Delirium is a depravation of the faculties of imagination and reasoning, arising from the internal representation of some absurd and unreal image to the mind✝."

" When the imagination and judgment are depraved, then exists what is called *delirium*,—or a deviation from the path of right reason, in which the sick talk and imagine absurd and improbable things‡."

BOERHAAVE and DE GORTER have ventured to strike out of the common beaten track ; with what success I shall not here examine ; but am

---

* " In genere delirium definiri potest, actio depravata phantasiæ et ratiocinationis, a spiritu impuro, phantasmati absurdo et inconvenienti occasionem præbente."—SENNERTI *Oper. Omn.* tom. iii. p. 84.

✝ " Delirium est phantasiæ et rationis depravatio, a phantasmatis absurdi et inconvenientis oblatione exorta."—JONSTONI *Ideæ Universæ Medicinæ Pract.* lib. viii. p. 388.

‡ " Cum imaginatio, et æstimatio depravatur, delirium accidit, quod dicitur,—declinatio a recta rationis semita, unde ægri absurda, et incongrua loquuntur, aut imaginantur."— TOZZI *Oper. Omn.* tom. i. p. 111.

inclined ·

inclined to suspect, that on a strict inquiry, they would be found to differ more in words, than in reality, from their predecessors:

The former says—" Delirium is the existence of ideas in correspondence with some internal disposition of the brain, and not with external causes; together with the judgment arising from such ideas, and the consequent affections of the mind and actions of the body: and as these exist in various degrees, and are solitary, or combined, they give rise to various kinds of delirium*."

De Gorter tells us that—" when the images arise in the mind while we are awake, in a manner similar to what we experience when dreaming; and it often happens that they do so, and are equally vivid with those which are excited by the senses, or by the will; we are then in a state of delirium. But the cause of delirium seems to be more powerful than that of dreams: for in sleep such erroneous images often present themselves in a state of health, but when we are waking, they always proceed from some morbid cause†."

The

---

* " Delirium est idearum ortus non respondens externis causis, sed internæ cerebri dispositioni, una cum judicio ex his sequente, et animi affectu motuque corporis inde sequente: atque his quidem per gradus auctis, solitariis, vel combinatis, varia deliriorum genera fiunt."—Boerhaavii *Aphor.* § 700.

† " Similia idola somniantium si vigilantes occupant, ut sæpe æque vivida sunt, quam per sensus offeruntur, vel quæ ex

mentis

The late botanical nosologists, if I may so call them, have all, except SAUVAGES, confined the term to the febrile delirium ; and affixed different generic names to the other species. They are almost the only writers who have materially deviated from the ancients ; and they differ from each other no less than from their predecessors. They have all, however, considerable merit ; but especially Dr. CULLEN, who has, in my opinion, greatly improved upon the rest, by an arrangement which is remarkable for the chaste simplicity, and philosophical precision, so conspicuous in whatever proceeds from the mouth or pen of that great modern improver of medical science.

The following definitions of melancholy and mania may serve as a specimen of the close adherence of even the most eminent among the moderns to their ancient masters.

" Melancholy is an alienation of mind, or privation of its faculties, without fever, accompained with fear and dejeétion without any manifest cause*."

---

mentis voluntate concitantur, faciunt hominem delirare : sed causa delirii plus valere videtur, quia in somno sine detrimento sanitatis sæpe, in vigilantibus autem semper a morbosa causa, aliena obrepunt."—DE GORTER *Medicinæ Dogmaticæ,* cap. i. § 5, p. 5.

* " Est autem melancholia mentis alienatio seu desipientia, sine febre, cum metu ac mœstitia sine causa manifesta conjunéta."—PISON. *de cogn. et curand. Morb.* lib. i. c. xxiii. p. 161, tòm. i.

" Melan-

" Melancholy is defined to be a delirium, or depravation of imagination and reason, without fever, and with fear and dejection*."

" Melancholy is a delirium without fever, with fear and dejection†."

" Melancholy is a delirium, arising from the internal representation of some melancholy image, in which the attention of the mind is rivetted to one subject, without fury or fever, and with dejection and fear‡."

" They who are melancholy fall into deep dejection and great fear. Their imagination and reason is also depraved; but in general this depravity is confined to some particular objects, and does not extend to all. The memory is unhurt, and there is no fever. The melancholy are distinguished from other madmen by the existence of fear and dejection, without any obvious cause; whence it has been observed by Hippocrates—that—' if fear and dejection continue for a long time, this is a symptom of melancholy§.' "

" That

---

* " Definitur melancholia quod sit delirium seu imaginationis et rationis depravatio, sine febre, cum timore et mœstitia."—Sennerti *Oper.* tom. iii. p. 90.

† " Melancholia est delirium sine febre, cum timore et mœstitia."—Riverii *Prax. Med.* lib. i. cap. xiv. p. 187.

‡ " Melancholia est dilirium, a phantasmate melancholico exortum, qua detentus, uni cognitationi, absque furore et febre, cum tristitia et metu, inhæret."—Jonstoni *Ideæ Univers. Medicinæ Pract.* lib. viii. p. 390.

§ " Melancholici in profundam mœstitiam, et ingentem timo-

rem

•" That disorder is by some physicians called *melancholy,* in which the patient is long and obstinately delirious, without fever, and almost always intent upon one and the same thought*."

" Melancholy is a fixed imagination, with alie‑ nation of mind, which dwells much upon certain objects, · with permanent anguish, inquietude, fear, and dejection, without any obvious cause; arising from the congestion and stagnation in the brain of a large quantity of blood, which passes with great difficulty through the vessels of that organ†."

" What the Greeks term *mania,* the Latins call *insania,* or more properly *furor,* or *rabies,*

_____

rem delabuntur. In his insuper imaginatio et ratiocinatio depravatur; non tamen plerumque in omnibus, sed in certis solum rerum generibus. Memoria autem firma manet, et fe‑ bris deest. Per id vero a cæteris insanis melancholici inter‑ noscuntur, quod timeant, et mœreant sine causa manifesta, un‑ de HIPPOCRATES, 6 Aph. 23. ' Si timor et mœstitia longo tempore perseverent, judica talem esse melancholicum.'"— TOZZI *Oper.* tom. i. p. 119.

* " Melancholia vocatur medicis ille morbus, in quo æger delirat diu, et pertinaciter, sine febre, eidem fere et uni cogi‑ tationi semper affixus."—BOERHAAVII *Aphor.* § 1089.

† " Melancholia—est firmior cum mente alienata phantasia, certis objectis valde inhærens, cum diuturno animi angore, in‑ quietudine, metu et tristitia sine ulla causa manifesta juncta, a valde difficili sanguinis copiosius in cerebro congesti ac stag‑ nantis per vasa ejus progressu oborta."—HOFFMANNI *Med. Rat. Syst.* tom. iv. p. 4. c. viii. § 7. *Operum.* tom. iii. p. 252.

because

because they who are ill of this disorder are raging, violent, and as ungovernable as savage beasts,—
in a word, mania is a violent alienation of mind,
or delirium, without fever*."

" Mania, or. fury, is a delirium, or depravation of the imagination and reason, without fear,
and rather with audacity, rashness, anger, contention, and violence, without fever, owing its origin
to a hot and fiery disposition of the spirits†."

" Mania is a delirium without fever, with fury
and audacity‡."

" Mania is a permanent emotion of the mind,
with audacity, and violence, without fever, arising from a fiery fervor of the spirits§."

" Though CICERO tells us that the Latins called this disorder *fury*, and the Greeks *melancholy;*

---

* " Μανίαν Græci, insaniam, vel magis proprie furorem, seu
rabiem latini vocant, quod eo malo detenti furibundi, temera-
rii, et ferarum instar effrenes sunt.—Est itaque mania alientio
seu delirium vehemens citra febrem."—PISON. *de cognos. et
curand. Morb.* lib. i. cap. xxiv. p. 173, tom. i.

† " Est—mania, seu furor, delirium, seu imaginationis et
rationis depravatio, sine timore sed potius cum audacia, temeritate, ira, jurgiis, et ferocia, sine febre, a dispositione spiri-
tuum fervida et ignea ortum habens."—SENNERTI *Oper.*
tom. iii, p. 108.

‡ " Mania est delirium sine febre cum furore et audacia."—
RIVERII *Prax. Med.* lib. i. c. xviii. p. 86.

§ " Mania est mentis diuturna, cum audacia et ferocia sine
febre, ab igneo spiritum fervore exorta, emotio."—JONSTONI
Ideæ Univ. Med. Pract. lib. viii. p. 394.

yet

yet physicians, in strictness of speech, give it the appellation of *insanity*, or that kind of delirium, in which the patient is not only affected with a depravity of imagination and reasoning, but is violent and outrageous, and fearing nothing, rashly dares, and indiscriminately attempts, every thing; yet is void of fever, and has the perfect use of his memory*."

" If melancholy increases to such a degree as to be attended with great agitation of the nervous fluid in the brain, by which violent fury is excited, the disorder is then called *mania*†."

" Mania is a violent insanity, accompanied with temerity, and vast exertions of muscular strength; proceeding from a forcible and copious transmission of thick, and melancholy blood, with great heat, through the vessels of the brain. Whereas phrensy is insanity with fever, arising from an inflammatory obstruction in the vessels of the brain‡." I shall

---

* " Quamvis Cicero hanc affectionem Latinos furorem appellasse, et Græcos melancholiam scripserit; proprie tamen medici ipsam dicunt insaniam, seu delirium illud, quo ægri præter imaginationis, et ratiocinationis depravationem, impetunt, furunt, ac nihil omnino formidantes, omnia temere audent, et indiscriminatim aggrediuntur: febre tamen carent, et memoria valent."—Tozzi *Oper.* tom. i. p. 114.

† " Si melancholia eousque increscit, ut tanta accedat agitatio liquidi cerebrosi, qua in furorem agantur sævum, mania vocatur."—Boerhaavii *Aph.* § 1118.

‡ " Mania—est violenta insania cum temeritate et ingenti membro-

I shall not trouble the reader with a minute criticism on these definitions. In what respects they are erroneous, or defective, will, I hope, be rendered apparent by what I shall hereafter advance in the course of these observations. A few cursory remarks, however, may not be improper in this place.

In all the definitions of insanity quoted, and most medical writers agree in giving pretty nearly the same definitions*, it may be observed that

---

membrorum robore conjuncta, a vehementiori sanguinis crassi, copiosi et melancholici per cerebri vasa cum magno æstu transpressione proveniens. Phrenitis denique est insania cum febre, a stasi sanguinis inflammatoria in vasis cerebri orta."—HOFF-MANNI *Med. Rat. Syst.* tom. iv. c. viii. § 7. *Oper.* tom. iii. p. 253.

* Such as choose to see more to the same, or nearly to the same purpose, may consult, among others, the following writers:—CELSI de Medicina, lib. iii. cap. xviii. p. 148, &c.— PAUL. ÆGINET. de re Medica, lib. iii. cap. xiv. p. 19, 39, and p. 20, 22.—PROSPERI ALPINI de Medicina Method. lib. x. c. x. p. 608, and cap. iv. p. 40,—MASSARIÆ Oper. lib. i. cap. xxi. p. 65, and cap. xxii. p. 74.—PLATERI Oper. Medic. tom. i. p. 84, 87, 85.—HORSTII (GEORG. senior) Oper. Medic. tom. iii. p. 38.—DOLÆI Encyclopæd. Medic. lib. i. cap. iii. p. 25, and cap. 22, p. 74.—WILLIS de Anima Brutor. cap. xi. p. 322, cap. xii. p. 344.—PITCARN. Element. Medicinæ, lib. ii. cap. vi. Operum. p. 103, 106.—BURNETI Thesaur. Medic. Pract. lib. xi. § 6. p. 602. § 9. p. 607.—BONETI Polyath. lib. ii. cap. xvii. tom. i. p. 671, and cap. xviii. p. 696.—DE GORTER Medicin. Dogmat. c. i. § v. p. 6.— HEISTERI Compend. Medicin. cap. xiv. § 23, 24, 25, p. 108. MEAD's Works, vol. iii. p. 41,—HOME Princip. Medicinæ, part ii. cap. vi. p. 225.

the

the term *delirium*, or something synonymous, is universally adopted. It is, however, as we have just seen, very differently defined by different writers ;—by many it is not defined at all ;—and by none so perfectly as might be wished. For most writers, while they adhere to the common definitions of delirium, and insanity, describe such sorts of insanity, in enumerating the particulars, as have nothing in common with the delirium of a fever: though none of them, in their definitions, except Aretæus, make any other difference between the delirium of a phrensy, and that of insanity, than what arises from the presence or absence of fever; as may be seen in the above extracts from Galen and his followers. Hoffman, in endeavouring to derive the distinctions from the difference of the proximate causes, has not perhaps done much better: and two other celebrated moderns, Boerhaave and De Gorter, in attempting to surpass, have rather fallen short of the ancients ; since their definitions, or at least that of De Gorter, are strictly applicable only to those species of delirium, which I shall hereafter define under the title of *ideal delirium*, whereas there are several species of insanity, which rank under another sort of delirium, in which there is nothing similar to what these writers have defined delirium to be.

It may be proper farther to observe, that there are species of insanity, and those not only fre-

quently

quently to be met with, but of various kinds, in which there is neither dejection nor audacity; and which consequently neither come under the description of mania, nor of melancholy. ·

· The learned Dr. Lorry has, indeed, attempted some new, and ingenious, definitions of insanity, in which he has taken no notice either of deli- rium, or fever, and though he has retained dejec- tion, or what he calls imbecility of mind, by which he means to express the αθυμία of Aretæus, as a specific symptom of melancholy, he has rejected audacity as not essential to mania.   But while he has in some respects laid aside the language of the ancients; his attachment to their opinions has so influenced his judgment, that his defini- tions will be found, on a close examination, to re- present, in fact, nothing more than the melan- cholia and mania of the Greek physicians, under the disguise of a new, and more showy dress.— They are as follows :—

" We shall define melancholy," says he, " to be an imbecility of mind, occasioned by a vitiated habit of body, in which we are so strongly af- fected, either by external objects, or by such as are formed merely by the power of imagination, as to be incapable of resisting, of withdrawing the attention from, or of overcoming by reason, the ideas thence arising*."

" Insa-

---

* " Melancholia—a nobis definietur, illa mentis imbecil-
                                                    litas

" Insanity, or mania, is that disordered state of
the body, in which the judgments arising from
the senses, in no degree correspond with each
other, or with the objects represented*."
But though insanity has almost universally been
divided into these two kinds, which have usually
been considered as so perfectly distinct, as to derive their origin from very different and distinct
causes ; one of which, according to GALEN, may
properly be called *atra bilis,*—" atque vomentibus
ipsam et olfacientibus videtur acida†,"—" and
when thrown up from the stomach, has an acid
taste and smell :"—while the other " is a kind of
feculent part of the blood, very thick, and not
unlike the lees of wine ; is without any acid quality,—and ought rather to be called *succus*, or
sanguis melancholicus, than *atra bilis‡ :"*—yet they

---

litas [αθυμία] a corporis vitiato habitu oriunda, in qua fortiter
concutimur ab objectis, aut externis, aut ab imaginandi vi ef-
fectis, ita ut jam impossibile sit ideis inde natis obsistere, ab
iis avelli, aut contra rationi tendere."—*De Melancholia, Intro-*
duct, p. 3,

    * " Insania, sive mania, est corporis ægrotantis conditio illa,
in qua judicia a sensibus oriunda nullatenus aut sibi inter se, aut
rei repræsentatæ responsant,"—*De Melancholia,* part ii. cap. vi.
Articul. prim. p. 361.

    † De Locis affect. lib. iij. cap. iii. LACUNÆ Epitom. p. 741,
l. 20.

    ‡ Est veluti fæx sanguinis, quæ admodum spissa existit,
fæcibus vidi haud absimilis—neque ulla acida qualitate partici-
pat ; et potius melancholicus aut succus aut sanguis, quam atra
bilis dicenda est."—*Ibid.* LACUNÆ *Epitom.* p. 741, l. 17 & 25.

                                                    are

are by no means so absolutely, and universally, distinct and unconnected diseases, as so distinct an origin, and such different symptoms, would lead one to imagine; and indeed it has been observed by ARETÆUS CAPPADOX*, ALEXANDER TRAL-LIANUS†, BOERHAAVE‡, and perhaps one or two more, that the one is frequently generated by the other.

Mania, however, is not always, as BOERHAAVE, after ARETÆUS and TRALLIAN, asserts, " *melan-choliæ proles*"—the offspring of melancholy;—since it often begins originally, without any pre-ceeding melancholy; and is on such occasions, sometimes the parent, instead of being the off-spring of that species of delirium.

Even during the course of the same illness, it not unfrequently happens that mania and melan-choly alternate repeatedly with each other; so that each in its turn generates, and is generated; is, in the language of BOERHAAVE, both parent and offspring.

Both also, notwithstanding that the definitions almost universally contain the words—" *sine fe-bre*,"—" without fever," or others to the same

---

* Δοκίει τὶ δὲ μοι μανίης τὶ ἔμεναι ἀρχὴ καὶ μέρος ἡ μελαχχολίη.—*Morb. Diuturn.* lib. i. c. v, p. 29, E.

† Nihil enim aliud est insania, quam melancholiæ ad majo-rem feritatem intensio.—*De Arte Medica*, lib. i. cap. xvii. HALLERI *Art. Med. Princip.* tom. vi. p. 86.

‡ Aph. 1119.

purpose,

purpose, are frequently accompained with fever, and have nightly exacerbations; especially mania. It is a fever, however, of a peculiar kind, and in no degree proportioned to the delirium.

And yet these definitions, as they have been so generally adhered to, must have been commonly looked upon as complete; or, at least, as very sufficient for the purposes of the practical physician. And, in fact, to one or other of these two genera, every species of madness has usually been referred;—with what propriety the reader will judge, after attentively considering what follows, and comparing it with the above definitions and observations.

It must be acknowledged, indeed, that there are some small deviations from these established definitions, besides those already mentioned, to be met with in the writings of practical physicians; especially when they come to enumerate the various symptoms of insanity. They have controverted the propriety of some parts of the definitions; and have hinted at a suspicion of a greater variety of species: but at the same time that they have perceived some few rays of truth, they have not had the courage to follow a light, of which they had discovered so small a glimmering*.

It appears wonderful that they did not examine

---

* BROEN Animadv. Medic. in REGII Prax. Med. lib. i. § 14, p. 137. Note a, § 15, p. 147. Note a, p. 148. Note i, BELLINI De Morb. capit. p. 508.

farther

farther—that they did not entirely reject definitions, and distinctions, so little consistent with appearances; which were originally built upon a
theory, of which the blindness of attachment
to established doctrines alone could prevent even
the earlier writers from perceiving the imper-
fection; and whicn the modern discoveries relative to the structure, functions, and economy of
the human body, might have taught them, have
but a very slender foundation in truth.

Having thus taken a general view of the definitions, and divisions of delirium, and insanity,
most commonly adopted; I shall now proceed to
inquire, how these disorders may be better defined, and the several species of insanity more
completely enumerated, and more accurately distinguished.

The sources of human knowledge have been
reckoned by the great Mr. LOCKE, to be two, *sensation*, and *reflection;* and consequently the objects about which the faculties of the human mind
may be employed, to be also of two kinds, one
comprehending, what may be called *objects of sensation*, and the other *objects of reflection**.

Objects of sensation are, all material objects and
their sensible qualities; and their representations
in the mind are properly called *ideas* or *images*.

Objects of reflection are, whatever the mind

* See LOCKE's Essay on Human Understanding, book ii.
chap. i. vol. i. p. 144.

perceives

perceives or discovers, or thinks it perceives or discovers, by the exercise of its faculties in considering the powers, properties, and relations, of material and sensible objects, or its own operations. Such perceptions and discoveries, real or imaginary, may with propriety be called *notions*.

This division, though apparently, and nominally, the same, is, in reality, considerably different from that of Mr. Locke; and nearly resembles that of Dr. Hartley, and though it may possibly be thought by some, to be less philosophical, it is, however, better adapted to explain my own particular views, in the present inquiry. The former derives from sensation,—ideas of sensation; and from reflection,—ideas of reflection: the latter calls those ideas which resemble sensations, *ideas of sensation:* and all the rest *intellectual ideas**. Whereas I confine the term *idea* to the immediate representation in the mind of objects of sensation only : and though I have adopted Locke's division into these two sources of knowledge, yet I am inclined to believe, with Hartley, that all we know is originally derived from sensation; which indeed Mr. Locke himself seems, in fact, to grant, in several parts of his essay ; and even of his second source, he observes, that " though it be not sense, as having nothing to do with external objects; yet it is very like it,

---

* Observations on Man, vol. i. Introduction, p. 2.

and

and might properly enough be called *internal sense**."

The following are HARTLEY's observations upon LOCKE's two sources of our ideas.

" First, says he, it appears to me that all the most complex ideas arise from sensation; and that reflection is not a distinct source, as Mr. LOCKE makes it.

" Secondly, Mr. LOCKE ascribes ideas to many words, which, as I have defined idea, cannot be said to have any immediate and precise ones; but only to admit of definitions. However, let definition be substituted instead of idea, in these cases, and then all Mr. LOCKE's excellent rules concerning words, delivered in his third book, will suit the theory of these papers.

" As to the first difference, which I think may be called an error in Mr. LOCKE, it is, however, of little consequence. We may conceive, that he called such ideas as he could analyze up to sensation, ideas of sensation; the rest ideas of reflection, using reflection as a term of art, denoting an unknown quantity. Besides which it may be remarked, that the words which, according to him, stand for ideas of reflection, are, in general, words that, according to the theory of these papers, have no ideas, but definitions only. And thus the first

---

* LOCKE's Essay on Human Understanding, book ii. chap. i. vol. i. p. 147.

diffe-

difference is, as it were, taken away by the second;
for, if these words have no immediate ideas, there
will be no occasion to have recourse to reflection as
a source of ideas ; and, upon the whole, there is
no material repugnancy between the consequences
of this theory and any thing advanced by Mr.
LOCKE.

" The ingenious Bishop BERKELEY has justly
observed against Mr. LOCKE, that there can be
no such thing as abstract ideas, in the proper
sense of the word idea. However, this does not
seem to vitiate any considerable part of Mr.
LOCKE's reasoning. Substitute definition for idea
in the proper places, and his conclusions will hold
good in general*."

We see, by this extract, that the difference between LOCKE and HARTLEY is not very great.
While the former makes two sources of our
ideas, sensation and reflection, he not only allows
that the latter is a kind of sensation, but even
makes it dependent on the other ;. since he asserts
that we can have no ideas till we begin to have
sensations.

But though it be granted, that sensation is the
instrument, which furnishes the mind with means
and materials, if not with the objects, of all its
knowledge ; without which it would be but like
" white paper, void of all characters, without any

---

* Observations on Man, vol. i. p. 360.

.. ideas,"

ideas," in a word, little better than a non-entity ;—
yet mere sensation is so .passive a thing, that a
very low degree of knowledge only could be derived
from so scanty a fountain ; and man without some
more copious source,—without some capacity of
turning to good account the information which he
receives from his senses,—would seem to be in a
state, and to possess powers, not at all superior to
those of the meanest animal.   Now man appears
to me to have such a capacity in what more peculiarly deserves the name of *reflection.*

For it may be observed of sensation and reflection, that the one seems to be merely a passive,
and the other partly a passive and partly an active
state of the mind : that when the latter is passive,
it might with more propriety be called internal
sensation or perception; and that only when active,
it can with strictness be denominated *reflection.*

And though it must be acknowledged that this
active state of the mind is much influenced by,
and seems, indeed, in a great measure, if not altogether, to owe its existence to the passive: yet
such is the nature and constitution of the mind,—
of this " *divinæ particula auræ*"—that while it is
capable of sensation and perception, that is, while
it can be said to exist, it can scarcely for a moment be merely passive ; for as whatever objects
present themselves to its view, whether externally
or internally, are all perhaps in some degree, directly, or by association, agreeable or disagree-

E 2   able,

able, the mind must have a perpetual motive, of some kind or other, for the exertion of its active powers, and must ever be engaged in the pursuit or avoidance of what it likes or dislikes, relative to knowledge, virtue, or pleasure.

In other words, the active state of the mind, and the active powers, in the immediate exertion of which such active state consists, seem originally, and perpetually, to depend on the passive, or perceptive, as an exciting cause, without the incessant instrumentality of whose stimulation and excitement, they would soon cease to be: the exercise of the understanding, will, and affections, all depending upon sensation, external or internal, of truth or falsehood, good or ill, pleasure or pain: in short, all our ideas or notions, however distant they may appear to be from any suspicion of such an origin, deriving their existence primarily from mere sensation.—"If it be asked," says that sagacious philosopher Mr. Locke, "when a man begins to have any ideas? I think the true answer is, when he first has any sensation. For since there appear not to be any ideas in the mind, before the senses have conveyed any in, I conceive that ideas in the understanding are coeval with sensation: which is such an impression or motion, made in some part of the body, as produces some perception of the understanding. It is about these impressions made on our senses by outward objects, that the mind seems first to employ itself

in

in such operations as we call *perception, remembering, considering, reasoning,* &c.*"

The faculty of perceiving material objects, and their grosser qualities, by means of the senses, we possess in common with brutes: but the power of comparing and arranging their several relations and properties, and of reasoning analogically concerning them ; the power of abstraction ; and that reflex action of the mind by which it is enabled to review its internal treasures, and to contemplate its own faculties and operations; which lead to the discovery of almost an infinity of new truths and probabilities; and are the inexhaustible sources of every species of knowledge ; are, in a great measure, the exclusive privilege of man.

About the former it is obvious that the mind can err, in any considerable degree, only by some defect in the bodily organs, whether natural or acquired, permanent or transient.

About the latter it may err from a variety of causes ; which might all, perhaps, not unaptly be arranged under the following heads:—a natural incapacity, or habitual deficiency of attention,—weakness of memory,—too great activity, and indulgence of imagination,—depravity of will,—excess of passion, which is the natural consequence of them all—and disease of body.

---

* Essay on Human Understanding, book ii chap. i. § 23, vol. i. p. 162.

These

. These errors may be very considerable, and unreasonable, without constituting madness :—to
deserve that appellation, they must appear of a
certain magnitude, and under certain circumstances and limitations, which I shall now proceed
to point out. It must, however, be acknowledged,
that it is frequently difficult, especially with regard to the latter sort of mental errors, exactly to
define where folly ends, and insanity begins.

" The mind may be said to be delirious when
it supposes sensible objects to exist externally,
which exist, as they then appear to the mind,
only in idea:—or as such notions about objects
which it sees, hears, or otherwise perceives, or
knows, as appear obviously false, or absurd, to
the common sense and experience of the sober
and rational part of mankind.—Delirium, therefore, may naturally be divided into two kinds:—
the one, arising from an error in our ideas, I call
ideal delirium; and the other, arising from an
error in our notions, I call *notional delirium.*"

The former kind of delirium is common both
to fever and madness;—the latter, I am inclined
to believe, is peculiar to madness,—and suspect
that whenever any degree of it is to be observed
in the delirium of a fever, it portends that it will
probably end in madness.

That the delirium of the true phrensy, and
other high degrees of febrile delirium, are of the
ideal kind, is obvious to the most superficial ex-
aminer;

aminer; but that the slighter degrees, which chiefly affect the patient, on first waking out of sleep, with absence, muttering, wandering, rage or terror; which greatly abate, or cease altogether, as the remaining effects of sleep are dissipated; are all likewise of the ideal kind, is not at first view so obvious: but upon a stricter scrutiny, we may perceive that these symptoms arise chiefly from delirious images in the brain, which being but slightly impressed, while the brain is but slightly affected, are only vivid during sleep, which shuts out the glare of external objects; and gradually vanish as sleep gives place to waking; just as dreams of children often continue for a while after they are apparently awake, their senses being with difficulty roused, and drawing off the attention by slow degrees from the ideal picture presented during sleep, to the real representation of surrounding objects.

If what has been advanced be just, I may now, with some degree of clearness and precision, proceed to define insanity; and to enumerate, and describe such of its species as have fallen under my own observation, or have been noticed by other medical writers.

Insanity, as well as delirium, may be considered as divisible into two kinds; one of which may be called *ideal*, and the other *notional insanity*.

" IDEAL INSANITY is that state of mind in which a person imagines he sees, hears, or otherwise per-

ceives, or converses with, persons or things, which
either have no external existence to his senses at
that time ;—or have no such external existence as
they are then conceived to have:—or, if he perceives external objects as they really exist, has yet
erroneous and absurd ideas of his own form, and
other sensible qualities:—such a state of mind
continuing for a considerable time; and being unaccompanied with any violent or adequate degree
of fever."

Insanity of this sort is sometimes attended with
fear, sometimes with audacity, sometimes with
neither; and may be either constant,—remittent,
—or intermittent.—The constant has no very ob-
servable, nor any regular remissions:—the remittent usually grows milder once in twenty-four
hours, generally in the day-time, and has exacerbations in the evening:—the intermittent has
considerable lucid intervals; and as the paroxysms
of this sort of madness have been commonly supposed to obey the full and change of the moon, it
has therefore been peculiarly distinguished by the
name of *lunacy*;—a name which has, however,
been indiscriminately extended to every species
of insanity.

" NOTIONAL INSANITY is that state of mind in
which a person sees, hears, or otherwise perceives
external objects as they really exist, as objects of
sense; yet conceives such notions of the powers,
properties, designs, state, destination, importance,

manner

manner of existence, or the like, of things and persons, of himself and others, as appear obviously,
and often grossly erroneous, or unreasonable, to
the common sense of the sober and judicious part
of mankind. It is of considerable duration; is
never accompanied with any great degree of fever,
and very often with no fever at all."

Notional, like ideal insanity, may be either
with 'or without fear or audacity: it is usually
constant;—but in some cases it remits—and
even intermits,—though for the most part with
great uncertainty and irregularity.

Insanity is easily distinguished from the temporary and transient delirium of intoxication, whether occasioned by wine, opium, or any other
inebriating substance,—from the delirium which
sometimes accompanies hysteric fits,—and others
of a like nature;—not by a knowledge of the
cause, but by the duration of the delirium:—for
even the delirium arising from any of these causes
becomes insanity, if it continue long after the original exciting cause hath ceased to act. Thus
intoxicating substances may not only produce
transient delirium, as is usually the case; but
sometimes, either in a brain predisposed to insanity, or when taken to great excess, or when the
intoxication has been frequently and habitually repeated, their pernicious effects may be more permanent; and indeed it too often happens that
actual madness, of various kinds, as circumstances
may

may chance to determine, is the dreadful consequence of this kind of intemperance.

IDEAL INSANITY may be either *phrenitic* or *not
phrenitic.*

In *phrenitic insanity* the mind may either be
employed about one set of ideas and notions, in
which case some particular affection is generally
concerned,—as love, avarice, fear, terror, and the
like;—or it may be agitated with various ideas,
notions, and affections indiscriminately.—The
latter state usually accompanies phrenitic insanity,
when it seizes suddenly, and is occasioned by some
bodily disorder.—The former most commonly attends it when it is the consequence of notional
insanity; or of any long continued and intense
attention, exertion, or passion of the mind.—But
both states are in some measure common to all
these sources of insanity; as is also a very high
degree of delirium, in which the patient's imagination has so lively an ideal picture for ever in
view, as overcomes, and confounds, the impressions made by external objects; so that he scarcely
perceives any person or object about him; or is
apt to perceive them erroneously, and to mistake
one person or object for another.

When ideal insanity is not phrenitic, it is either
maniacal, or incoherent, or sensitive.

In *maniacal insanity* the mind may, in like
manner, be employed either about one set of
ideas, or about more than one;—but in this
                                              respect

respect it essentially differs from phrenitic insanity, that though the patient raves, and has a world of images floating in the brain, which, as in a dream, or in a reverie, appear to be real objects; yet when he attends to the external objects which surround him, he readily distinguishes every thing, and every person about him.

In *incoherent insanity* the trains of ideas are either sluggish and interrupted, or too slightly connected, or pass in too rapid a succession. The mind is seldom, if ever in this species of insanity, confined to any one particular set of ideas; in the two first of these states it borders upon idiotism, or has actually arrived at it; and in the last, in some instances, it approaches to phrenitic insanity, and in others is but an aggravation of some of the species of notional insanity.

When ideal *insanity* is *sensitive*, as in lycanthropia, cynanthropia, and in some cases of what is commonly called hypochondriacal melancholy, in which the diseased imagines himself to be a wolf, or a dog, or a tea-pot, or fancies that he is made of glass, or of wax, or the like, the mind is chiefly employed about one idea.

In NOTIONAL INSANITY the mind may either be employed about one particular notion, or passion; or may take a larger scope, and range through a variety of absurd notions and affections. And in both cases may be either cheerful, or melancholy, according to the nature of its object.

In

In the former kind, or when the mind is employed about one object, the delirium may, in some instances, appear glaringly absurd;—as when a man supposes himself, though a mortal, to have the command and regulation of the elements,—to be a dead corpse,—to have no soul like other men,—to be capable of flying,—of working miracles,—or the like; in all which cases it usually borders upon ideal insanity :—or it may appear plausible ; so that not only the mind may impose upon itself,—but, when the disorder is not very violent, or extravagant, even others may be imposed upon, by the apparent reasonableness of the notion, or affection, which possesses it, and which arises from some seemingly real and just cause, and appears, at most, only to err in being quite disproportioned to it ;—as in love, jealousy, suspicion, timidity, irresolution, superstition, despair, avarice, misanthropy, nostalgia, and all inordinate desires and affections :—or it may obviously arise from a diseased state of the natural appetites, producing an ungovernable inclination to indulge them, and incessantly exciting in the mind a lively notion of the felicity of such indulgence.

The latter, or that kind of notional insanity which is not confined to any one particular notion, or passion, may likewise be considered as either plausible, or grossly absurd ; and comprehends all the varieties of what I shall hereafter describe under the names of whimsical, fanciful, impulsive, scheming,

scheming, self-important, and hypochondriacal insanity; which manifest themselves in almost every
kind of unaccountable whim, or wild and extravagant fancy; in an invincible inclination to pursue
every impulse of passion, or imagination; in self-
importance, and vanity; in wit, vivacity, and cunning; in laughing, singing, talking, waggery, bragg-
ing, and lying; in fondness for scheming and traffic of the most romantic, extravagant, childish,
or absurd kind; in attributing great effects to little
causes, and great causes to little effects; in melancholy without any fixed, and determinate object, or what is called *tædium vitæ*, arising from a
general impression of dejection on the mind, which
renders it totally incapable of relishing any of
those things whence mankind usually derive their
happiness.

Insanity, or delirium, according to the above
account of them, cannot with propriety be said to
exist, but where the JUDGMENT is deceived, the
AFFECTIONS are misguided, or the CONDUCT is
perverted by some delusive perception, or some notion palpably erroneous, or absurd; but the several faculties of the mind are liable to various other
disorders, of no inconsiderable magnitude and importance, besides those which, strictly speaking,
deserve these appellations.

The MEMORY may be defective, and even sometimes almost annihilated, either from a diminished,
or from an increased activity of certain fibres and
vessels

vessels of the brain, on whose prompt and regular
vibrations, in due subserviency to the sound operation of all the faculties of the mind, the perfection of its exertions in a great measure consists.
Their diminished activity may either consist in
an almost total privation of power ; or in a languid
uniformity of action : and their increased activity
in such quick transitions as give rise to ideas in
such order and succession that they appear to have
little or no proper connexion ; or in such vigorous exertions as produce rapid, but naturally and
obviously connected trains of ideas. .In the one
case there exists a stupid vacancy, or an indolent
uniformity ; and in the other a busy incoherency,
or an animated velocity of ideas. Hence arise four
different states of the mind, all of which are apt,
more or less to affect the memory, and some of
which universally, and infallibly, impair it. Either
there is almost a total incapacity of receiving, at least
of retaining, any idea at all, much more of receiving,
and retaining, any thing that deserves the name
of a train of ideas :—or the mind is in such a tor-
pid state, as disposes it indolently to dwell on some
one object, which has at present obtained its attention, or something like its attention, keeping
it perpetually in the same point of view, rarely
turning it into any new position, and never so far
exerting itself as to bring its different views and
positions together in review, and to compare them
with each other,—a state of which every man
must

must have had some little experience, either in the
absence of a reverie, on the approach of sleep, or
in those disagreeably uniform dreams which often
attend on fevers, or other disordered states of
the body :—or the original associations of the
mind may be so deranged, and its ideas incessantly obtrude themselves with so little connexion,
as may be altogether incompatible with that due
command of recollection in which memory properly consists:—or the mind may be so fully employed by its own rapid succession of ideas, as
scarcely to attend to any thing else but the fleeting
images of the passing instant.

The MEMORY and IMAGINATION are so nearly
alike in their operations, so intimately connected,
and so perfectly dependent on each other, that in
many respects they are scarcely to be distinguished,
and are, consequently, often confounded : it is,
therefore, no wonder, that faculties so similar
should be liable to similar disorders ; and that in
all the cases just enumerated, the memory and
imagination should suffer together, and both faculties be in like manner affected.—In the first case,
as there are few ideas, and still fewer, and those
very imperfect trains ; so there may truly be said to
be no imagination.—In the second, the inactive
state of the brain, as it is unfavourable to the memory and recollection, so it stupifies and deadens
the imagination.—In the third, there is an activity
of the imagination of a peculiar kind, in which the
ideas

ideas are so slightly connected, and seem so little
indebted for their appearance to the usual ties of
association, and so almost totally free from the
control of the other powers of the mind, as to appear for the most part perfectly incoherent.—In
the fourth case, as there are often appearances of
surprising memory, at the same time that there
can be no dependence on the certainty of the
operations of that faculty, while they are so little
under the influence of the governing powers of the
mind; so, for the same reason, in similar states of
mental activity, we are often astonished with the
wonderful effulgence of sudden flashes of a rapid
imagination, but rarely delighted with the steady
light, and permanent splendor, which are displayed
in a regular and vigorous, but not too accelerated,
exertion of that faculty.

All these states may be connected with, but
do not constitute an essential part of madness.
When they are either constantly, or occasionally,
accompanied with absurd notions, or delusive
images, they are then to be arranged under some
of the species of that disorder, as the symptoms may
happen to determine. Otherwise, the three first
states are to be considered as so many distinct
kinds of idiotism :—and may be termed the *stupid*,
in which scarcely the trace of a thinking soul remains ;—the *absent*, in which the mental powers
are benumbed, and the attention is with difficulty
removed from one object to another ;—and the

inco-

incoherent, in which the associated trains of ideas
are deranged and confounded, and the powers and
operations of the mind weakened, and obstructed,
by the disorderly intrusion of ideas which are very
slightly, or improperly, or not at all connected.—
The *fourth state* is an approach to madness.

The three first states of the imagination, or the
stupid, absent, and *incoherent idiotism,* though
essentially different from insanity, yet so far agree
with it, that arising nearly from the same causes
with some of its species, hereafter to be mentioned,
they are to be cured, if curable, by the same means.

The fourth, or *usually active state of the imagination,* so often to be met with in men of
genius, and of lively feelings;—or the ridiculous
absences of literary and studious men, more conspicuous for their attachment to science and lite-
rature, than for real abilities to comprehend and
improve them, which have some resemblance to
the third state;—though bordering upon madness,
or idiotism, in which they are but too apt to terminate; are yet readily distinguishable from madness by the circumstances already mentioned; and
the latter from idiotism by the degree, the causes,
and the remissions of the malady: as are the common follies and absurdities of mankind from notional insanity, by their frequency, and almost uni-
versality;—unless we are disposed to think that
in reality there is no essential difference, that all
mankind deserve to be reckoned in the same class

of

of insanity, and that it was not more severely, than truly, asserted by a very able satirist—that—

" Tous les hommes sont fous : et malgre tous leurs soins,
" Ne different entre eux que du plus ou du moins *."

" All men are mad, and, spite of all finesse,
" The madness differs but in more or less."

But, however this may be, it is certain that there is a great similarity between folly, and notional insanity ; and especially that species of it which I have denominated pathetic. For as ideal insanity consists in the appearance of unreal, or erroneous images, to the mind; so notional insanity is owing to erroneous associations, in which consists the very essence of the erroneous notions both of the madman and of the fool :—but, perhaps, with this difference, that the erroneous notions of the fool are confined to the estimation of good and evil, only; whereas those of the madman extend to the estimation of cause and effect, and, indeed, to that of every other relation of things, about which a disordered brain is liable to form erroneous associations.

All the kinds of insanity, above enumerated, may be variously combined, and frequently interchange one with another. If of long standing, they are generally incurable ; and in a course of time, unless death prevent the melancholy spectacle, usually degenerate into idiotism ; a most pitiable privation of the human faculties, in which

* BOILEAU, Satire iv, tom i. p. 27.

the

the memory and imagination, as we have just seen,
are often so debilitated, and irregular, as to sink
the man, in almost every respect, even below the
level of the brute creation ; not only by depriving
him of reason, but even in a great measure of the
proper use of his senses, and of instinct, which,
so far as the well being of mere animal life is concerned, might in some degree supply its place.

Notional delirium, as I have already observed,
seems to be peculiar to madness ; and I am sorry to
find myself under the necessity of so far agreeing
with the satirist, as to assert, that the bulk of
mankind, morally, at least, I will not say medically speaking, are more or less affected by it.—
There is, indeed, some difficulty in determining
the boundaries between what may not improperly
be called *moral* and *medical* insanity. Several of
the ancient philosophers, and particularly Socrates, and the stoics, considered every foolish, or
vicious person, as insane, or morally mad ; and only
to be distinguished from the actually and medically mad, by the degree of disorder*,—the symp-

* " Hanc enim insaniam, quæ juncta stultitiæ patet latius,
a furore disjungimus.—Insaniam enim censuerunt [duodecim
tabulæ] constantia id est sanitate vacantem : posse tamen tueri
mediocritatem officiorum, et vitæ communem cultum, atque
usitatum."—*See the passage from* Cicero, *at length, immediately following in the text.*
" For we separate from fury, this sort of insanity," &c.

toms

toms of fury*, by which they understood what I
have called *ideal madness*, and especially those
species termed *phrenitic, incoherent*, and *maniacal*,—and the obvious existence of some bodily
cause†:—as may be collected, to mention no
other authorities, from the following passage of
Cicero's third book of Tusculan Disputations‡.

" All fools are disordered in mind ; all fools,
therefore, are insane: for it is the opinion of
philosophers, that sanity, or health of mind, consists in a certain tranquility, and equanimity, or,
as they term it, constancy; and they consider
the mind, when void of these qualities, as insane ;
since sanity can no more exist in a disordered
mind, than in a disordered body.—Nothing, therefore, can be better than the common mode of

---

.* " Furorem autem esse rati sunt mentis ad omnia cæcitatem. Quod cum magis esse videatur quam insania; tamen
ejusmodi est, ut furor in sapientem cadere possit, non possit insania."—*Ibid.*

" But they esteemed fury to be an universal blindness of
mind, with regard to all sorts of objects. Now though fury
appears to be of greater magnitude than insanity, it is yet of
such a nature, that a wise man may become furious, but cannot be insane."

† Which they termed *atrabilis.*—" Quasi vero atra bili solum mens, ac non sæpe vel iracundia graviore, vel timore, vel
dolore moveatur !"—*See the same passage from Cicero.*

" As if the mind could be deranged only by atrabilis." &c.

‡ Cap. iv, and v.

speaking

speaking in the Latin language, when we say, that they who are carried away either by ungovernable desire, or by immoderate anger, are out of their own power.—They, therefore, who are said to be out of their own power, are for this reason said to be so, because they are not under the controul of reason, to which Nature has allotted the supreme government of the mind. How the Greeks came to give to this the appellation of *mania*, might not be very easy to determine. But I may venture to affirm, that we distinguish in this matter better than they; for we separate from fury this sort of insanity, which being of the nature of folly, is of greater extent and magnitude; the Greeks wish to do the same, but are unhappy in the choice of an inadequate term. What we call *fury*, they call *melancholy*. As if the mind could be deranged only by atrabilis, and was not frequently in the same manner affected by violent anger, or fear, or distress; as in the case of ATHA-MAS, ALCMÆON, AJAX, and ORESTES, to all of whom we give the appellation of *furious*. Whoever is so affected, the twelve tables forbid that he should have the management of his own affairs. It is not written, if he begins to be insane, but if he begins to be furious. For they considered insanity as void of equanimity, that is, of sanity; but thought, notwithstanding, that the insane were capable of fulfilling tolerably well the ordinary duties of life, and of going through the com-

F 3   mon

mon and familiar forms of social intercourse. But
they esteemed fury to be an universal blindness of
the mind, with regard to all sorts of objects.
Now though fury appears to be of greater magnitude than insanity, it is yet of such a nature, that
a wise man may become furious, but cannot be insane*."

---

* " Omnium insipientium animi in morbo sunt : omnes insipientes igitur insaniunt : sanitatem enim animorum positam
in tranquilitate quadam constantiaque censebant [philosophi] :
his rebus mentem vacantem, appellarunt insanam : propterea
quod in perturbato animo, sicut in corpore, sanitas esse non
possit.—Itaque nihil melius, quam quod est in consetudine ser-
monis Latini ; cum exisse ex potestate dicimus eos, qui ecfre-
nati feruntur aut libidine aut iracundia.—Qui igitur exisse ex
potestate dicuntur ; idcirco dicuntur, quia non sunt in potestate mentis : cui regnum totius animi a natura tributum est.
Græci autem μανίαν unde appellant non facile dixerim. Eam
tamen ipsam distinguimus nos melius, quam illi ; hanc enim
insaniam, quæ juncta stultitiæ patet latius, a furore disjungimus : Græci volunt illi quidem, sed parum valent verbo :
quem nos furorem, μελαγχολίαν illi vocant. Quasi vero atra
bili solum mens, ac non sæpe vel iracundia graviore, vel timore, vel dolore moveatur ! quo genere ATHAMANTEM, ALC-
MÆONEM, AJACEM, ORESTEM furere dicimus. Qui ita sit
adfectus, eum dominum esse rerum suarum vetant duodecim
tabulæ. Itaque non est scriptum, si insanus, sed si furiosus
esse incipit : insaniam enim censuerunt constantia, id est sanitate, vacantem : posse tamen tueri mediocritatem officiorum,
& vitæ communem cultum atque usitatum : furorem autem
rati sunt mentis ad omnia cæcitatem. Quod cum majus esse
videatur quam insania : tamen ejusmodi est, ut furor in sapientem cadere possit, non possit insania."

This

This passage, I must own, is not to be met with, as it here stands, in any one edition of the Tusculan Disputations in my possession, or which I have had an opportunity of consulting; but the *disjecta membra* of it are all to be found, some in one copy, and some in another. The reading which I have chosen is exactly the same with that which is given by some of the best editions, excepting in one word;—for where I read, " *insaniam*, enim, censuerunt constantia, id est sanitate vacantem,"· they adhere to the common reading, and retain *stultitiam;* which I have changed for *insaniam:* for as the sense absolutely requires *insaniam*, and we actually meet with it in some editions, though not, as I can discover, on the authority of any manuscript, yet on that of NONIUS*, which may, I think, be esteemed in this case as little, if at all, inferior, I have ventured to receive it as the true reading; and am persuaded that the text, as it is here set down, may be safely considered as restored to its primitive purity.

The learned MERCURIALIS† wonders that CICERO should be so much a stranger to the real sense in which these words, *mania* and *melancholia*, were used by Greek writers long before his time, as in this passage, in his opinion, he appears to be.

---

* Vide NONIUM, de varia significatione verborum, in voce furor.

† Hieron. MERCURIALIS Variar. Lection. lib. vi. cap. xvi. Opuscul. Aureor. p. 475.

But

But such a writer as CICERO ought not lightly to
be censured. He seldom discovers himself to be
either ignorant, or inaccurate: and it is certain
that the old Greek writers did not unfrequently
confound these terms; as even MERCURIALIS himself acknowledges that HIPPOCRATES has done in
one instance; to which he might have added,
had he been at the trouble of examining his works
with this intention, several others: his words are,
—" though I do not deny that HIPPOCRATES has
used *mania* for *melancholia*, in the twenty-first
Aphorism of the sixth book*."

But the truth, I believe is, that MERCURIALIS
did not perfectly enter into the views of that elegant writer in this passage, in which it must be
acknowledged, he has not delivered himself altogether with his wonted perspicuity.—In order to
understand him, two things are to be attended
to: the one is, that he is endeavouring to prove
the natural connexion between folly and madness; and the other, that he wishes to show the
superior excellence of the Latin language, in more
exactly distinguishing the several kinds of madness; in more clearly pointing out their relation
to folly; and in making use of terms whose philosophical and vulgar senses perfectly coincide.—
He had said a little before,—" omnes insipientes
esse non sanos†."—" that all fools are insane;"—a

---

* " Quanquam non inficior semel HIPPOCRATEM, xxi libri
sexti Aphorismo, maniam pro melancholia usurpasse."—*Ibid.*

† Id. ib.

few

few lines after he adds—" Hence wisdom is sanity
of mind, and folly is insanity, which is likewise
called *dementia,* and is that state in which a man
may be said to be out of his mind. These circumstances are much better pointed out in the
Latin language, than in the Greek ; an observation
which may be made on many other occasions, as
well as on this*."—He then subjoins the following
observation in favour of his native language:—
" The very meaning, therefore, of the word itself,
completely illustrates the object of our present inquiry, and clearly explains the true nature of insa-
nity†."—After a few obsevations on the strict propriety of the common modes of expression in the
Latin language on this subject of moral insanity,
most of which have been quoted above, he adds,
as we have already seen,—" how the Greeks
came to give to this the appellation of *mania,*
might not be very easy to determine :"—and that
with very good reason ; since none of its uncertain etymologies render it strikingly applicable to
this moral insanity of the philosophers : since it is
commonly used, by writers of every class, to express impetuosity of passion ; and by medical wri-

---

* " Ita fit ut sapientia sanitas sit animi : insipientia autem
quasi insanitas quædam, quæ est insania, eademque dementia:
Multoque melius hæc notata sunt verbis Latinis, quam Græcis :
quod aliis quoque multis locis reperietur."—*Id. ib.*

† " Totum igitur id, quod quærimus, quid et quale sit,
verbi vis ipsa declarat."—*Id. ib.*

ters to denote violence of delirium, whether of a
fever, or of madness:—and yet it is certain that μανία, μαίνομαι, or the like, are the very words made
use of by the old Grecian philosophers, when
speaking of the identity of folly and insanity.
SOCRATES in PLATO's Alcibiades Secundus*, tells
us that—ἀφροσύνη ἄρα καὶ μανία κινδυνεύει ταυτόν εἶναι
—" folly and madness seem to be the same
thing."—DIOGENES LAERTIUS† informs us that
ZENO, the founder of the stoic philosophy, taught,
that " a wise man could never be mad"—ἔτι δὲ ἰδὲ
μαινήσεσθαι ;—" that he might experience the representation of delusive images in his mind, either through melancholy or delirium,"—διὰ μελαγχολίαν ἢ λήρησιν ;—" not in consequence of any error in his notions and estimation of things, but of
some natural disorder of his body."—And CICERO
himself has placed the following Greek aphorism
—ὅτι πᾶς ἄφρων μαίνεται—at the head of his fourth
paradox in support of the doctrine—" that every
fool is insane."—Had MERCURIALIS attended to
these facts, he would not have charged CICERO
with being ignorant of the meaing of the Greek
word μανία ; and would have acknowledged that
his reflections are not less just, than the circumstance on which he grounds them is true. Nor
is CICERO the only Latin writer who uses *insania*

---

* Sect. 2.
† Lib. vii. in Vita ZENONIS, p. 509.

in

in the same manner, as corresponding to the μανία, or moral insanity, of the Greeks, SENECA,
in his second book De Beneficiis*, has the following passage :—" We say that every fool is insane: we do not, however, attempt to cure them
all with hellebore; but even trust those very men
whom we call insane, to vote in our assemblies,
and to fill the most important offices of the
state†."

After this observation, that he could not see
any reason, in the etymology of the word, why the
Greeks made use of the term *mania* to signify
what the Latins, in a moral sense, termed *insanity*;—he adds—" but we distinguish in this matter [of insanity] better than they: for that kind
of insanity which being of the nature of folly, only
differs from it in magnitude"—" quæ juncta stultitiæ patet latius"—" we separate from fury,
which we define to be"—" mentis ad omnia cæcitatem"—" an universal blindness of the mind;"
—" forbiding the latter"—" dominos esse rerum
suarum"—" to have the management of their
own affairs;"—while we allow that the former,
though insane even in a medical sense, are able—
" tueri mediocritatem officiorum, et vitæ commu-

---

* SENECÆ Oper. tom. i. p. 651. De Beneficiis, lib. ii.
cap. xxxv.

† " Insanire omnes stultos diximus: nec tamen omnes cu-
ramus elleboro; his ipsis quos vocamus insanos, et suffragium
et jurisdictionem committimus."

nem

nem cultum et usitatum,"—" to fulfil tolerably
well the ordinary duties of life, and to go through
the common and familiar forms of social intercourse."—" The Greeks wish to do the same, but
are unhappy in making choice of an inadequate
term:" for their melancholia, instead of specify-
ing something totally distinct from their mania,
and our insania, and exactly corresponding to our
furor, corresponds in some cases to mania, and insania, as well as to furor;—and being injudici-
ously taken from a supposed cause, which, however real, is a partial one, betrays a want of precision, where precision was particularly aimed at,
since the same symptoms, whether of insania,
mania, or furor, may equally arise from other
causes, as well as from atrabilis,—such as—" iracundia gravior, vel timor, vel dolor,"—" violent
anger, or fear, or distress."

The Greeks, in short, he observes, have been
less fortunate than the Latins in the choice of their
terms in these respects,—that their mania is not
so strikingly applicable, from its obvious meaning,
to that kind of mental disorder which is strictly
moral, and is properly denominated *stultitia*, or
folly, as the *insania* of the Latins is ;—that they
have no term by which they distinguish that kind
of insanity—" quæ juncta stultitiæ patet latius,"
—" which being of the nature of folly, is of
greater extent and magnitude," and answers
pretty exactly to what I call *notional insanity*.

and

and that their melancholia, at the same time that it corresponds to the furor of the Latins, does not properly comprehend those kinds of furor which arise from excess of passion, and not from atrabilis.

Thus CICERO, we find, reckons three kinds of insanity ;—the *first*, simple stultitia, folly, or moral insanity ;—the *second*, that kind of insanity which, " being of the nature of folly, is of greater extent and magnitude ;" and corresponds to such species of notional insanity as arise from the affections of the mind ;—the *third*, what he calls *fury*, which answers to those species of ideal insanity which can be conceived to come within the definition of " an universal blindness of mind, with regard to all sorts of objects."

The following passages from CÆLIUS AURELIANUS may serve still farther to corroborate CICERO's observations relative to the mania and melancholia of the Greeks,—to show the injustice of MERCURIALIS's charge of ignorance in these matters,—and to confirm the truth of the explication which I have above advanced.—It may be proper to observe, that he generally uses the Latin word *furor* either as synonymous to the Greek *mania*, or to the Latin *insania*.

"The stoics," says he, "have asserted that there are two sorts of fury; one of which ranks under folly, and this they prove to be a kind of insanity inherent in every man who is not wise; and the other is is owing to an alienation of mind, united with a bodily disorder. They who follow EMPEDOCLES, say that the first arises from a corruption of the soul; and the latter from an alienation of mind, occasioned by a cause, or disorder, residing in the body. Of this last I am now about to write; which, as it produces great anxiety, the Greeks call *mania;* either because it immoderately relaxes the soul, or the mind ; for μανόν· in Greek signifies depressed, or softened: or because, &c.*"

" For fury possesses the mind sometimes with anger, sometimes with mirth, sometimes with dejection, or with vanity, sometimes with empty fear of threatening danger, &c†."

Afterwards, in treating of melancholia, he has the following remarkable passage :—

" But the followers of THEMISON, and many

---

* " Stoici duplicem furorem dixerunt, alium insipientiæ genus, quo omnem imprudentem insanire probant; alium ex alienatione mentis et corporis compassione. EMPEDOCLEM sequentes alium dicunt ex animi purgamento fieri, alium alienatione mentis, ex corporis causa sive iniquitate, de quo nunc scripturi sumus: quem Græci, siquidem magnam faciat anxietatem, appellant μανία vei quod animum sive mentem ultra modum laxet ; μανόν enim demissam sive mollem appellant; vel quod," &c.—*Morb. Chronic.* lib. i. c. v. § 144, p. 325.

† " Nam furor nunc iracundia, nunc hilaritate, nunc mœstitudine, sive vanitate occupat mentem, nunc timore comminante inanium rerum," &c.—*Morb. Chronic.* lib. i. cap. v. § 144, p. 327.

others,

others, have called this affection a species of fury. It differs, however, from fury in this, that in melancholy the stomach is principally affected; and in fury the head*."

Let me add one more authority to show that melancholia sometimes means the same with the furor of CICERO.

"For mania, insanity, or fury," says ZACUTUS LUSITANUS, " is a kind of melancholy†."

It has been commonly asserted, that persons of great abilities, and genius, are more liable to madness than men of inferior understandings.— That, whether wise men are of a melancholy temperament, has long been a subject of inquiry, which has been determined in the affirmative, is evident from the following passage of ZACUTUS LUSITANUS :—

" Whether wise men are of a melancholy temperament ? is a proper subject of inquiry in this place. For ARISTOTLE asserts,—that all who have been famous for their genius, whether in the study of philosophy, in affairs of state, in poetical composition, or in the exercise of the arts, have

---

* " Sed hanc passionem furoris speciem alii plurimi, atque THEMISONIS sectatores vocaverunt. Differt autem, siquidem in ista principaliter stomachus patitur, in furiosis veto caput." —*Morb. Chronic.* cap. vi. § 183, p. 340.

† " Mania enim, insania, seu furor, quædam est melancholia."—*Praxis Historiar.* lib. i. cap. viii. p. 204, col. 2, C.

been

been inclined to melancholy; as HERCULES, AJAX, BELLEROPHON, LYSANDER, EMPEDOCLES, SOCRATES, and PLATO. But why melancholy should contribute to wisdom, is difficult to explain, of which GALEN was not ignorant; for in the first book of his Treatise on Human Nature, in which he supposes that the disposition of mind is determined by the temperament of the body, he advances that quickness and penetration of mind proceeds from the bilious humour, as equanimity and firmness do from the melancholy. If, therefore, these two humours are exactly attempered, they render a man wise; since he may be called a wise man who reasons with ease and celerity, and determines with judgment*."·

---

* " Verum melancholici sint sapientes? hoc loco a nobis enucleandum.   Nam ARISTOTELES lib. xxx. prob. i. omnes qui ingenio claruerunt, vel in studiis philosophiæ, vel in republica administranda, vel in carmine pangendo, vel in artibus exercendis, melancholicos fuisse perhibet, quales HERCULEM, AJACEM, BELLEROPHONTEM, LYSANDRUM, EMPEDOCLEM, SOCRATEM, atque PLATONEM extitisse affirmat.   Cur autem melancholia ad prudentiam conferat, explicatu difficile est, quod GALENUM non latuit : hic enim lib. i. de natura human. com. 39. supponens animi mores corporis temperamentum sequi, docet quod animi acies, et intelligentia ab humore bilioso emanet, quemadmodum constantia, et firmitas a melancholico. Si ergo prædicti duo humores exacte attemperantur, hominem sapientem reddunt, cum sapiens ille dicatur, qui facile ac cito discurrit, ac graviter discernit."—ZACUT. LUSITAN. Prax. Historiar. lib. i. cap. viii. Oper. tom. ii. p. 206, col. 2, E.

The

The very just observation of one of the best of our English poets, in the following couplet, is frequently quoted in favour of the natural con-. nexion between wisdom and madness :

" Great wits are sure to madness near allied,
" And thin partitions do their bounds divide*."

And, indeed, it is true, that persons of great inventive genius, of fine imagination, and of lively feelings, if not blessed with great judgment, as well as with the best moral dispositions, are so situated upon the very verge of madness, that they easily fall into it, if pushed forward by any considerable accidental cause†. What, in-deed,

---

* DRYDEN's Absalom and Achitophel.

† Of this we have a remarkable instance in the celebrated poet TASSO ; on whose fine imagination the passions of hope-less love, and of grief occasioned by ill treatment, seem to have generated ideal madness, of such a kind as might be ex-pected in a sublime poet, who had indulged his fancy so wildly, and so exquisitely, as he had done, in the visionary creation of witchcraft and enchantment.—Of this insanity we meet with the following anecdote in the Life of TASSO prefixed to HOOLE's translation of his Jerusalem Delivered.

" In this place [at Bisaccio near Naples] MANSO had an op-portunity of examining the singular effects of TASSO's melan-choly ; and often disputed with him. concerning a familiar spi-rit, which he pretended to converse with. MANSO endea-voured in vain to persuade his friend that the whole was the illusion of a disturbed imagination : but the latter was strenu-ous in maintaining the reality of what he asserted ; and, to convince MANSO, desired. him to be present at one of these

deed, can be a nearer approach to madness, than
that of a man of genius, in the act of poetical invention, when, as SHAKESPEARE inimitably ex-
presses it,—

" The poet's eye, in a fine phrensy rolling,
" Doth glance from heav'n to earth, from earth to heav'n;
" And, as imagination bodies forth
" The forms of things unknown, the poet's pen
" Turns them to shape, and gives to aiery nothing
" A local habitation and a name*."

mysterious conversations. MANSO had the complaisance to
meet him next day, and while they were engaged in discourse,
on a sudden he observed that TASSO kept his eyes fixed upon
a window, and remained in a manner immoveable : he called
him by his name several times, but received no answer : at
last TASSO cried out, ' There is the friendly spirit who is come
to converse with me : look, and you will be convinced of the
truth of all that I have said.'—MANSO heard him with surprize; he looked, but saw nothing except the sun-beams dart-
ing through the window : he cast his eyes all over the room,
but could perceive nothing, and was just going to ask where
the pretended spirit was, when he heard TASSO speak with
great earnestness, sometimes putting questions to the spirit,
and sometimes giving answers, delivering the whole in such a
pleasing manner, and with such elevated expressions, that he
listened with admiration, and had not the least inclination to
interrupt him. At last the uncommon conversation ended with
the departure of the spirit, as appeared by TASSO's words, who
turning to MANSO, asked him, if his doubts were removed.
MANSO was more amazed than ever ; he scarce knew what to
think of his friend's situation, and waved any farther conversation on the subject."—*Life of* TASSO, p. xlviii.

* Midsummer Night's Dream, act v. scene 1.

It

It is also true, that the ablest heads, and sound-est judgments, may be deranged by too intense application of mind :—and that madness from bo-dily causes has little, if any relation, to the greater or less extent of the original powers of the soul, and may equally seize on the wise man and on the fool.

But, setting aside these considerations, I may venture, I think, from much experience in these cases, to affirm—that men of little genius, and weak judgment, especially if to a small degree of capacity be joined a lively and active imagination, strong passions, or absurd and gloomy notions of God and religion, derived from vulgar prejudices, and a very defective, or an injudicious education, are, when certain circumstances co-operate, pecu-liarly liable to every species of notional insanity.

In short, as, in a moral sense, every fool is with propriety said to be insane ; so, in a natural and medical sense, it may truly be asserted, that fools are [most liable to madness : so far from true is the common notion ; which has been adopted by a very ingenious poet, and thus poeti-cally expressed in the following lines of his beau-tifully descriptive ode on this subject :

" Hail, awful madness, hail !
" Thy realm extends, thy powers prevail,
" Far as the voyager spreads his vent'rous sail.
" Nor best nor wisest are exempt from thee ;
" Folly—folly's only free*."

---

* PENROSE's Flights of Fancy, p. 16.

As

As notional delirium is peculiar to madness, so, on the other hand, ideal delirium is common both to fevers and madness; but with this difference, that in fevers it is generally pure, and unmixed; whereas in madness it seldom occurs without some mixture of notional delirium.

In notional madness the patient properly perceives, and distinguishes, surrounding objects, knows where he is, and who are about him: but a person labouring under ideal madness knows no more of these matters, under equal degrees of delirium, than one in the delirium of a fever;—and the cause is obvious: for both in the delirium of a fever, and in that of ideal madness, the mind is nearly in the same state as that of a person in a dream,—has a world of images within itself, which are so forcibly obtruded upon its observation, and so vividly perceived, as in a great measure to prevent the perception of those which are offered by the ministration of the senses, as immediately acted upon by the then present material objects of the visible, audible, and tangible world without.— In all these cases, in proportion as the senses are affected, or, in other words, as they affect the mind, by the perception of present external objects, the deception of the febrile and maniacal delirium, and of the dream, is incomplete*.

So

---

* ADDISON, in the Spectator, has a very just observation, among many others, on the subject of dreams, which is equally applicable to the delirium of some species of ideal madness, and

of

So that the distinction of ARETÆUS, which must be acknowledged to be plausible; because founded on real, though partial observation; is yet far from true. After relating a very curious case of madness, he adds,—" The cause of this disorder is in the head and the hypochondria, which sometimes begin to be affected both at once, and at other times one disorders the other. But the principal seat of the disease in mania and melancholy is in the viscera; as that of the phrenitis is, for the most part, in the head and the senses. For in the latter, or phrenitis, they have erroneous sensations, and see things as present which are not so; objects being represented to their sight which do not appear to those about them:—whereas they who are maniacal see only as they ought to see; but do not judge of what they see as they ought to judge*."

Hippo-

---

of fevers. " The soul," says he, " in dreams converses with numberless beings of her own creation, and is transported into ten thousand scenes of her own raising. She is herself the theatre, the actors, and the beholder. This puts me in mind of a saying which I am infinitely pleased with, and which PLUTARCH ascribes to HERACLITUS, That all men whilst they are awake are in one common world; but that each of them, when he is asleep, is in a world of his own.—The waking man is conversant in the world of nature; when he sleeps, he retires to a private world that is peculiar to himself."—*Vol.* vii. *No.* 487.

  * Ἴσχυσι δὲ τὴν αἰτίην τᾶ νοσήμαῖος, κεφαλὴ καὶ ὑποχόνδρια, ἄλλοτε μὲν ἅμα ἄμφω ἀρξάμενα· ἄλλοτε δὲ

                 ἀλλή-

HIPPOCRATES, or whoever was the author of the Treatise De Morbis, which is to be found in all the collections of his works, justly observes, that the delirium of a phrenitis and of madness, are alike.—" There is a great similarity," says he, " as to the disorder of mind, in those who are ill of a phrensy, and those who are afflicted with melancholy: for they of a melancholy temperament become diseased, and are delirious, and some of them maniacal, whenever the blood becomes corrupted with bile and phlegm. And it is the same in the phrensy. And in both, the mania and the delirium, are less in proportion as the bile is less predominant than the phlegm*."

GALEN says, in effect, the same thing:—" For by the constant presence of fever, alone, can we

---

ἀλλήλοισι ξυντιμωρᾶντα· ·ὸ δὲ κῦρος, ἐν τοῖσι σπλάγχνοισί ἐςι ἐπὶ μανίη καὶ μελαγχολίη, ὅκωσπερ ἐν τῇ κεφαλῇ καὶ τοῖσι αἰσθήσεσι τὰ πολλὰ τοῖσι φρενητικοῖσι· οἵδε μὲν γὰρ παραισθάνονται, καὶ τὰ μὴ παρεόντα ὁρέασι δῆθεν ὡς παρεόντα, καὶ τὰ μὴ φαινόμενα ἄλλῳ κατ' ὄψιν ἰνδάλλεται· οἱ δὲ μαινόμενοι ὁρέασιν μόνως ὡς χρὴ ὁςῆν, ὰ γιγνώσκασι δὲ περὶ αὐτέων, ὡς χρὴ γιγνώσκειν.—De Causis et Sign. Morb. Diuturn. lib. i, cap, vi. p. 32, C.

* Προσεοίκασι δὲ μάλιςα ὁι ὑπὸ τῆς φενίτιδος ἐχόμενοι, τοῖσι μελαγχολῶσι κατὰ τὴν παράνοιαν. οἵτε γὰρ μελαγχολώδεες ὁκόταν φθαρῇ τὸ αἷμα ὑπὸ χολῆς καὶ φλέγματος, τὴν νᾶσον ἴχασι καὶ παράνοοι γίνονται. ἔνιοι δὲ καὶ μαίνονται. καὶ ἐν τῇ φρενίτιδι ὡσαύτως. οὕτω δὲ ἧσσον ἡ μανίη τε καὶ ἡ παραφρόνησις γίνεται, ὅσωπερ ἡ χολὴ τᾶ φλέγματος ἀσθενεσέρη ἐςίν.—Vide Foesii HIPPOCR. Oper, Qma. p. 460, 50.

distin-

distinguish a phrensy; which differs from mania
in nothing but this circumstance: for they are
both disorders of the mind; but the absence of
fever is charaƈteristic of the latter, as is its presence of the former*."

It may not be amiss here to oberve, that though
GALEN in this, and other passages, calls mania
a delirium without fever; yet he acknowledges
that the term is used by HIPPOCRATES, in several
places, as indeed it is in that just quoted above,
only to express a violent degree of delirium,
whether it be with, or without fever. In
commenting upon a passage in which μανικόν†,
or maniacal, is used by HIPPOCRATES when

---

* Ἐν τέτῳ γὰρ μόνῳ διηνεκῶς ὑπάρχοντι μέ[α πυρετᾶ
τὴν· φρενίτιν νοᾶμεν, ᾶδενὶ διαφέρᾶσαν ἄλλῳ τῆς μανίας
πλὴν τῷ πυρετῷ· φρενῶν μὲν γὰρ ἄμφω βλάᾶαι, τὸ δὲ χω-
ρὶς πυρετᾶ τῶν μαινομένων ἴδιον, ὥσπερ τὸ σὺν πυρετῷ φρε-
νιτιχῶν.—Vide Foesii Œconom. HIPPOCRAT. art. Μανία; where
more may be seen to the same purpose.

† " In febribus autem dentibus stridere, quibus a puero minime est consuetum, μανικον καὶ θανατῶδες;."—" Grating the teeth
in a fever, when the patient has not been accustomed to do so
since his childhood, foretells a violent degree of delirium, and
even death itself "—HIPPOCT. Prænotion. lib. i. p. 37, l. 52.
And a little after, still speaking of fevers, he says,—" Quod si
etiam pulsus in præcordiis insit θόρυᾶον ἢ παραφροσύνην indicat.
Verum etiam eorum oculos intueri opportet. Si namque oculi
crebro moveantur μανῆμι τότοις ἐλπίς."—If there be a pulsation
about the præcordia, it denotes simply an approaching perturba-
bation of mind, or delirium. But it is also proper to observe
the eyes; for if the patient moves them frequently about, a
violent delirium may soon be expeƈted."—Ibid. p. 38, l. 37.

speaking

speaking of delirium in a fever, he observes,—
μανικόν μὲν, ὡς εἰ καὶ παρακοπλικὸν ἰσχυρῶς εἰρήκει :—
"that in using the term *maniacal*, he means the
same thing as if he had said—highly delirious."

I cannot in this place forbear taking notice of
the latitude which the ancients often allowed
themselves in the use of words: in which, indeed,
too many of the moderns, partly from the poverty of language, partly from a desire to avoid
the charge of an affectation of singularity, or a
fondness of innovation; but more, I suspect, from
inattention, indolence, and habit, have followed
their example. This latitude of language is often
the occasion of much confusion, and apparent inconsistency, in the writings of the ancient Greeks
and Romans; has greatly diminished the value of
even their best compositions, relative to natural
science, by rendering them frequently obscure,
and sometimes perfectly unintelligible; and has, I
believe, been as much instrumental to the decline
of classical learning in this philosophical age, as
any other cause whatever. Had they been as accurate as they are elegant, they would have been
more valued, and more generally read; but nothing can compensate, in the estimation of a philosopher, for want of precision; since there can
be no sound philosophy, where there is no precision in the use of terms.

This want of precision, by throwing over a
composition the dark veil of obscurity, is as unfa-
                                    vourable

vourable to the reputation of an author, as a man
of real science and genius, as it is injurious to the
advancement of knowledge:—since, as we are
usually unwilling to take much pains to understand a writer in whose works we frequently meet
with the unpromising appearance of obscurity and
inconsistency ;—and, as we cannot be supposed to
enter much into the spirit and meaning of what
we read without pleasure, and without attention ;
or to be much instructed by what we do not understand :—so, we are not very ready to give a writer credit for much science, or any deep views
into the secret operations of Nature, who has not
sagacity, or attention, sufficient to enable him to
affix determinate, and appropriate ideas, to the
terms he makes use of ;—and are apt to suspect
that he has no very clear head, or bright genius,
who is unable to communicate his own notions,
whatever they may be, at least for the most part, ·
with perspicuity and precision :—for, as HORACE
very justly observes,—

" Scribendi recte sapere est principium et fons.
* * * * * * *
" Verbaque provisam rem non invita sequentur*."

" Good sense the fountain of the muses art.
* * * * * * *
" And if the mind with clear conceptions glow,
" The willing words in just expressions flow†."

---

* De Arte Poetica, v. 311.
† FRANCIS.

There

.. There is not, perhaps, a more striking instance
of this latitude in the use of words, than in the
variety of significations in which the ancient physicians have employed the terms *melancholia* and
mania.

, Melancholia is sometimes employed to signify a certain temperament, or morbid disposition
of body* ;—sometimes to express madness in ge-
neral†, of which this temperament, or atrabilis,
was almost universally supposed to be the cause,—
in which view Horace, speaking of a happy madman, says—

> " Expulit ellebbro morbum bilemque meraco ;"—
> " And with strong hellebore drove out the disease and the
>   bile together;"

—most commonly to discriminate that kind
which is attended with dejection and fear‡, as has
already been abundantly proved ;—and sometimes, as Cicero has observed, to denote even
fury ; and that either in proper madness §, or in
the

---

* Hippocr. De Aere, Locis, et Aquis. p. 288. 6.—De
Victus Ratione in Morb. Acut, p. 404. 39.—De Affection.
p. 325. 21.—De Morbis Vulgaribus, p. 1090, G.

† Hippocr. De Morbis, p. 460. 48.

‡ Ibid. sect. 6, Aphorism 23.—See also the definitions
already transcribed from the writings of the ancient physicians.

§ Ibid. De Morbis, p. 460. 45.—This may be farther confirmed by the following passage of the *Capteivei* of Plautus :

" Tynd.

the delirium of a· fever*.—In like manner, by mania sometimes is understood madness· in ·general†;—most frequently madness with fury and audacity, in which sense, as has been fully shown already, it is opposed to melancholia‡.;—sometimes no more than a high degree of delirium in a fever § ;—and sometimes even · to denote that kind of ·madness which is accompanied with fear

---

TYND.· " Ardent oculi, fune opu'st Hegio,. Viden' tu illi macularj totum corpus maculis luridis ? Atra bilis agitat hominem."

TYND. " His eyes flash fire; 'twere fit he were confin'd. See you not how his body is o'erspread With livid blotches ? 'Tis black bile disturbs him."

And a little after TYNDARUS says—

" Jam deliramenta loquitur : larvæ stimulant virum."

" Hark how he raves ! some ghosts unseen torment him." Act iii. scene 4. v. 63—67.

* HIPPOCR. Prorrhet, lib. i. No. 14, 15, 18.—Coac. Prænot. p. 130. No. 88, 93, 94, 95.

† HIPPOCR. De Morbo Sacro, p. 308, 309.—Prorrhet. lib. ii. p. 83.—Insaniæ Tractatio, p. 1286.—HIPPOCRATIS et DEMOCRITI Epist. p. 1285.

‡ HIPPOCR. Aphorism, § 3. Aphor. 20, 22, § 6. Aphor. 56. —De Victus Ration. lib. ii, p. 352. 30.

§ HIPPOCR. De Judicationibus, p. 55. 41.—De Morbo Sacro, p. 460. 49.—JACOTIUS, speaking of three kinds of phrenitis mentioned by HIPPOCRATES, says the second is μανιώδης, melancholica.—Vide HOLLERII et JACOTII Comment. in HIPPOCRAT. Coacas Prænot. lib. ii. n. 30, p. 101.

and

and dejection, and is usually distinguished from
mania by the opposite term, *melancholia**.

I shall now proceed to arrange the various *species* of madness according to the above definitions; and for the sake of placing them in a clear
point of view, shall throw them together into the
form of a *table*; which shall be followed by such
descriptions, illustrations, and authorities, as shall
appear to me necessary to explain, and confirm,
whatever may stand in need of explanation, or
confirmation.

---

* HIPPOCR. De Victus Ration. lib. ii. p. 351. 50—Aphorism. § 6. Aphor. 21, as explained by GALEN; and acknowledged by MERCURIALIS. Variar. Lection. lib. vi. p. 475.
The same writer has, in another work, the following observation; which seems scarcely to be consistent with his censure of
CICERO above-mentioned:—" Per maniam, omnia deliria.
Nam ut GALENUS scribit, hæc vox mania significat aliquando
melancholiam, jam maniam, jam omnia deliria."—" By mania," says he, " he means all sorts of delirium. For as we
learn from GALEN, this word mania signifies sometimes melancholy, sometimes mania, and sometimes every kind of delirium."—Vide Hieron. MERCURIAL. in secund. Lib. Epidem.
HIPPOCRAT. Prælection. Bononiens. P. 238.

A TABLE

A TABLE OF THE SPECIES OF INSANITY.

One Genus, ... INSANITY.

Two Divisions, ... IDEAL—and—NOTIONAL.

I. IDEAL INSANITY.

INSANITY .... 1. Phrenitic.
                2. Incoherent.
                3. Maniacal.
                4. Sensitive.

II. NOTIONAL INSANITY.

INSANITY .... 5. Delusive.
                6. Whimsical.
                7. Fanciful.
                8. Impulsive.
                9. Scheming.
                10. Vain, or self-important.
                11. Hypochondriacal.
                12. Pathetic.
                13. Appetitive.

I. IDEAL INSANITY.

1. In PHRENITIC INSANITY the patient raves incessantly, or -with short, and those rarely lucid intervals, either about one*, or various
ous

---

* " Curiosius inquisivi," says VAN HELMONT, " plures amen-tes, et non paucos sanavi, tam qui a magnis perturbationibus, pas-sionibus, aliisque morbis, quam qui absumptis dementes facti erant, narraruntque mihi, se incidisse sensim in maniam, cum prævio sensu ex hypochondrio illis ascendere solitam, veluti obscuram phantasiam et nubilam tentationem amentiæ, qua primum vel inviti premebantur, donec idea tandem, plenum sibi dominium acquisivisset. In se autem reversi, erant acto-rum omnium memores. Fidenter enim conquesti sunt de om-nibus. Quod nimirum spoliarentur primum omni discursus consecutione, seque mansisse in punctuali immersione unius conceptus : extra quam nihil aliud cogitarent, cum mœrore, molestia, et importunitate. Cogitarent non secus ac si in spe-culo illum semper conceptum fuissent intuiti. Imo nec scie-bant se tum illud cogitare, vel suo conceptu sic aspicere : quan-quam sic immobiliter cogitarent, ut tandem sub ingressum et dominium maniæ, si contingeret illos stare, stetissent per dies aliquot, absque lassitudine, nec scirent se stare."—VAN HEL-MONT *Demens Idea. Operum*, p. 174.

" I have minutely examined many madmen, and have cured not a few ; as well such as have been rendered insane by great uneasiness, violent passions, or by other diseases, as by sub-stances of an injurious nature taken into the stomach ; and they have all told me that they became gradually maniacal, having a previous sensation of a kind of obscure ideal picture, a sort of a faint approach of insanity, which seemed to ascend from the region of the stomach : that this troublesome representation
was

ous[b] objects; and laughs, sings, whistles, weeps,
laments, prays, shouts, swears, threatens, attempts
to

---

was at first yielded to with reluctance, but the idea insensibly
gaining strength, acquired at length perfect dominion over
them. When they came, however, to themselves, they remembered all that they had experienced in their illness; and
gave an exact relation of all their distresses;—as that they were
at first deprived of all the connexions of association and reasoning,
so that the mind remained fixed on the individual point of one
single object, beyond which it could not think, and which it
dwelt upon with grief, uneasiness, and solicitude; that in this
intense act of thinking they seemed for ever to behold one
object; as it were in a glass;—and that they were not even
conscious that they were merely thinking of such object, or
that they only beheld it in imagination; though they were so
immoveably rivetted in thought, that if they happened to be
standing, at the first attack, or at least during the violence of
a maniacal paroxysm, they would continue standing for some
days, without weariness, and yet not be aware that they were
standing."

"Quidam senex nobilis, quandoque a sede exiliens subito,
ab hostibus se impeti credebat: quos arreptos, retro se in fur-
num confertim, sua quidem opinione, intrudebat."—WIERI
De Præstigiis Dæmonum. lib. iii. *De Lamiis,* cap. vii. § 2.
Operum, p. 180.

"A certain elderly nobleman would sometimes, on a sudden, fancy that he was attacked by an enemy; and springing
from his seat, would, in imagination, thrust together such as
he could seize upon, into an oven which was at his back."

[b] "Juvenis robustus, viginti quatuor annos natus, biliosus,
et poculis largioribus quotidie indulgens, nuper magna contu-
melia fuit affectus, quæ ipsum, hinc ira valde perturbatum, diu
de vindicta magnopere habuit solicitum. Post aliquot dies cœpit

to commit violence either to himself or others, or
does whatever else the nature of his delirium
prompts

---

pit ferocior videri, et cum quovis de rebus leviculis rixari,
noctes pene totas insomnes ducere, et miris imaginationibus
infestari. Cumque malum deinde ingravesceret, diluculo quo-
dam invigilans, e lecto nudus exiliit: indusium et lodices dif-
fregit, clamoribus furiosis totam domum replevit, et in occur-
rentes domesticos tantum impetum fecit, ut uni, renitentibus
aliis, gulam manibus fortissime comprehensam, pene totam
confregit. A pluribus itaque viris robustis comprehensus, et
vinculis in lecto dententus: ubi jam per biduum clamans, absurda loquens, cantillans, ridens, dejerans, torvum videns,
perpetuo vigilat. Cibos oblatos satis avide ingerit. Potum ore
haustum, in adstantium vultum, si non attendant, labris in
fistulæ modum arctatis impudenter nonnumquam ejaculatur.
Sæpissime nudo jacet corpore, nec ullum frigus sentit, nec ab
ullo læditur. Nullis blandimentis, nullis objurgationibus, nec
ullis admonitionibus, ejus ferocia frænari vel leniri hactenus
potest."—Brown *Animad. Med. in Regii Prax. Med.* lib. i.
§ 15.

" A robust young man, of twenty-four years of age; of a
bilious constitution, and used to a daily indulgence in hard
drinking, received lately a violent affront, at which he was so
enraged, that he thought of nothing but how he might be re-
venged. After some days he began to be morose, to quarrel
with any body about the merest trifles; to pass almost whole
nights without sleep, and to be troubled with strange fancies.
The disorder increasing, one morning early, as he was lying
awake, he suddenly started, naked, out of bed, tore his shirt,
and his bed-clothes, filled the whole house with the noise of
his violent raving, and attacked with such fury the servants
who ran to him, that seizing one by the throat, he almost
strangled him, notwithstanding the assistance given him by the
rest. He was, therefore, secured by several stout men, and
fastened

prompts him to do ;—or is as incessantly employed
about some one thing, which is either absurd or un-

---

fastened down in his bed; where he has now lain, without
sleep, for two days, incessantly shouting, talking nonsense,
singing, laughing, swearing, and expressing in his looks the
sternness of revenge. He eats his food somewhat greedily.
Sometimes, contracting his lips so as to form a kind of tube,
he will rudely spirt out of his mouth a part of his drink, into
the faces of his attendants, if they are not careful to avoid it.
He often lies quite naked, and neither perceives, nor is injured
by cold. Neither persuasion, chiding, nor admonition, have
hitherto had the smallest effect in restraining, or soothing his
ferocity."

" Vidi maniacum omnia corporis integumenta lacerasse, et
nudum stramini incubuisse in loco lapidibus strato, dum asper-
rima sæviebat hyems, per plures septimanas; quandoque per
octo dies omni cibo abstinuisse, deinde oblata quævis ingurgi-
tasse avidissime, imo et fœdissimo spectaculo, proprias fæces
alvinas devorasse, licet optimi cibi suppeterent. Per plures
septimanas noctes et dies pervigil. Horrendis clamoribus totam replebat viciniam; et tamen per plures annos supervixit,
sedato quidem furore, sed fatuus, et omnium rerum immemor."
—Van Swieten Comment. Aph. 1120, tom. iii. p. 521.

" I have seen a maniac tear all his clothing from his body;
lie naked upon straw, on a stone pavement, for many weeks,
during the severity of a cold winter; sometimes abstain from
food for eight days together; then greedily swallow whatever
was placed before him; and, what was shocking to behold,
devour his own excrements, even when he had the best of food
at hand. I have known him to have no sleep for many weeks
together; to fill the whole neighbourhood with his dreadful
cries; and yet he survived for several years, the fury in the
mean time abating, and being succeeded by idiotism, and a
total inattention to every thing." — Vide etiam, Schenkii
Observ. Medic. Barier. lib. i. De Mania. Causæ, Obs. 1, 2,
p. 132. &c.

                 common;

common[c]; and is almost wholly intent on the solitary idea, or on the world of ideas within; and scarcely

---

[c] Dies ac noctes cursitabat [maniacus], subsultu tam pernice, et agitatione tam perenni, ut præ defatigatione deflueret undequaque sudoribus: neque tamen propterea, vel tantulum quiesceret, homo volaticus, et irrequietæ huic revolutioni, tam stricte addictus, ut nunquam se dederit ulli quieti, nisi quam invito extorqueret, inevitabilis dormiendi necessitas."

" A qua insania, haud multum certe ablusit, illa, læsæ imaginationis, species: quam a mallei similitudine, lubuit malleationem vocare. Nam velut fabri ferrarii, iteratis ictibus, incudem suam tundunt: sic vidimus mulierem Campensem, insania hac percitam, percussisse indesinenter genu suum; modo dextro, modo vero brachio sinistro: sed ictu tam vehementi, ut quilibet ipsam maximopere læsisset: nisi verberantis manus impetum fregissent domestici, interposito molliori pulvinari.

" Brachium quidem elevabat, ac deprimebat satis distincte: sed motum ejus inchoatum, vel incitare, vel retardare, non videbatur, in manu ipsius esse, multo minus integre cessare, ab hoc feriendi studio. Quod sane lubens intermisisset (jam enim quinque menses, incudem hanc tutuderat) nisi ipsam potenter eo pertraxisset, falsa imaginatio."—Tulpii *Observ. Medic.* lib. i. cap. xvi. and xvii. p. 34.

" A certain maniac ran backwards and forwards day and night, with such persevering agility; and such incessant hurry, that he was usually in a profuse sweat from fatigue : he would not, however, rest a moment, but, flying about, so strictly persisted in this restless revolution, that he never allowed himself the shortest repose, but when, overcome by sleep, he could no longer avoid it."

" From this instance of insanity that species of depraved imagination was not widely different, which, from its resemblance to beating with a mallet, I have taken the liberty to call *malleation.* For as blacksmiths repeat the strokes upon their anvils,

so

scarcely knows[d], or attends to external objeᏜs about him ; and when he does perceive external objeᏜs, is apt to perceive them erroneously ;—thus I have

so have I seen a woman of Campen, affeᏜed with this sort of madness, strike upon her knee without ceasing, sometimes with her right hand, and sometimes with her left; and that with such violence, that she must have received much pain from every stroke, had not her attendants broke their force, by interposing a soft pillow to receive them.

" She appeared evidently to lift up, and bring down her arm, in the same manner as in common voluntary motion; but seemed not to have the power either of quickening, or retarding the motion, when it was once begun ; much less could she cease altogether from striking in this manner; which, doubtlessly, she would willingly have laid aside (for she had now in this way beat the anvil for five months), had she not been violently impelled to it by some erroneous appearance in the imagination."—*Vide etiam* BARTHOLINI *Hist. Anat. Rar.* Cent. 2. Hist. 69, p. 258.

d " Novimus quendam in Creta. religiosum, habitudinis cholericæ, ætate juvenem, subita furiosa dementia correptum, qui domesticos omnes gladio persequebatur, a pluribus captus, manicis et compedibus in carcerem intrusus est: faᏜis et sermone delirabat, neminemque neque amicum, neque sodalem noverat, audax, furiosus, &c."—SCHENCKII *Obs. Med. Rar.* lib. i. *De Melancholia, Symptomata,* Obs. i. p. 124.

" I knew a certain person in Crete, of a religious order, young, and of a choleric temperament, who was suddenly seized with a furious madness, and pursued the servants of the house with a drawn sword; till being overcome by numbers, he was secured with handcuffs, and fetters, and confined in prison. His delirium discovered itself both in aᏜions and discourse; he knew nobody, not even his nearest friends and companions; was daring, furious, &c."

known

known a patient, in this state, in the clearest day-
light, so grossly to mistake certain objects, as to
imagine bricks, stones, logs of wood, sticks, or
straws, to be kings, princes, generals, instruments
of war, horses, and other things; to describe
their dress and appearance; and to be quite angry
at the blindness, or perverseness, of those who
could not, or, as he rather imagined, pretended
they could not see the same objects:—or he is
apt erroneously to connect them with other
images; which exist, as he supposes them to
exist, only in his distempered brain ; as when a patient, of this sort, imagined that the physician
who came to attend him had arrows sticking in
his eyes; but, in general, all the varieties of phrenitic insanity agree in this, that the patient sleeps
very little.

    I have called this species *phrenitic insanity*, be-
cause this kind of insane delirium is similar to
that of the phrenitis, of which, as has already been
observed, ARETÆUS says,—" For in the latter, or
phrenitis, they have erroneous sensations, and see
things as present which are not so ; objects being
represented to their sight which do not appear to
those about them[c]."

    It is usually attended with some degree of red-

---

[c] Οἱδὲ μὲν γὰρ παραισθάνονται, καὶ τὰ μὴ παρεόντα
ὁρίεσι δῆθεν ὡς παρεόντα, καὶ τὰ μὴ φαινόμενα ἄλλῳ,
κατ᾽ ὄψιν ἰνδάλλεται.—*De Causis et Sign. Morb. Diuturn.*
lib. i. cap. vi. p. 32, C.

ness,

ness, more or less, in proportion to its violence, of the tunica albuginea of the eyes; with rather a florid countenance; heat of the head; a quick and sometimes a full pulse; whiteness of the tongue; foulness of the teeth and lips; and often with a copious discharge of mucus, or rather of inspissated lymph, from the mouth, throat, and trachea, which is generated, or much increased, by incessant raving; with rather a preternatural heat; often a dry and harsh, but sometimes a moist skin; moisture of the eyes; a thick sordid rheum adhering to the edges of the eyelids, and in the corners of the eyes; and rather a greasy appearance of the face. Patients of this sort, are sometimes thirsty; seldom have much appetite; too often obstinately refuse both meat and drink; and not unfrequently are as obstinately bent upon destroying themselves in some other way; the cause of which fatal inclination is, in some cases, obvious, from the nature and cause of the delirium; as when, though arising from a bodily disorder, it is visibly accompanied with great anxiety, fear, distress, and horror[f]; or, being generated

---

[f] " Ubi insania vehementer aucta sit, hanc Græci tyrioden [θυριώδη, ut videtur] appellarunt : in hac ingentia quævis mala maniaci perpetrant. Eadem symptomata apparent etiam ex humore melancholico vehementer putrefacto, sed cum iis adest quoque timor cum moestitia: unde isti melancholici furentes præ timore plerumque se ex præaltis locis præcipitant, atque

ita

nerated by the pusillanimous passions, it has proceeded through the antecedent stages of religious,
or some other of the distressful species of notional,
to phrenitic insanity[r].—In other cases it appears
quite

---

ita moriuntur. Qua morte Franciscus a Ponte olim pictor
excellentissimus, atque Delphinus a Como, ambo Bassanien-
ses, præteritis annis interierunt."—Alpini *de Medicina Method.*
lib. x. c. x. p. 610.

"When insanity becomes violent," says Prosper Alpinus,
"the Greeks give it the appellation of *savage*. Maniacs of this
sort are apt to perpetrate every kind of desperate mischief.
The same symptoms may arise from the melancholy humour,
when greatly corrupted ; but are in this case accompanied with
fear and dejection : hence it happens that those melancholy
madmen, who become furious through fear, generally throw
themselves down from some eminence, and so destroy themselves. In this manner Franciscus a Ponte, and Delphinus
a Como, both natives of Bassano, put an end to their lives some
years ago."

Cases of this kind are very common.

[s] "Contigit Antverpiæ, quod faber lignarius, sibi persua-
dens, se noctu spectra horrida vidisse, quorum terrore est totus
amens factus. Missusque ad tumulum S. Dympnæ virginis,
ubi solent obsessi a cacodæmone, liberari ;—Faber ergo, toto
anno alitur, et amens utcunque solita implorarenter remedia :
cumque nummi non mitterentur Antverpia, pro semestri ul-
timo, remiserunt maniacum in curru vinctum. Qui cum vin-
cula sibi solvisset, e plaustro dissiliit, in stagnum profundum
et vicinum. Tandem extractus ; pro cadavere ; in currum
depositus. At deinceps per annos 18 a mania liber vixit."—
Van Helmont, *Demens Idea,* § 49. *Operum,* p. 175.

"A certain carpenter at Antwerp fancied he had seen some
frightful spectres in the night, which so terrified him, that he
entirely

quite unaccountable; arising from bodily disease; and being unaccompanied with any such visible and permanent appearances of anxiety, or anguish, as seem sufficient for the production of such an effect; so that it is impossible to discover any adequate motive for so horrid a deed. This disposition is often as obstinate, and constant, as it is unaccountable; and is, in such cases, accompanied, for the most part, with a gloomy silence and reserve:—sometimes it is sudden, and unexpected, and seems to arise from some temporary feeling of extreme distress, or some momentary impulse of the imagination, which can rarely be exactly investigated:—and in no case, can we clearly discover any distinct, and habitual passion, to which it can be attributed; much less can it be traced up to any such obvious antecedent cause as the distress of disappointed love, inconsolable grief, reli-

---

entirely lost his senses. He was, therefore, sent to the tomb of the holy virgin St. Dympna, where they profess to cure those who are possessed by evil spirits. The carpenter was boarded there for a whole year; and, though evidently a madman, the usual means were employed; but no money being remitted from Antwerp for the last six months, he was sent home, bound, in a carriage. Having found means, by the way, to extricate himself from his confinement, he jumped out of the carriage, and threw himself into a deep pool which happened to be near: from whence, after some time, he was got out, and replaced, as dead, in the carriage. He recovered, however, and lived for eighteen years after, perfectly free from mania."

gious

gious despair, or to any other of the desponding, and unmanly affections, which so frequently urge unhappy mortals to rush upon the greatest of evils to escape from a less; irrevocably to plunge into the very ills they dread; and to seek by death an immediate entrance into that eternal misery, the apprehended certainty of which is the cause of all their horror; a strange inconsistency which did not escape the observation of GALEN, who remarks:—" There are some whose disorder is accompanied by the fear of death, and who yet procure for themselves the very death they fear[h]."

The same unaccountable inclination to suicide sometimes exists in the delirium of a fever, of which we have an instance in BARTHOLINE's Historiarum Anatomicarum rariorum, Centuria secunda:—" A certain person was ill of a fever, and in consequence of petechiæ became so highly delirious, that he hung himself up, one morning early, in the absence of the nurse who was hired to attend him, by means of a string which he fixed to the top of his bed[i]."

2. Of INCOHERENT INSANITY there are several varieties. Its characteristic is an incoherency of

---

[h] " Sunt qui simul et mortem metuant, et mortem sibi consciscant."

[i] " Quidam—febricitat et tanto ex petechiis delirio furit, ut absente muliere conductitia custode, ipsum se summo mane injecta fascia ad lectum suspenderit."

ideas,

ideas, occasioned by an excessive, perverted, or defective activity of the imagination and memory, accompanied with images existing in the mind, which do not exist externally.

This species of ideal insanity displays itself in four different ways, constituting four varieties, which are owing to so many different states of the brain, all capable of producing either real, or apparent, incoherency of ideas. For incoherent insanity may arise—from a too active, and almost phrenitic state of the brain;—from that kind of active state of the brain which occasions a flightiness of imagination, without any tendency to a phrenitic state;—from such a state of the brain as produces, perpetually, trains of apparently unconnected, or very slightly connected, ideas;—and from that state of the brain, in which there is a great defect of memory, occasioned by an almost total privation, or by a fixed, and senseless uniformity, of the mental operations.

Of the four varieties of incoherent insanity, proceeding from these four different states of the brain, the *first* is a near approach to, and often merely an incipient state of phrenitic insanity, and might be termed *ardent*, or *raving* incoherent insanity:—the *second* is that state of incoherent insanity, which exhibiting sudden transitions, and rapid flights, of imagination, might very properly be called *flighty:*—the *third*, which peculiarly deserves the appellation of *incoherent*, and might therefore

therefore be properly distinguished from the other
varieties by the additional title of *unconnected*,
is nearly related to the third species of idiotism:—
the *fourth* is of two sorts, *stupid*, and *absent* or mu-
sing; of which the first, or stupid, is more especially accompanied with great defect of memory;
they resemble the first and second species of idiotism, and the delirium of old age, which, as ARE-
TÆUS defines it, is—" a delirium [λήρησις] which
has no resemblance to mania; being a stupefaction of the senses, of reason, and of the other faculties of the mind, from refrigeration: whereas
the cause of mania is of a hot and dry nature, and
its symptoms are turbulent[k]."

SAUVAGES's *amentia* seems to comprehend the
third, and the two sorts of the fourth variety of
incoherent insanity. For though in describing
amentia, he distinguishes it from *morosis*, or idiotism, yet he afterwards makes the latter a species
of the former; as he does likewise the *delirium
senile*.

" Amentia is an inability to reason and judge
aright: it differs from morosity, or stupidity, in
this, that they who are troubled with amentia, have
a proper perception of the impressions of objects,
which the stupid have not; they do not, however,
attend to, or regard them; but view them with
indifference, slight their consequences, and give

---

[k] Vide ARETÆI CAPPAD. Morb. Chron. lib. i. c. vi.
p. 31, B.

them-

themselves no trouble about them:—they disregard all things alike, and laugh and sing, when men in their right minds would make heavy complaints of hunger, thirst, or cold:—they are neither furious, nor audacious, like maniacs ; nor perpetually dejected, and thoughtful, like those who are afflicted with melancholy[1]."

The two first varieties are usually accompained with incessant talking, or raving, either on the same subject, or with the sudden transitions from one subject to another, as images and fancies arise,—the former with symptoms of approaching phrenitic insanity ; and the latter without such symptoms, and resembling impulsive, whimsical, flighty, or some other species of notional insanity, with the addition of ideal delirium:—the third with calmer, and less perpetual, but frequent incoherent talking, or muttering; without the least tendency to a phrenitic state, or any flightiness of imagination:—the two divisions of the fourth va-

---

[1] " Amentia est ineptitudo ad recte ratiocinandum, et judicandum : differt a morosi seu stupiditate mentis, quia amentes objectorum impressiones sentiunt apprime, non vero stupidi, ast amentes eas non attendunt, non curant, sed quasi omnino indifferentes praetermittunt, harum consequentias flocci faciunt, harum minime satagunt;—omnia perinde neglígunt, rident, cantillant, in iisdem circumstantiis in quibus sani de fame, siti, frigore gemebundi conquererentur; minime iracundi, audaces, ut maniaci, nec tristes constanter et meditabundi, ut melancholici."—Sauvagesii *Nosolog. Method.* tom. iii. Part. Prim. p. 374.

riety,

riety, are usually remarkable for obstinate and invincible silence, and stupid inattention, which in
some cases is almost inviolably preserved for a
long course of time*; in others it is sometimes
interrupted, and enlivened, by transient ramblings,
low unintelligible mutterings, and even by momentary gleams of intelligence, and attention.

They are all to be distinguished from notional
insanity, and the two last from idiotism, by the
obvious existence, at some period or other of the
disorder, of erroneous images.

Both phrenitic and incoherent insanity, together
with the species immediately following, to which I
have limited the appellation of *maniacal*, might
not improperly be considered as constituting a
larger subdivision of ideal insanity, and be called,
in a more extended sense of the term, *maniacal*;
since all these species are, in most instances, attended with such symptoms as have usually been
thought to lay claim to that title.—But this distinction I have waved;—because even this exten-
sion

---

* " When you see a man for months (I may say years) together, not suffering even a rag of clothes on him, lying in straw;
and without showing any signs of discontent, or attempting
to do mischief, maintaining an inviolable silence against all the
applications of persuasion and force; what reason have we for
calling this a deluded imagination? Those who have been so
happy as to recover from this state, describe it no otherwise
than a total suspension of every rational faculty. Their recovery

sion of the term *maniacal* would not bring it to a perfect correspondence with, and enable it exactly to comprehend neither more nor less than, just those cases of insanity which have commonly been ranked under it; but would exclude some which have generally been taken in, and admit others which have as generally been excluded; the several varieties of sensitive insanity, which have commonly been reckoned maniacal, would still be excluded, though they have frequently maniacal, and sometimes even phrenitic symptoms; and all the species of notional insanity, many of which have been as commonly excluded, and referred to melancholy, would occasionally be admitted, as they all have a tendency to acquire these symptoms;—because it would oblige me to change two very proper, and significant specific terms, *maniacal* and *sensitive*, which would in such case become the titles of a general division, for terms less proper and significant, if I would wish to avoid the confusion, which might arise from applying the same term to a species, and to an assemblage of species, which could no way be avoided but by striking out those specific names, and putting others in their stead, were I to adopt such a subdivision,—and because the same end

---

very seems like the awaking from a profound sleep, having seldom any recollection, or at least a very confused one, of what has passed during their illness."—MONRO'S *Remarks on Dr.* BATTIE'S *Treatise on Madness*, p. 6.

may

may be answered, and the above-mentioned inconi‑
veniences avoided, by barely pointing out the
analogy between phrenitic, incoherent, and ma‑
niacal insanity, as I have defined them, and what
is usually understood by the latter term; and
showing that these three species of ideal insa‑
nity form a collection of species, which, ex‑
cepting in a few instances, perfectly resemble, and
nearly comprehend, all those symptoms of insa‑
nity which have, by the bulk of medical writers,
been, strictly speaking, denominated *maniacal*.

3. Maniacal Insanity, properly so called,
as a species, is of all others, perhaps, the most
comprehensive; since it extends its dominion
over the whole internal world of ideas, and com‑
prehends every possible combination of sensible
images which can enter into, and delude, a dis‑
tempered brain. To enumerate all its varieties
would not only be difficult, but impossible: nor
indeed would it be of any material advantage; as
it will be perfectly sufficient, for every practical
purpose, to know that—this species contains what‑
ever comes under the definition of ideal insanity,
and is at the same time, neither phrenitic nor in‑
coherent, nor sensitive:—and that, while in phre‑
nitic insanity, the patient scarcely knows, or at‑
tends to external objects; in incoherent, attends
to them but little, and remembers them very im‑
perfectly, and at best, casually and uncertainly;

in

in most, if not in every instance of purely maniacal insanity, the patient perceives for the most
part,—that is, whenever he is not under the actual
influence of very strong impressions of delusive
images ; or, if the disorder arises from, or is connected with, notional insanity, is not under the
immediate, and powerful imposition, of false, and
absurd notions ; neither of which happen in all cases,
or at all times; but both the one, and the other, in,
comparatively, but few cases; and in these few
only at intervals, of uncertain frequency, and duration ;—excepting in these circumstances, the
patient perceives such external objects as are not
immediately connected with his delirium, for the
most part as they really exist; and consequently
knows, in a great measure, the true appearance,
and situation, of surrounding objects; knows
what kind of place he is in, what persons, and
what objects, are about him, and what he says, and
does; but yet has, at times, and in certain respects, ideas, or images, in the mind, of things as
really existing externally, which do not, and which,
in many cases, could not possibly so exist ; it being
not only contrary to the real present appearances,
but inconsistent with the very nature of things. A
maniacal patient, for instance, may not only imagine that he sees flasks of oil, which he does not
see; like him mentioned by Aretæus[n], who

---

[n] De Causis et Signis Morb. Acutor. lib. i. cap. vi. p. 32, A.

was

was in perpetual fear lest they should fall, and
be broken; or that he is continually haunted by a
dreadful spectre°; or sees persons who are dead,
or

---

* "Diabolos præcipitatos spinxit SPINELLO, et tam atrocem
vultum Lucifero tribuit, ut et ipse horrore perculsus, hunc dæ-
monem sævam exprobrantem pictaram, quod vixit tempus,
oculis continuo portaverit."—TISSOT Serm. Inaug. de Literatorum Valetudine, p. 20.

"SPINELLO, in painting the casting the fallen angels out of
heaven, gave so fierce and dreadful a countenance to Lucifer,
that being shocked at it himself, he had continually before his
eyes, during the rest of his life, the image of that devil, up-
braiding him for the horrible countenance which he had given
him in this picture."

A curious instance of maniacal insanity, just bordering upon,
if not actually become phrenitic, accompanied with extreme
terror arising from the perpetual image, in the mind, of a horrid spectre; occasioned by a suppression of the menses; is described at length in SCHENCKIUS's Observationes Medicæ Ra-
riores; of which the following are a few of the circumstances:
—" De phantasmate conquerebatur [virgo quædam] magnitu-
dinis inusitatæ,—adeo truculenti vultus, horrendique, ut cujus
intuitu illa horrescat—et perpetuo contremescat, ejusdemque
præsentiam conspectumque refugiat:—illique tandem incessit
exclamandi vociferandique permagna cupiditas: phantasma
denique eam crudelius propiusque premit, agitat, consectatur:
—obnixe rogat supplex, ut herus phantasmati nequissimo insidias paret, ipsumque confodiat.—Nos ægrotantem ad parentes
deducendam esse percensemus. Ita fore ut loci et aeris mu-
tatione fortasse illud prægrande phantasma dispareat, et eva-
nescat. Eo cum ventum est, ecce propere phantasma præcur-
risse conqueritur misella."—Lib. i. p. 126, Obs. 1.

"A young woman complained of being terrified by a spectre
of

ór absent[p]; or hears voices, and sounds, which he does not hear[q]; or that he is a king[r]; prince,

---

of unusual magnitude, with so cruel and horrid a countenance, that she perpetually shuddered and trembled when it seemed to look upon her, and endeavoured to fly from its presence, and from its sight :—at length she was seized with a vast propensity to cry out, and make great exclamation : the spectre seemed to press nearer upon her, to pursue, and cruelly distress her :— and she earnestly entreated that her master would surprize the wicked phantom, and run it through with his sword. I advised that she should be sent home to her parents : supposing that the change of place, and of air, might occasion this monstrous illusion to vanish, and disappear. But when the unhappy young woman arrived at home, she complained that the phantom had been too nimble for her, and was got thither before her."

[p] " Novi qui se fratrem multis inde miliaribus degentem videre diceret."—WIERI de Præstig. Dæmon. lib. iii. de Lamiis, cap. vii. § 3. Operum, p. 182.

" I knew one who said he saw his brother, notwithstanding that he was dwelling, at that time, at the distance of many miles."

[q] " Novi,—qui suis auribus semper obstrepere masculorum concubitor, quemcunque obvium, etiam conjunctissimum, quereretur."—WIERI de Præstig. Dæmon. lib. iii. de Lamiis, cap. vii. § 5. Operum, p. 182.

" I knew a man who complained that every one he met, even his most intimate friends and acquaintance, shouted in his ears, and called him a sodomite."

[r] " Qui se totius mundi monarcham et imperatorem esse, ad se solum id spectare nomen crederet, novi melancholicum Italum : alioqui bene habitum, eloquentem, nec alio morbo læsum : mire interim in suis Italicis rythmis de statu christianismi,

prince, hero, orátor, tragedian', a man endowed
with wonderful science, extraordinary learning, or
by the especial favour, and inspiration, of heaven,
with preternatural power, or a knowledge of future events : — but some have fancied that a
knife, or any other inanimate thing; or any of

---

nismi, de religionis dissidiis, de bellis in Gallia exortis et Belgio
componendis, tanquam divinis effatis, sibi placentem : passim
vero suum titulum hisce literis evulgabat, R. R. D. D. M. M. id
est, rex regum, dominus dominantium, monarcha mundi."—
WIERI *de Præstig. Dæmon.* lib. iii. *de Lamiis,* cap. vii. § 2.
Operum, p. 180.

" I knew an Italian, troubled with melancholy, who believed
that he was monarch, and emperor, of the whole world; and
that he alone had a right to that appellation : in other respects
he was quite rational, was eloquent, and did not labour under
any other disease: at the same time he was wonderfully amused
with composing verses, in Italian, relative to the state of christianity, to the differences about religion, and to the putting an
end to the war which then existed between France and Holland, all which he delivered as so many divine oracles. He
every where made known his title by means of these letters,
R. R. D. D. M. M. or, rex regum, dominus dominantium,
monarcha mundi, that is, king of kings, lord of lords, and
monarch of the world."

• " Sic denique furens alius se—deum [existimavit], alius
oratorem, alius tragœdum, vel comœdum, aliùs stipulam fe-
rens mundi se sceptrum tenere."—CÆL. AUREL. *Morb. Chron.*
lib. i. cap. v. p. 328.

" Thus one, in his raving, has imagined himself a god; another, an orator; another, a tragedian, or a comedian; another, carrying a straw in his hand, has imagined that he held
the sceptre of the world."

the

the animal race, by nature void of reason and speech ; has held conversation with them, or exerted some other power, or faculty, inconsistent with its nature.—One imagined the whole surface of the earth to be formed of very thin glass, under which he could plainly perceive serpents without number ; and would, by no means, be persuaded to get out of his bed ; which he conceived to be an island, situated in the midst of this immense glassy expansion ; and which, therefore, he dared not to quit, lest, if he should tread on this thin brittle surface, it should break, and suffering him to fall through, he should be devoured, or stung to death, by the serpents underneath[t].—The amiable, and learned, HARRINGTON, author of Oceana, " was observed to discourse of most things as rationally as any man, except his own distemper, fancying strange things in the operation of his animal spirits, which he thought to transpire from him in the shape of birds, of flies, of bees, or the like. And those about him reported, that he talked much of good and evil spirits, which made them have frightful apprehensions.—He used—sometimes to argue so strenuously that this was no depraved imagination, that his doctor was often put to his shifts for an answer. He would on such occasions compare himself to DEMOCRITUS, who for his admirable discoveries in anatomy

---

[t] SCHENCKII Observ. Medic. Rarior. lib. i. p. 124, Obs. 1.

was

was reckoned distracted by his fellow-citizens, till
HIPPOCRATES cured them of their mistake".".—
A woman, mentioned by TRALLIAN, continually
held up her middle finger, on which she imagined
she was supporting the whole earth, and was in
perpetual anxiety lest she should suffer her finger
to give way, and destroy the world, with its inhabitants".—Some have imagined themselves to be
God the Father", others Jesus Christ, and others
the Holy Ghost[x]:—and I have known some who

" British Biography, vol. v. p. 405.

ᵛ TRALLIAN. de Arte Medic. lib. i. cap. xvii. HALLERI
Art. Medic. Princip. tom. vi. p. 91.

ʷ Vide BOERH. de Morb. Nervor. tom. ii. p. 404.

ˣ " Tres in Frisia non procul a Groninga eo correptos enthu-
siasmo intellexi, ut se Deum Patrem, Filium, et Spiritum Sanctum crederent, horreumque in quo subsistebant, esse Noe ar-
cam, ad quam multi similiter fere affecti, salutis ergo conflue-
bant."—WIERI de Præstig. Dæmon. lib. iii. de Lamiis,
cap. vii. § 2. Operum, p. 180.

" Three men in Friesland, not far from Groeningen, as I
have been informed, were possessed with so great a degree of
fanaticism, that they imagined themselves to be the Father,
Son, and Holy Ghost; and the barn in which they lived to be
Noah's ark : to which many others, in like manner affected,
resorted, that they might obtain salvation."

" Alius se spiritum Sanctum profitebatur."—HOFFMAN.
Oper. vol. vi. p. 342, § 8. Vide BORELL. Cent. 1. Obs. 37.

" Another thought himself the Holy Ghost."

" Quædam infernam se furiam esse voce intentissima asse-
ruit."—BONET. Med. Sept. Coll. lib. i. § 19, cap. ix. sub fin.
tom. i. p. 188.

" One cried with a loud voice that she was an infernal fury."

have

have conceived themselves, or others, to be more than one being at the same time, or at such small intervals, and in so quick and rapid a succession, as amounted nearly to the same thing.—And yet, notwithstanding these delusions, many of these persons, as was remarkably the case with HARRINGTON, think, and converse, as rationally in most other respects, as any man, of similar knowledge, and capacity, in his right and perfect mind.

Of this species was the insanity described by HORACE:—

   " At Argos liv'd a citizen, well known,
   " Who long imagin'd, that he heard the tone
   " Of deep tragedians on an empty stage,
   " And sat applauding in extatic rage:
   " In other points a person, who maintain'd
   " A due decorum, and a life unstain'd,
   " A worthy neighbour, and a friend sincere,
   " Kind to his wife, nor to his slaves severe," &c.[y]

FRANCIS.

Madmen of this sort sometimes imagine that they are conversing with absent people, with gods, angels, or devils: though it must be acknowledged that this is more frequently a symptom of phrenitic insanity.

---

[y] ——" Fuit haud ignobilis Argis,
   " Qui se credebat miros audire tragœdos,
   " In vacuo lætus sessor plausorque theatro ;
   " Cætera qui vitæ servaret munia recto
   " More ; bonus sane vicinus, amabilis hospes,
   " Comis in uxorem, posset qui ignoscere servis," &c.
       HORATII *Epist.* lib. ii. Ep. 2. v. 128, &c.

An

An instance of this conversation with an absent person in phrenitic insanity, is furnished by the following case ; in which the disorder, taking its rise from the passion of love, seems to have been at first notional, then maniacal, and in the end to have become phrenitic :—

" A certain merchant," says VALERIOLA, as quoted by SCHENCKIUS[*], " becoming insane, in consequence of love, grew quite melancholy ; was agitated by the appearance of wonderful phantoms in the day-time, as well as in the night ; would sometimes break out into rage and fury, and presently becoming mild and gentle, would indulge in immoderate laughter. He always affirmed that his mistress was present with him ; and while at some times, both his conversation, and gestures, were expressive of that tender attention which a lover displays when happy in the conversation of a mistress who is not insensible to his addresses ; at others, he would severely chide her for not favouring him with a proper return of affection. In short, all his discourse was about her : his whole days were spent in lamentation, he passed his nights without sleep, in grief and distress, and would have laid violent hands upon himself, had not his friends and domestics made use of force to prevent him[*]."

TASSO's

---

[*] Obs. Medic. Rar. lib. i. p. 134. Obs. 5.

[*] " Vir quidam mercator ex amore in insaniam deductus, melan-

TASSO's disorder, however, the description of which has been already quoted[b], is an instance in which the symptom above-mentioned, of conversation with a being which was present only in imagination, was purely maniacal; as is that of LUTHER and SWEDENBORG, hereafter to be noticed, and of many other enthusiasts[c].

This species of insanity often approaches near to, and is readily convertible into, phrenitic insanity. And as every other species of insanity is liable to become maniacal and phrenitic; so both these, besides their own peculiar symptoms, may be accompanied with the symptoms of any of the others.

In some cases which properly come under this species, it is difficult to discover any direct, and positive, evidence of the existence of ideal symptoms, except when the disorder is arrived at

---

melancholicus effectus est, mirisque visis etiam interdiu, nedum noctu agitabatur, modo in iram ac furorem concitus, mox placabilis in risum effusus, amatæ speciem se in momenta singula in conspectu habere affirmabat, illi blandiebatur, ac si præsens fuisset: mox quod se amantem redamare nollet, miris increpabat modis, omnis de amata sermo, omnis inter luctus ibat dies, noctem sine somno, tristitia mœrorque consumebant; et sibi ipsi injecisset manus, ni suorum vi prohibitus fuisset."

[b] See above, p. 81.

[c] Vide etiam BONETI Med. Sept. Coll. lib. i. § 19, cap. ix. tom. i. p. 188. N. B. The patient thought herself dead; and conversed with beings which were present only in imagination.

I 4   such

such a height, as to be bordering upon phrenitic
insanity: for, till they are thrown off their guard
by the very frequent, and vivid, appearance of delusive images, patients of this kind have often too
much remaining sense, and caution, to discover
to those about them, such visionary scenes, or
ideas, as they themselves scarcely know whether
to consider as realities, or illusions ; and which,
in whatever light *they* may view them, they are
very sensible that their friends will look upon as
no more than the delirious impressions of a distempered brain.   These cases, we must either
refer to some of the species of notional insanity,
till ideal symptoms actually discover themselves ;
or, where appearances are very strong, and especially where the eyes are in any degree suffused,
we may be content to rely upon circumstantial
evidence ; in which we shall seldom be deceived ;
the obvious appearances being generally sufficient,
under such circumstances, to point out the actual
existence of real, though latent, ideal symptoms.
It can scarcely, for example, be supposed, that a
man of ordinary birth, and in a private station,
should imagine himself to be a king, a prince, or
a hero, characters to which he has not the faintest
shadow of pretension ; or, that an ignorant, and
illiterate man, should fancy himself an admired
orator, or a celebrated actor, as I have sometimes
known, at the same time that he has never
actually sustained any such character ; or should

conceive

conceive himself, without even the slightest ground for such a fancy, to be a man of prodigious science, and learning, possessed of preternatural power, or favoured by Heaven with a knowledge of future events ;—we can scarcely suppose a man to be persuaded of the truth of such impossible things, without supposing, at the same time, that such visionary scenes have frequently presented themselves to his imagination, as are adequate to the production of such a deception, and sufficient to raise in him a firm persuasion so little consistent with reality. Indeed such delusive images are usually, sooner or later, actually discovered to exist ; and till they really make their appearance, while there remains the least doubt about the matter, they may with propriety be referred to their corresponding species of notional insanity.

4. By SENSITIVE INSANITY I mean that in which the disorder shows itself chiefly, or remarkably, in the erroneous images which are excited in the mind, relative to the person's own form, substance, or other sensible qualities, or contents ; and which are not only contrary to truth, but often inconsistent with the nature of things, and almost always contradictory to the testimony of the senses of those about them.

I call this *sensitive insanity*, because I imagine that such erroneous images are presented to the mind,

mind, for the most part, if not altogether, in consequence of erroneous sensation.

The absurd imaginations of persons afflicted with this species of insanity are almost innumerable. They have thought themselves transformed into wolves[e], dogs[f], lions[g], cats[h], cows[i], oxen[j], game-

---

[e] " Qui lycanthropia detinentur, noctu domo egressi, lupos in cunctis imitantur, et donec illucescat, circa defunctorum monumenta plerumque vagantur. Hæ comites ipsorum notæ sunt. Facies pallida, oculi sicci, et ad videndum imbecilli, lingua aridissima, nulla in ore saliva, sitis immodica, tibiæ sine remedio exulceratæ, quod frequenti per noctem ejus partis offensione accidit."—PAUL ÆGINET. de Re Medica, lib. iii. cap. xvi. p. 22, l. 15.

" They who are affected with that kind of insanity called *lycanthropia*, leaving their habitations in the night-time, imitate in every thing the actions of wolves, and usually ramble among the tombs till day-light appears. The concomitant symptoms of this disorder are,—a pale face ; dry eyes, with weakness of sight ; a parched tongue ; no saliva in the mouth ; incurable ulcerations in the legs, occasioned by the frequent injuries which they receive in these nightly excursions."

" Literarum monumentis tradit GULIELMUS Brabantinus in sua historia, virum prudentem diaboli arte eo perductum fuisse, ut aliquibus anni temporibus non secus sciverit quam se rapacem esse lupum, qui per loca sylvestria et specus oberraret, ac maxime pueros persequeretur, et eum sæpe velut amentem per nemora vagari inventum fuisse: qui tandem dei gratia ad mentem rediit."

" Ad hæc Patavii lupus sibi videbatur agricola, anno millessimo quingentesimo quadragesimo primo : multosque in agris insiliit, trucidavitque. Tandem non sine multa difficultate captus, confidenter asseveravit se verum esse lupum, discrimen

solum

game-cocks[k], sparrows[l], cuckoos[m], nightingales,

---

solum existere in pelle cum pilis inverso."—WIERI *de Præstig.*
Dæmon. lib. iv. cap. xxiii. p. 335, &c.

" WILLIAM of Brabant in his history, tells us of a man of
good understanding, who was so deluded by the artifice of the
devil, that, at certain seasons of the year, he imagined himself
to be a ravenous wolf, wandered about among woods and
caves, chiefly pursuing children, and was often found, like a
madman, rambling through the forests. At length, by the
grace of God, he was restored to his right mind."

" Also, a countryman, at Padua, in the year 1541, fancied
himself to be a wolf: and attacked many people in the fields,
and killed them. Being at length caught, not without a good
deal of difficulty, he confidently affirmed that he was a real
wolf; and that he differed in nothing from other wolves, but
in having the hair of his skin turned inwards."—*Vide etiam,*
cap. xxv. p. 339.—See another case of this sort in ZACUT.
LUSITAN. de Prax. Medic. admirand. lib. i. Obs. 51, p. 12,
col. 2, B, C. Oper. tom. ii. And two other curious ones in
SCHENCKII Obs. Med. Rar. lib. i. p. 129.—See also VAN
SWIETEN Comment. Aph. 1120, tom. iii. p. 521. BARTHO-
LINI de Morbis Biblicis, cap. xiii. p. 68, et ejusdem Epistol.
Medic. Cent. 2, Epist. 100, tom. i. p. 732.

f AETII Tetrabib. lib. vi. cap. xi.

g AVICENNA; quoted by WIERIUS, de Præstig. Dæmon.
loco supra citato, p. 336, § 5.

h RIVERII Prax. Medic. lib. i. cap. xiv. p. 188, col. 1.

i Of this kind was the madness of the daughters of PRŒ-
TUS, a king of the Argives, who were cured by MELAMPUS,
as mentioned by PLINY in his Natural History, lib. xxv. cap. v.
p. 457, l. 16.—VIRGIL alludes to their insanity in the following lines :—

" Prœtides implerunt falsis mugitibus agros :

" At non tam turpes pecudum tamen ulla secuta est
                                                    Concu-

gales", earthen vessels°, pipkins, jars, tea-pots⁹,

" Concubitus : quamvis collo timuisset aratrum,
" Et sæpe in levi quæsisset cornua fronte."
                                        Bucolic. Eclog. vi. v. 48.

" The maids of Argos (though with rage possess'd,
" Their imitated lowings fill'd the grove)
" Yet shun'd the guilt of thy prepost'rous love.
" Nor sought the youthful husband of the herd,
" Though lab'ring yokes on their own necks they fear'd ;
" And felt for budding horns on their smooth foreheads
. rear'd."
                                        DRYDEN.

ⁱ BARTHOLINI de Morb. Biblic. loco supra citato, de NE-
BUCODONOSORIS mania seu melancholia.—MEAD's Medica Sa-
cra, chap. vii. On the Disease of King NEBUCHADNEZZER.—
Works, vol. iii. p. 182.

ᵏ CÆL. AUREL. Morb. Chron. lib. i. cap. v. p. 328,
§ 152.
" Alii [se—esse putant] gallum etiam ut vocem illius imi-
tantor."—TRALLIAN. de *Arte Medic.* lib. i. cap. xvii. inter
HALLERI *Art. Med. Princip.* tom. vi. p. 91.
" Some have imagined themselves cocks, and imitated their
crowing."
" Alter gallos cantare audiens, ut hi alarum ante cantum,
sic ille brachiorum plausu latera quatiens, animantium sonum
imitatus est."—GALEN. de *Locis affect.* lib. iii. cap. vi. as
quoted by SCHENCKIUS *Obs. Medic. Rar.* lib. i. Obs. 1, p. 123.
" Another hearing the crowing of cocks, imitated their noise,
clapping his arms, and shaking his sides, as those animals clap
their wings before they crow."

ˡ CÆL. AUREL. Morb. Chron. ib.
ᵐ RIVERII Prax. Medic ib.

ⁿ TRALLIAN. de Arte Medic. ib.
ᵖ CÆL. AUREL. Morb. Chron. ib.

bricks,

bricks[q], candles[r], or the like. Some have imagined themselves to be made wholly, or in part,
of wax[s], butter[t], glass[u], leather[v], or straw[w].
One

---

[p] For this instance, and for that of male pregnancy, I have
only the authority of the poet; but have as much reason to believe them to be facts, from the consideration of their relative
probability, as that of the goose-pye, which we are told in Bishop Warburton's note on the passage,—" alludes to a real
fact, a lady of distinction imagined herself in this condition :—
and it is no diminution of their credibility, that they are of a
similar nature to others, for which we have more grave authority; and that several of the poet's other instances allude to
well attested facts. They are introduced in a description of the
Cave of Spleen, the whole of which is as just, as it is poetical.
He concludes as follows :—

" Unnumber'd throngs on every side are seen,
" Of bodies chang'd to various forms by spleen.
" Here living tea-pots stand, one arm held out,
" One bent; the handle this, and that the spout:
" A pipkin there, like Homer's tripod walks ;
" Here sighs a jar, and there a goose-pye talks ;
"· Men prove with child, as pow'rful fancy works,
" And maids turn'd bottles, cry aloud for corks."

Pope's *Rape of the Lock*, cant. iv. l. 47, &c. Works,
vol. i. p. 164.

I have since met with a well attested instance of male pregnancy.

[q] Cæl. Aurel. Morb. Chron. ib.—One thought himself a
brick, and obstinately refused to drink, lest he should be dissolved by the moisture."—Aræt. Cappad. de Causis et Sign.
Morb. Diuturn. lib. i. cap. vi. p. 32, A.

[r] Tissot de Valet. Literator. p. 22.

[s] Riverii Prax. Med. ib.—Tulpius relates a curious case,
which

One fancied that his head was cut off[x]; another
that

---

which fell under his own inspection, and which he cured by
an ingenious artifice, of an eminent painter who confined himself for a whole winter in bed, imagining all his bones to be as
soft and flexible as wax, and not daring to rise, lest, being unable to support his weight, they should give way under their
load, and his whole body should sink down into a mis-shapen
globular mass.—*Observ. Medic.* lib. i. cap. xviii. p. 36,—VAN
SWIETEN *Comment.* Aph. 1113, tom. iii. p. 513.

t " Orator, poeta, medicus GASPER BARLÆUS, non peri-
culi ignarus,—nimiis studiis, vim sensorii adeo fregit, ut suam
corpus butiraceum crederet, et ignem ne liquesceret anxie fu-
giebat, donec, sævorum pertæsus metuum, sese in puteum
præcipitem egit."—TISSOT, *de Valet. Literator.* p. 20.—*Vide*
BROEN *Animad. Medic.* p. 142.

" CASPER BARLÆUS, an orator, poet, and physician, who
was not ignorant of the danger of such a conduct, so injured
the *sensorium commune* by too intense application to study, that
he believed his body to be made of butter, and anxiously
avoided going near a fire, lest he should melt away; till being
wearied out with these dreadful apprehensions, he put an end
to his life, by throwing himself into a well."

u " Dum eruditus vir ex immodicis studiis in hunc morbum
inciderat, credebat se habere crura vitrea, hinc nullo modo illis
audebat insistere, sed de lecto ad focum deferebatur, cui tota
die assidebat. Ancilla, dum ligna adferebat foco alendo, ruditer illa projecit, unde territus herus, et cruribus suis vitreis
metuens, illam acriter objurgavit : morosa ancilla, et herilis insaniæ pertæsa, ligno percussit rudius heri tibiam, unde acrem
quidem dolorem sensit, sed simul iratissimus exiliit, ut illatam
hanc contumeliam ulcisceretur; paulo post, defervescente ira,
gavisus fuit, se cruribus insistere posse, et deleta fuit de
mente ejus vana hæc imaginatio."—VAN SWIETEN *Comment.*
Aph. 1113, p. 514.

" A learned

that he had lost his thighs[v] ; " ARTEMIDORUS
the grammarian, as we are told by CÆLIUS AURE-

" A learned man who fell into this disorder in consequence
of immoderate study, fancied that his legs were nothing but
glass, and for that reason dared on no account venture to stand
upon them ; but was carried from his bed to the fire-side, and
there sat from morning till night. His maid bringing one day
some logs of wood to mend the fire, threw them carelessly
down; for which her master, who was terrified for his legs of
glass, severely reprimanded her. The surly maid, who was
heartily tired of her master's insanity, gave him a smart blow
on the leg with one of the logs, which hurt him a good deal,
and so provoked him, that he rose from his seat in a violent
hurry, to revenge the insult. Soon after, when his anger was
abated, he was happy to find that his legs were able to support
him ; and his mind was from that time perfectly freed from this
absurd imagination."

" Quidam opinatus est ex vitro sibi conflatas clunes, sic ut
omnia sua negotia, atque actiones stando perficeret, metuens
ne si in sedile se inclinaret, nates confringeret, ac vitri frag-
menta hinc inde dissilirent.—ZACUTI LUSITANI de Medicor.
Princip. Hist. lib. i. Hist. 37. Paraphras. tom. i. p. 74,
col. 2, E.

" A certain person imagined his posteriors were made of
glass ; and therefore transacted all his business, and did every
thing else, standing ; for fear lest, if he should sit down, his glassy
foundation should break, and be shivered into fragments."—
See also SCHENCKII Obs. Med. Rar. lib. i. p. 124, col. 1.—
BARTHOLINE tells a similar story of a celebrated poet of Amsterdam.—Hist. Anat. Rar. Cent. 1. Hist. 79, p. 114.

[v] TRALLIAN. de Arte Med. lib. i. cap. xvii. inter HAL-
LERI Art. Medic. Princip. tom. vi. p. 91.

[w] VAN SWIETEN Comment. Aph. 1113, tom. iii. p. 513.
Straw (legs made of), BOERH. de Morbis Nerv. tom. ii. p. 409.
BONETI Med. Sept. Collat. lib. i. § 19, cap. i. tom. i. p. 182.

LIANUS,

LIANUS, being terrified by the unexpected appearance of a crocodile, was so much disordered by
the fright, that he not only imagined the animal
had devoured his left leg, and hand, but even forgot all that he had learned[x]."—Some have believed that they were incumbered with enormous
noses[a]; others have supposed themselves to be

grains

---

[x] TRALLIAN. ib.

[y] TISSOT de Valetud. Literator, p. 22.

[z] " Artemidorum grammaticum APOLLONIUS memorat
nitente gressu crocodilum in harena jacentem expavisse, atque
ejus metu percussa mente, credidisse sibi sinistrum crus atque
manum a serpente commestam, et literarum memoria caruisse
oblivione possessum."—Morb. Chron. lib. i. cap. v. p. 328,
§ 151.

[a] " Plebeius apud nos vir sanguine melancholico turgens,
nasum sibi in eam magnitudinem excrevisse imaginabatur, ut
publico abstineret, ne nasus a transeuntibus conculcaretur."—
BARTHOL. Hist. Anat. Rar. Cent. 1, Hist. 79, p. 114.

" A man of the lower order here, whose vessels were replete
with melancholy blood, imagined his nose to be grown to such
a size, that he was afraid of stirring out of doors, lest people
should tread upon it as they passed by him."

" Alius, referente QUERCATANO, tom. ii. p. 209, nasum
urnæ magnitudine sesé habere autumabat."—HOFFMANI Oper.
vol. vi. p. 342, § 8.

" Another, according to QUERCATANUS, fancied he had a
nose as large as a pitcher."

" Cuidam persuasum erat nasum sibi excrevisse in immen-
sum, atque in prodigiosam longitudinem, exporectum sic, ut
elephantis proboscidem circumferre visus sit, qui nusquam non
esset

grains of wheat, and have been for ever in apprehension lest they should be so unfortunate as to be eaten up by fowls [b]; and we are told of a lady who conceived that she was a goose-pye: one thought he had an immense pair of stag's horns branching from his forehead [c]; a man, as we are informed by CÆLIUS AURELIANUS, imagined himself a helpless infant, and cried to be led by the hand [d]; and some men, if we may believe the poet, have fancied themselves pregnant; SCHENCKIUS relates the case of a married woman, who was persuaded that she was very large about the waist, and in the last stage of pregnancy, when, in reality, she had been delivered but little more than a month, and did not appear to be larger than her natural size [e]; and I have known a young woman, who being insane, in consequence of the terror occasioned by

---

esset impedimento adeo ut subinde patinis, ut illi creditum est, innataret."—SCHENCKII *Obs. Medic. Rar.* lib. i. p. 124, col. 1.—Vide etiam BROEN. *Animad. Medic.* p. 142.

" A certain person was persuaded that his nose was grown to an immense magnitude, that it seemed, as he went about, to dangle from his face like the snout of an elephant, and to be always so much in his way, that he fancied as he sat at table, that he could not prevent it from floating in the dishes."

[b] RIVERII Prax. Med. lib. i. cap. xiv. p. 188, col. 1.— BROEN. Anim. Med. p. 142.—A grain of mustard. BONETI Med. Sept. Coll. lib. i. § 19, c. v. tom. i. p. 185.

[c] SCHENCKII Obs. Med. Rar. lib. i. p. 124, col. 2.

[d] CÆL. AURELIAN. loco citato.

[e] SCHENCKII Obs. Med. Rar. ib. p. 128, Obs. 8.

K an

an attempt made upon her person, imagined that
she was for ever bringing forth children, and had
a fresh delivery almost every instant: the celebrated Mons. PASCAL was persuaded that he had
a ball of fire sticking in his side[t]; and ZACUTUS
LUSITANUS tells us of a man who imagined himself
to be so intensely cold, that nothing could restore
him to his native heat, but actual burning in the
fire[s]: many have conceived that they had living

animals,

---

[t] " Post graves studendi, cogitandi et imaginandi exantlatos
labores, sic vitiabatur cerebrum BLASII PAACHALII, ut indefi-
nenti motu nonnullæ fibræ agitatæ hanc sensationem, animam
perpetuo experire cogerent, quam impressisset globus igneus a
latere positus, et nervis victa ratio vix ac ne vix præsentis globi
ideam deponere potuit."—TISSOT de Valet. Literat. p. 20.

" The brain of the celebrated Mons. PASCAL, was so much
injured by the severe labours of study, reflection, and imagination, which it had undergone, that certain of its fibres
were agitated with a perpetual vibration, which excited incessantly the same sensation in the soul, as would have been
produced by a ball of fire fixed in his side; and reason, overcome by the influence of the nerves, could scarcely ever lay
aside the idea of the actual presence of such a ball."

[s] " Quidam in vanam incidit imaginationem, ut se frigere
perpetuo arbitraretur, sicque ardente sirio ad ignem continuo
sedens, se non posse calefieri prædicabat, nisi toto corpore ure-
retur. Quumque clam, furtimque ter in ignem se projiceret;
tandem vinctus catenis, sedens semper juxta ignem, hac miserabili
imaginatione detentus, diem, noctemque miser ducebat insom-
nis."—ZACUT. LUSITAN. Prax. Medic. Admirand. lib. i.
Obs. 48, p. 11. ad fin. tom. ii. et ejusdem de Medicor. Princip. Histor. lib. i. Obs. 38, p. 75.

" A cer-

animals, men, devils, or other dreadful, or uncommon things within them[h] ; not a few have
fancied

" A certain person fell into the vain imagination that he was
perpetually affected with intense cold, so that, even in the
heat of the dog-days he would for ever sit at the fire, and
declare that it was impossible he should ever become warm,
unless his whole body were burned: and, having three times
privately and by stealth thrown himself into the fire, the unhappy man was at length secured with chains ; and sitting
always close to the fire, passed his miserable days and nights
without sleep, under the influence of this tormenting imagination."

[h] *Devils.*—" Bonarum literarum studiosus—mœrore ex
morte sororis fractus et lucubrationibus attritus, de diaboli insi-
diis apud me conqueritur. Affirmat sentire se malum spiritum
per anum ingredi cum vento sursumque in corpore suo repere
donec caput occupet, ne sacris solita devotione vacare possit ;
eundem vero eadem via descendere et exire quando ad preces
et lectiones sanctas accingitur. Ante hæc se inaudita lætitia
fuisse perfusum ex assiduis precibus et vigiliis, ut concentum
etiam cœlestem exaudiverit, spretisque mortalibus omnia in
pauperes erogasse : nunc defervente pietate ob nimium cibi ap-
petitum, ob turbatum isto vento cerebrum, cujusdam in cerebro
vocem se exaudire, βλασφημίαν exprobrantis, tundentes pugnos
se sensire, et fœtorem ante nares obversantem."—BARTHO-
LINI *Histor. Anat. Rarior.* Cent. 1, Hist. 85, p. 122.

" A certain student——dejected with grief for the death of
his sister, and worn out with study, complained to me of the
stratagems of the devil. He assured me that he could perceive the evil spirit to enter into him, accompanied with wind,
by the fundament, and to proceed upwards in his body till he
arrived at his head, so as to prevent him from attending to
sacred matters with his usual devotion : and to descend, and

fancied that some external part, or parts, of the
body, have been much altered in their form,
bulk,

---

pass out, by the same way, whenever he betook himself to
praying, and reading the scriptures. That before this, through
constant praying and watching, he had been filled with such
inexpresssible joy, as to hear the harmony of the heavenly
choir; and that despising mortal things, he had given away
whatever he had to the poor: but that now, since the fervour
of his piety was abated, by the violent cravings of hunger, and
the disturbance which this wind had produced in his brain,
he seemed to hear a voice proceeding from his brain, as of
somebody accusing him of blasphemy, felt the strokes of fists
on his body, and his nostrils were offended by a fetid smell."

" Accepi—a viro fide digno, quendam sibi persuasisse, tribus
dæmoniis agitari, in corpore latere, indicabat in scapulis, et in
fronte."—SCHENCKII *Obs. Med. Rar.* lib. i. p. 137, Obs. 11.

" I have been informed by a gentleman of credit, that a
certain person persuaded himself that he was possessed by
three devils, which were lodged in his body; and pointed out
his shoulder-blades, and his forehead, as the places of their residence."

" *Knights.*—" A fido didici teste, celebrem quondam acri-
tate disputationum PETR. JURIEU, et scriptis pugnando, et in
exponenda Apocalypsi laborando, sic cerebrum turbavisse, ut,
cætera sat sapiens, firmiter crederet sævas quibus premebatur
colicas, oriri ex continua dimicatione inter septem equites in-
testinis suis inclusos."—TISSOT. *de Valetud. Literatorum,* p. 22.

"I have learned from good authority, that PETER JURIEU, once
so famous for the acrimony of his disputes, so disordered his
brain by writing books of controversy, and by the labour of
composing an exposition of the Revelations, that, while in his
right mind in other respects, he firmly believed that the violent
colics with which he was tormented, arose from the continual
engagements of seven knights who were shut up in his bowels."

A Ser-

bulk, or appearance, by disease, when in reality
they were in a perfectly sound, and unaltered state[i];
one believed himself to be ATLAS, carrying the
world on his back ; and was in much anxiety lest
it should fall, and not only crush himself, but all
mankind, to atoms[j]; another imagined that he-

A Serpent.—TRALLIAN. de Arte. Med. lib. i. cap. xvii. inter HALLERI Art. Med. Princip. tom. vi. p. 91.—ALPINI de
Medicina Method. lib. x. cap. xi. p. 613.

Frogs and Toads.—SCHENCKII Obs. Med. Rar. lib. i.
p. 121, col. 1.—ALPINI de Med. Meth. ib. p. 614.—HOFF-
MAN. Suppl. secund. Part. secund. Prefatio, p. 227.

Mice.—RIVERII Prax. Medic. lib. i. cap. xiv. p. 188. col. 1.

A living Mole, or False Conception.—TUPLII Obs. Med.
lib. i. cap. xix. p. 39.

A Spike-nail.—BARTHOLINI Hist. Anat. Rar. Cent. 1.
Hist. 79, p. 114.

[i] " Scio quoque, ubi sulphur et picem redolere maritum oc-
clamaret melancholiæ vitium patiens conjux, et cibum oblatum
piper resipere judicaret ; quæ quam alienissima esse a rei veri-
tate cognoscebantur. Partes item pudibundas inflammatione pu-
toreque ita vitiatas asserebat, ut gangrænam suboriturum perti-
mesceret, his interim locis ab omni vitio immunibus."—WIERI
de Præstig. Dæmon. lib. iii. *de Lamiis,* cap. vii. § 6, p. 182.

" I know a married woman, disordered with melancholy,
who cried out that her husband smelt of sulphur and pitch ;
and declared that the food which was set before her tasted of
pepper ; though it was certain that nothing could be farther
from the truth. She also asserted that certain parts of her
body, which were in a perfectly sound state, were so inflamed,
and putrid, that she was terrified lest a mortification should
succeed."

TRALLIAN. de Arte Med. lib. i. cap. xvii. inter HALLERI
Art. Med. Princip. tom. vi. p. 91.

had

had so vast a quantity of urine within him, that
he was afraid of making water, lest his friends and
neighbours should be drowned in the deluge it
might produce[k].

---

[k] BROEN Animad. Medic. p. 142.

II. NOTIONAL INSANITY.

5. I have placed first in order under this division, that species of insanity which I have denominated *delusive*, because it nearly approaches to the two last-mentioned species of ideal insanity. It has a peculiar title to the appellation of *delusive*, because, without the smallest distinguishable trace of ideal delirium,—the images in the mind, so far as can be discovered, perfectly corresponding to the present external objects of sense, and to the natural, and real, state of his own body,—and with the sound ·and unimpaired use, in every other respect, of the rational faculties, which in some cases have even been observed to be remarkably acute, the patient, in relation to some particular subject, or subjects, is under the influence of the most palpable, and extraordinary delusion.

Of this species there are two varieties; the one nearly related to maniacal, and the other to sensitive insanity; but it is free, in the former case, from maniacal delirium, and in the latter, is never obviously accompanied with any erroneous ideas of the patient's own form, or other sensible qualities.

In the first-mentioned variety, the patient has such notions relative to his own powers, properties, and relations, as are incompatible with his state and nature, or inconsistent with fact and

K 4 reality;

reality; appears, for the most part, to derive these
erroneous notions rather from the suggestions of
fancy, than from the illusion of feeling; and generally discovers some degree of self-complacency, on
account of this imaginary possession of a supposed
excellency:—as when he imagines that he has the
power of working miracles[a];—of directing the
action of the elements, regulating the weather,
and distributing the seasons[b];—the power of
flying

---

[a] " Mens autem—erat læsa—illi, qui pollicebatur se GA-
BRIELEM aut MICHAELEM coacturum, ut ad se venirent, et
illos de rebus magnis interrogatos responsum daturos. Sed
cum ille rogaretur a Cardardinale TOURNONE, ut id efficeret:
respondebat se non posse, nisi præparato prius corpore multis
jejuniis et orationibus, nec nisi pro rebus reipublicæ chris-
tianæ."—WIERI de Præstig. Dæmon. lib. iii. de Lamiis,
cap. vii. p. 182.

" His mind was disordered, who pretended that he could
compel the angel GABRIEL, or MICHAEL, to come to him, and
to answer such questions as he should put to them about things
of high importance. But when he was asked by Cardinal TOUR-
NON to do so, he answered, that he could not, without first
preparing himself with much fasting and praying, nor unless
the common advantage of christianity required it."

[b] Though I can produce nothing better than poetical authority for this instance, yet as it is perfectly consonant to what I
myself have experienced to be fact, I have ventured to set it
down as such. The authority I allude to, is that of Dr. JOHN-
SON, in his Rasselas; where he has beautifully illustrated this
variety, in the character of an astronomer, who fancied he had
such a power. The whole story, and the observations upon
insanity which accompany it, are as just, and philosophical, as
they

flying through the air, from one place to another,
without the aid of wings ;—of hanging suspended,

they are elegant ; and are worthy of the pen from which they
proceeded. I shall only make a short extract.—" About ten
years ago," said the astronomer, " my daily observations of
the changes of the sky led me to consider, whether, if I had
the power of the seasons, I could confer greater plenty upon the
inhabitants of the earth. This contemplation fastened on my
mind, and I sat days and nights in imaginary dominion, pour-
ing upon this country and that showers of fertility, and se-
conding every shower of rain with a due proportion of sun-
shine. I had yet only the good will to do good, I did not
imagine I should ever have the power.

" One day as I was looking on the fields withering with
heat, I felt in my mind a sudden wish that I could send rain on
the southern mountains, and raise the Nile to an inundation.
In the hurry of my imagination, I commanded rain to fall, and
by comparing the time of my command, with that of the inundation, I found that the clouds had listened to my lips.—I
reasoned long against my own conviction, and laboured
against truth with the utmost obstinacy. I sometimes suspected myself of madness, and should not have dared to impart the secret but to a man like you, capable of distinguishing
the wonderful from the impossible, and the incredible from the
false.

" Why Sir, said I, do you call that incredible, which you
know, or think you know, to be true ?"

" Because," said he, " I cannot prove it by any external evidence ; and I know too well the laws of demonstration, to
think that my conviction ought to influence another, who
cannot, like me, be conscious of its force. I, therefore, shall
not attempt to gain credit by disputation. It is sufficient that
I feel this power, that I have long possessed, and every day
exert it."—*Rasselas, Prince of Abyssinia*, chap. xli. p. 253.

for

for any length of time, without the assistance of
any mechanical means;—of discharging blood
from any part of the body, and especially from
the urinary passage, or of retaining it; of emptying
the vessels to any degree, or of keeping them
full; by the sole direction of the will;—and of
performing a variety of other wonders—merely
by blowing with the breath,—by a particular motion of the leg, or foot,—posture of the body,—inclination of the head,—and a thousand other inadequate means, equally trifling, and ridiculous:—
or when he imagines that he possesses great authority, large domains, or abundant riches, when
possessed in reality of no such thing[e].

In

---

[e] " THRASYLAUS PYTHODORI filius, hac Insania correptus
fuit, ut æstimaret esse suas quæcunque in Piræeum naves ap-
pellarent, illas recenseret, demitteret, deduceret, in portum
subeuntes exciperet, tanto gaudio, quam si dominus earum
mercium esset, de his quæ perierant, nihil requireret, de iis
quæ allata et salva fuissent vehementer gauderet, sic multa cum
voluptate vitam agens. Ubi vero frater ejus CRITON ex Sicilia
reversus prehensum medicis tractandum commisit ab illa sana-
tus dementia lætius ac jucundius se nunquam vixisse affirmabat, quoniam et omnis molestiæ prorsus expers esset, et pluri-
mis interea voluptatibus frueretur."—ATHENÆI *Deipnosoph.*
lib. xii. Vide SCHENCKII *Obs. Med. Rar.* lib. i. p. 123, col. 2.

" THRASYLAUS, the son of PYTHODORUS,—was seized
with such an insanity, that he imagined all the ships which
came into the Pyræeus were his own; reviewed, dismissed,
and launched them; received those which arrived in port with
as much joy as if he were the proprietor of the merchandize they
                                                    brought

In the second variety the patient is deluded probably by something very strange and singular in his feelings, so as to form the most erroneous, and absurd conceptions of the state, and manner of existence of his own soul, or body, but without discovering any obvious indications of the presence of erroneous images in the mind, relative to his own form, substance, or other sensible qualities, or contents; and is usually, more or less, dejected, and distressed, on account of the supposed imper-fection of his unparalleled, and pitiable state.

Under this variety may be enumerated the cases of such as have imagined themselves to be dead[d],—to be deprived of their proper nature as

human

---

brought home: of which, if any were lost, he made no inquiry about it; but rejoiced greatly for whatever came safe. Thus he passed a life of much pleasure. But his brother CRITO, returning from Sicily, had him secured, and put under the care of the faculty; when, being cured of his insanity, he declared he had never lived with so much satisfaction, and pleasure, before; since he had nothing to disturb him, and a multitude of things to afford him delight."

[d] " Qui gravius laborant, sese—vel vita defunctos credunt." —" Alii epulas pertinacissime recusant, amissam esse vitam rati."—NICOL. PISONIS de cognosc. et curand. Morb. lib. i. cap. xxiii. tom. i. p. 163.

" They who are more violently affected—imagine themselves dead."—" Others obstinately refuse refreshment, conceiting that they have departed this life."

" A young hypochondriac had a strong imagination that he was dead, and did not only abstain from meat and drink, but

impor-

human beings*,—to have been once dead, and though restored to life again, to be sent back into the

---

importuned his parents that he might be carried to his grave, and buried before his flesh was quite putrified. By the counsel of physicians, he was wrapped in a winding-sheet, laid upon a bier, and so carried on men's shoulders towards the church; but on the way two or three pleasant fellows (hired for that purpose) meeting the hearse, demanded aloud of them that followed it, whose body it was that was there coffined and carried to burial? They said it was a young man's, and told his name: surely, replied one of them, the world is well rid of him, for he was a man of a very bad and vitious life, and his friends have cause to rejoice that he hath rather ended his days thus, than at the gallows. The young man hearing this, and not able to bear such injury, roused himself up on the bier, and told them they were wicked men to do him that wrong he had never deserved; that if he were alive again, he would teach them to speak better of the dead. But they proceeding to defame him, and to give him much more disgraceful and contemptuous language, he not able to suffer it, leaped from the bier, and fell about their ears, with such rage and fury, that he ceased not buffeting them till quite wearied; and by the violent agitation of the humours, his body being altered, he returned to his right mind, as one awakened out of a trance; and being after brought home and refreshed with wholesome diet, within few days he recovered both his health and his understanding."

" A noble person fell into this fancy, that he verily believed he was dead,—insomuch that when his friends and familiars besought him to eat,—he still refused all, saying it was in vain to the dead; but when they doubted not but that this obstinacy would prove his death, and this being the seventh day from whence he had continued it, they bethought themselves of

the world without a heart, and to exist in a manner totally different from all other mortals[f],—to have no

---

of this device: they brought into his room, which on purpose was made dark, some personated fellows wrapped in their winding-sheets, and such grave-clothes as the dead are appareled with: these bringing in meat and drink, began liberally to treat themselves. The sick man seeing this, asks them who they are, and what about. They told him they were dead persons: what then, said he, can the dead eat! Yes, yes, say they, and if you will sit down with us, you shall find it so: straight he springs from out of his bed, and falls to with the rest. Supper ended, he drops into a sleep, by virtue of a liquor given him for that purpose."—TURNER *of Diseases incident to the Skin,* p. 167.

The last of these stories is related by SCHENCKIUS, from LEMNIUS.—Vide *Obs. Med. Rar.* lib. i. p. 123, col. 2.

A similar imagination in an ardent fever, is related by SCHENCKIUS from HOLLERIUS, without any clear account of ideal delirium; at least the patient appears—" to see as he ought to see, but not to judge as he ought to judge."—" In febre ardente Burgundus quidam Lutetiæ—multis clarissimis medicis adstantibus mortuum se affirmabat simul cum fratre ibi decumbente. Postea phantasia mutata declamabat, precabaturque medicos, ne amplius animæ impedimento essent, quo minus e purgatorio evolaret ad deum : aliquando imitabatur moribundum, quasi efflaret animam, monebat ut spectarent expiratum ; postea summo timore et omnium desperatione corripiebatur. Tandem, opportunis adhibitis remediis, et hæmorrhoidum profluvio liberatus est."—SCHENCKII *Obs. Med. Rar.* lib. i. p. 124, col. 1.

" A certain Burgundian, at Paris, in an ardent fever—declared, in the presence of many eminent physicians, that he, and his brother who was lying ill at the same time, were both dead.

no rational soul, it having gradually decayed and
perished, so as to leave a living man indeed, but
perfectly empty of all thought[e],—and whatever

---

dead. Afterwards, the delirium taking a different turn, he
talked much, and begged that the physicians would no longer
hinder his soul from escaping from purgatory to God. Sometimes he imitated a dying person, pretended to be breathing
his last, and desired they would observe him expire. Afterwards he was seized with extreme terror, and despair. At
length he was freed from his disorder, by the proper use of
medicines, and a copious discharge of blood from the hæ-
morrhoidal veins."—*Vide etiam* BONETI. *Med. Sept. Coll.*
lib. i. § 19, cap. ix. tom. i, p. 188.—N. B. This case was
become maniacal.

e " Eo usque delirabat [juvenis ditissimi mercatoris filius] ut
sese hominem esse haud agnosceret."—SCHENCKII *Obs. Med.*
Rar. lib. i. p. 127, Obs. 7.

" A young man, the son of a rich merchant, was delirious to
such a degree, that he could not be satisfied that he was any
longer a man."

f " [Quædam]—incidit in insaniam—credens firmiter, se
fato functam, ea conditione a DEO in mundum remissam, ut
viveret deinneps excors. Corde enim suo, a DEO, retento,
doluit impense, aliamque sibi, quam aliorum mortalium vitam :
afflixit quidem ipsam aliquandiu hæc tristitia : sed tandem licet
tardius, discessit."—TULPII *Obs. Med.* lib. i. cap. 19, p. 39.

" A certain woman became insane—and firmly believed that
she had been dead, and by God sent back again into the world,
on condition that she should for ever after live without a heart.
But she was exceedingly grieved that God had withheld her
heart, and that her life was of so different a nature from that
of other mortals :—in this manner she was afflicted for some
time; at length, however, though slowly, her disorder left
her."

other

other cases may occur, of the like wonderful and
unaccountable delusions.

Though

₵ This is strikingly exemplified in the case of Mr. Simon
Browne; who, at the same time that he was firmly persuaded of the truth of so absurd a notion as " that his soul had
long been annihilated," does not appear to have discovered the
smallest degree of ideal insanity. As the history of his disorder
is very circumstantially related; is as well attested, as it is
extraordinary; and is at present buried amidst the multifarious
contents of so miscellaneous a repository as a voluminous
Monthly Magazine; I shall make no apology for transcribing
it here at length. It stands in the Gentleman's Magazine as
follows :—

Oct. 19th, 1762.

MR. URBAN,

" You have been so kind as to oblige your readers, by in-
serting many curious anecdotes and letters of deceased persons,
some of which I have sent you. This gives me encouragement
to hope that you will publish the following epistle, which I can
warrant an original. It was written by the Rev. Mr. Simon
Browne (who was many years ago a minister and an author in
this city) to the Rev. Mr. Read, of Bradford, Wilts, deceased, from whom I received it. It is well known, that for
several years Mr. Browne had a peculiar and unhappy turn
of mind concerning himself, imagining that he had no rational
soul; at the same time he was so acute a disputant, that his
friends said he could reason as if he was possessed of two souls.
Your publishing this letter, as it may be useful to some persons, will oblige, Sir, yours, &c. R. W."

" REV. SIR,

" I doubt not you have been earnest with God in my be-
half, since you left the city, who expressed so much tender
concern

Though both these varieties of delusive insanity are, in many cases, obviously distinct from
the

---

concern for me while you were in it. I wish I could write
any thing to you that might turn your compassion into thanks-
giving, and your prayers into praises. But alas! nothing of
that kind is to be expected from one who has lived a life of de-
fiance to God, under a christian profession, and a sacred character; and is now, through his just displeasure, in the most
forlorn state a man can be on earth, perfectly empty of all
thought, reflection, conscience, or consideration; destitute,
entirely destitute of the knowledge of God, Christ, and his
own soul, and the things both of time and eternity, being unable to look backward or forward, or inward or outward, or
upward or downward; having no capacity of reviewing his
conduct, or looking forward with expectation of either good
or evil; and, in a word, without any principles of religion, or
even of reason, and without the common sentiments and reflections of human nature; insensible even to the good things
of life, incapable of tasting any present enjoyments, or expect-
ing future ones; dead to his children, friends, and country;
having no interest, either bodily or spiritual, temporal or eternal, to value or mind, but converted into a mere beast, that
can relish nothing but present bodily enjoyments, without
tasting them by anticipation or recollection.

" This is my true condition, thus am I thrown down from
my excellency. Because I had not, God has taken away the
things that I had. Indeed I have not those horrors on my
mind to which you was a witness; I am grown more calm, because more insensible, and every day since you saw me, has
this insensibility been growing upon me; nor can it be removed without a miracle of grace, and for this grace I cannot
pray, having lost all sight of God, and tenderness of soul towards him. Such an instance of divine displeasure, the world
hardly

the two species of ideal insanity to which, as I have said, they are so nearly allied; yet in others, it

---

hardly ever saw, much less one recovered by divine grace out of such a condition. I doubt whether you have room to pray, but if you think you have, I doubt not that you will be fervent at the throne of grace in your requests. But I am so changed that I must first be made a man, before I can be made a christian; having now none of that knowledge or common sentiments on which a saving change must be founded. I am utterly incapable of any business in life, and must quit my present station, and think as soon as I can to be retiring into my own country, there to spend out the wretched remains of a miserable life, which yet I am continually prompt to destroy. I thought you would be willing to hear from me; and though you cannot be pleased with the account, I am obliged to give you a true one, and beg an interest in your prayers, which will turn to your own account, if it avails nothing towards the salvation of the most wretched and wicked sinner, who would yet, if he was able, be

" Your friend and servant,

" SIMON BROWNE."

" The following account of this extraordinary man we have taken from the Adventurer, No. 88, as a proper supplement to this letter; for which we are greatly obliged to our correspondent.

" Mr. SIMON BROWNE was a dissenting teacher, of exemplary life, and eminent intellectual abilities; who, after having been some time seized with melancholy, desisted from the duties of his function, and could not be persuaded to join in any act of worship, either public or private. His friends often urged him to account for this change in his conduct, at which they expressed the utmost grief and astonishment; and after much importunity, he told them, ' that he had fallen under

it must be acknowledged, they approach so near,
the one to maniacal, and the other to sensitive
insanity,

---

the sensible displeasure of God, who had caused his rational
soul gradually to perish, and left him only an animal life in
common with brutes ; that it was therefore profane in him to
pray, and incongruous to be present at the prayers of others.'

" In this opinion, however absurd, he was inflexible, at a
time when all the powers of his mind subsisted in their full vigour, when his conceptions were clear, and his reasoning
strong.

" Being once importuned to say grace at the table of a friend,
he excused himself many times ; but the request being still repeated, and the company kept standing, he discovered evident
tokens of distress, and, after some irresolute gestures, and he-
sitation, expressed with great fervor this ejaculation : ' Most
merciful and Almighty God, let thy spirit, which moved upon
the face of the waters when there was no light, descend upon
me ; that from this darkness there may rise up a man to praise
thee.'

" But the most astonishing proof of his intellectual excellency and defect is, A Defence of the Religion of Nature and
the Christian Revelation, in answer to Tindal's Christianity
as old as the Creation, and his Dedication of it to the late
Queen. The book is universally allowed to be the best which
that controversy produced, and the dedication is as follows :

" MADAM,

" Of all the extraordinary things that have been rendered to
your royal hands since your first happy arrival in Britain, it
may be boldly said, what now bespeaks your Majesty's accept-
ance is the chief.

" Not in itself indeed ; it is a trifle unworthy your exalted
rank, and what will hardly prove an entertaining amusement

to

Insanity, as to render it sometimes no very easy matter to distinguish them.

The

---

to one of your Majesty's deep penetration, exact judgment, and fine taste.

" But on account of the author, who is the first being of the kind, and yet without a name.

" He was once a man; and of some little name; but of no worth; as his present unparalleled case makes but too manifest; for by the immediate hand of an avenging GOD, his very thinking substance has for more than seventeen years been continually wasting away, till it is wholly perished out of him, if it be not utterly come to nothing. None, no not the least remembrance of its very ruins remains, not the shadow of an idea is left, nor any sense that, so much as one single one, perfect or imperfect, whole or diminished, ever did appear to a mind within him, or was perceived by it.

" Such a present from such a thing, however worthless in itself, may not be wholly unacceptable to your Majesty, the author being such as history cannot parallel; and if the fact, which is real, and no fiction, or wrong conceit, obtains credit, it must be recorded as the most memorable, and indeed astonishing event in the reign of GEORGE the Second, that a tract composed by such a thing was presented to the illustrious CAROLINE; his royal consort needs not be added; fame, if I am not misinformed, will tell that with pleasure to succeeding times.

" He has been informed that your Majesty's piety is as genuine and eminent, as your excellent qualities are great and conspicuous. This can, indeed, be truly known to the great searcher of hearts only: He alone, who can look into them, can discern if they are sincere, and the main intention corresponds with the appearance; and your Majesty cannot take it amiss, if such an author hints, that his secret approbation is of

L 2　　　　infinitely

The celebrated VAN HELMONT seems to have been affected with a temporary delusive insanity, of

---

finitely greater value than the commendation of men, who may be easily mistaken, and are too apt to flatter their superiors.

"But if he has been told the truth, such a case as his will certainly strike your Majesty with astonishment, and may raise that commiseration in your royal breast which he has in vain endeavoured to excite in those of his friends; who by the most unreasonable, and ill-founded conceit in the world, have imagined that a thinking being could, for seven years together, live a stranger to its own powers, exercises, operations, and state, and to what the great GOD has been doing in it and to it.

" If your Majesty, in your most retired address to the King of Kings, should think of so singular a case, you may, perhaps, make it your devout request, that the reign of your beloved sovereign and consort may be renowned to all posterity, by the recovery of a soul now in the utmost ruin, the restoration of one utterly lost at present amongst men.

" And should this case affect your royal breast, you will recommend it to the piety and prayers of all the truly devout, who have the honour to be known to your Majesty: many such, doubtless, there are: though courts are not usually the places where the devout resort, or where devotion reigns. And it is not improbable, that multitudes of the pious throughout the land may take a case to heart, that under your Majesty's patronage comes so recommended.

" Could such a favour as this restoration be obtained from heaven, by the prayers of your Majesty, with what a transport of gratitude would the recovered being throw himself

of this second variety, when, after tasting of a pre-paration of the *napellus,* or monkshood, he could plainly perceive, as he imagined, that the seat of his intellectual, and reasoning faculty, was not in his brain, but in his stomach.

The passage in his works, which I here allude to, is of so curious a nature, and his whimsical, and eccentric writings, though interspersed with many ingenious, and some useful observations, are so little read; and indeed, upon the whole, so little deserve to be read; that I presume there are many, who neither are conversant with his works, nor desire to be so, to whom a pretty long extract

---

at your Majesty's feet, and adoring the divine power and grace, profess himself,

" MADAM,

" Your Majesty's most obliged and dutiful servant."

" This dedication, which is no where feeble or absurd, but in the places where the object of his phrensy was imme-diately before him, his friends found means to suppress; wisely considering, that a book to which it should be prefixed, would certainly be condemned without examination; for few would have required stronger evidence of its inutility, than that the author by his dedication appeared to be mad. The copy, however, was preserved, and has been transcribed into the blank leaves before one of the books, which is now in the library of a friend to this undertaking, who is not less distinguished by his merit than his rank, and who recommended it as a literary curiosity, which was in danger of being lost, for want of a repository in which it might be preserved."—*Gentle-man's Magazine for October,* 1762, vol. xxxii. p. 453, &c.

relative

relative to this very singular discovery, may not be unacceptable, or unentertaining.

"I began," says he, "to treat monkshood in a variety of ways. And once, after slightly preparing the root, I tasted it with the tip of my tongue. But though I did not swallow the smallest particle, and spit a good deal after it, yet I soon perceived my skull to be externally bound tight, as with a broad bandage. Just then intervened a hurry of family affairs; I settled an account, went about the house, and did such other business as was requisite. At length, what I had never observed before, I was sensible that I neither understood, conceived, nor in any respect exercised the powers of understanding or imagination, in the usual manner, in the head: but perceived, with admiration, plainly, clearly, reflectively, and constantly, that this whole business was performed in the breast, and seemed to be expanded about the mouth of the stomach: and this I perceived so sensibly, and distinctly, and even so attentively noticed, that though I at the same time was conscious that sensation and motion continued to be distributed to every part of the body from the head; yet the whole discursive, or reasoning faculty, as if the mind was then holding its deliberations there, evidently and sensibly resided in the breast, to the total exclusion of the head. Full of admiration, and astonishment, at this uncommon sensation, I strictly attended to
                                                            my

my own conceptions, and began to examine both
them, and myself, with more precision. And I
plainly discovered, and was satisfied, that during
all that time I comprehended and reflected with
more than my usual perspicuity; insomuch that
no words can describe that sensation by which I
perceived that I performed the offices of the understanding, and imagination, in the breast, and
not in the head. There was a kind of joyful delight
in that intellectual illumination. Now it was not
an affair of short duration, nor did it happen to
me while I was sleeping, or dreaming, or in any
respect disordered; but while I was fasting, and
in good health. And though I had before experienced several ecstasies, yet I remarked that they
had no resemblance whatever to this sensation
of reasoning and understanding in the breast,
which thus excluded all co-operation of the head.
For I found by sensible reflection, which I exercised with as much attention as if I had been fore-
warned so to do, that, so far as the imagination
was concerned, the head was totally unemployed;
for, I remember, I wondered that the operations
of the imagination should, with a sensible exulta-
tion, be performed out of the brain, and in the
neighbourhood of the breast. In the mean
time I was sometimes held suspended, in the
midst of my delight, with the fear lest these unusual
perceptions should be but the prelude to insanity;
since they took their rise from a poison: but this

fear

fear was counteracted, by reflecting on the preparation which the poison had undergone, and the
very slight taste I had taken of it. But though
this unexpected brightness, or joyous illumination
of my understanding, gave me reason to be suspicious of this new mode of perception; yet a free
and full resignation of myself to the divine will,
at once restored me to my former happiness. At
last, after about two hours, I was twice seized
with a kind of slight vertigo. In consequence of
the first, I perceived that my intellectual faculty
was returned; and of the second, that its operations were performed in the usual manner.
Though, after this, I several times tasted of this
same monkshood, yet I never again experienced
any thing similar. And, indeed, I learned abundantly enough from this one experiment only[b]."

It

---

[b] "Coepi diversimode napellum agitare. Ac semel, cum
ejus radicem ruditer præparassem, degustavi in apice linguæ.
Etenim quanquam nil deglutiveram, multumque salivæ sputi-
taveram, sensi tamen mox abinde, cranium velut zona forinse-
cus stringi. Tum demum præcipitanter aliquot mihi negotia
familiæ obvenere, computum quendam solvi, per ædes ober-
ravi, atque singula pro requisito peregi. Tandem obvenit
mihi (quod nunquam alias) quod sentirem, me nil intelligere,
concipere, sapere vel imaginari in capite, pro more alias solito;
sed sensi (cum admiratione) aperte, dilucide, discursive, atque
constanter, totum istud munus obiri in præcordiis, et expandi
circa os stomachi, idque adeo sensibiliter et clare sensi, imo
attente notavi, quod quamvis etiam sentirem sensum et motum,

﹀ It must appear something extraordinary, after
reading the above account of the excessive activity.

---

tum, sospites, a capite in totum dispensari: quod tota discur-
suum facultas notorie et sensibiliter in præcordiis esset, cum
exclusione capitis, quasi tunc mens consilia sua ibidem meditaretur. Admirationis itaque et stuporis, insolitæ illius sensa-
tionis, plenus, notabam mecum meas notiones, et examen earundem, atque mei ipsius, præcisiori modo, instituebam. Et
luculenter inveni, ac trutinavi, me, illo toto spatio, intelligere
et meditari, longe perspicacius. Adeoque non potest sensus
ille, quo perspiciebam me intelligere et imaginari in præcordiis, et non in capite, ullis exprimi verbis. Eratque gaudium
quoddam, in ista intellectuali claritate. Etenim non erat res
exiguæ durationis; nec mihi dormienti, aut somnianti, aut
alioqui morbido, advenerat : sed jejuno et benevalenti accide-
rat. Imo quamvis ecstases aliquot antea expertus fueram, notavi tamen, illas nil commune habere cum hoc præcordiali dis-
cursu et sensu intelligendi, omnem capitis co-operationem ex-
cludente. Quippe quod cum reflectione sensibili (tanquam
antea præmonitus essem) caput prorsus feriari, respectu phantasiæ, deprehendi : quia mirabar, quod phantasia extra cerebrum, in præcordiis, sensibili operationis festivitate celebrare-
tur. Interim quandoque in gaudio illo suspensus timui, inso-
litus ne casus in amentiam deduceret : eo quod a veneno ince-
pisset : sed præparatio veneni, et ejusdem levicula tantum de-
gustatio, aliud insinuabant. Interim quanquam claritas, sive
illuminatio gaudiosa mei intellectus, inauspicata, suspectum
illum intelligendi modum redderent : attamen resignatio liber-
rima mei, in voluntatem divinam, me restituit in sabbatismum
priorem. Tandem, post binas circiter horas, levicula quædam
vertigo, bis repetita, me invasit. A priore enim rediisse intelligendi facultatem percepi : et altera, sensi me intelligere more
solito. Deinde, tametsi postmodum aliquoties de eodem na-
pello degustaverim, attamen nunquam amplius quicquam tale
mihi contigit. Perfecte enim multa exinde didici."—VAN HEL-
MONT *Demens Idea*, § 12, *Operum*, p. 171.

of

of the monkshood, when only tasted by the tip of the tongue, and carefully spit out again ;—if we allow that these wonderful sensations were not produced by some other cause, but were really occasioned by the virulence of this poisonous plant ;—that it should since have been so strongly recommended by STORCK, under the name of *aconite*, as—" innocuum, et valde efficax medicamentum"—" an innocent, and very powerful medicine ;"—the extract of which, as he informs us, he has given in so large a dose as twenty grains, and has sometimes repeated it three times in the short space of four and twenty hours.

6, In WHIMSICAL INSANITY the patient is possessed with absurd, and whimsical fancies[i], aversions[k], fears[l], scruples, and suspicions ;[m] of which

he

---

[i] ANTONII STORCK libellus, quo demonstratur, stramonium, hyoscyamum, aconitum, non solum tuto posse exhiberi usu interno hominibus; verum et ea esse remedia in multis morbis maxime salutifera. P. 51, Experim. 14.

[j] " Refert unius historiam AVENZOAR—" Qui cum probus esset, armis minitabatur servos, ut farinam in puteum injicerent, et pedibus malaxarent, et facerent placentulas."— ZACUT. LUSITAN. *de Med. Princip. Hist.* lib. i. Hist. 37, *Paraphr. Operum;* tom. i. p. 74, col. 2, E.

[k] " AVENZOAR tells us the story of one, who, though a very good sort of man, obliged his servants, by force of arms, to throw flour into a well, and to tread and mix it with their feet, in order to make pancakes."

" Nobilis fœmina ex hypochondriorum vitio diuturno in melancholiam

he is sometimes the sport of an endless variety; and is peculiarly apt to imagine ridiculous, improbable,

---

lancholiam tandem incidit, gravem illam et pertinacem; sed quæ tamen usque eo expugnari se pharmacis passa est, ut raro nunc interpellet, uno symptomate excepto, quod tenaciter adhuc adhærescit. Quotiescunque etiam inter preces et maxime seria versatur, omnes stipulas, et plumas per totum conclave anxie vestigat, colligit, et sibi seponit. Accedit et mirum calceorum novorum desiderium : nam quemcunque, et ubicunque reperit novis calceamentis indutum, ad illum tacite se confert, solvit corrigias, et calceos clam suis pedibus aptat."—BARTHOLINI *Acta Medica et Philosophica Hafniensia.* Volum. iv. n. 45, p. 148.

" A lady of a noble family, having long been troubled with an hypochondriacal disorder, fell at length into deep, and obstinate, melancholy; which, however, has so far given way to medicines, that it now rarely shows itself, except in one symptom, which yet remains unmoved. Whenever she is engaged about the most serious matters, not excepting even her prayers, she anxiously searches about the room for straws, and feathers, which she collects, and carefully lays by themselves. She has also, a wonderful fondness for new shoes: and whenever she finds persons with new shoes on, be they who or where they will, she approaches them with caution, unbuckles their shoes, and carefully puts them upon her own feet."

* A very curious instance of this variety of whimsical insanity is minutely related by SCHENCKIUS, of a lady of a good family, whose insane aversion had gradually extended almost to every thing; and in the midst of plenty, had left her scarcely a rag to her back, through her antipathy to the makers of all kinds of apparel; had deprived her of every kind of aliment, whether solid or fluid, excepting the milk of one cow which she kept

probable, or impos:
great, important, c

---

kept .for her own sole u
her aversion; and had
for she had an aversion t
out of which she woulc
The whole history is w
place.—*Vide* SCHENCK
Obs. 5.

" Alii mingere non
RIVERII *Prax. Med.* p.
" Some dare not ma
deluge by so doing."

" In Anglia quidam n
corporis per urinam exce
aliquot constrinxit, quo
a fratre vi vinculum f
Anat. Rar. Cent. 1. His

" Fuit autem alter tin
dicitur, gravatus sub ta
ipse cum illo collideretur
—GALENI *de Locis affe*
Obs. Med. Rar. p. 123,

" Another feared les
world, should become w
from him; and he, and
its ruins."

" Memini me sapien
qui dum audivisset plure
hydrophobos, licet et v
tentata fuissent, incidi
num, dum forte j
sectonibus in

little, insignificant, and altogether inadequate causes; or, on the contrary, to imagine causes

of

---

posse, atque denuo aliis communicari. Hinc a nullo mortalium tangi se patiebatur, ut tantam calamitatem vitaret. Nec conjugis aut liberorum amor a severo hoc proposito abducere poterant prudentem in reliquis virum."—VAN SWIETEN *Comment.* tom. iii. Aph. 1094, p. 475.

" I remember to have seen a man, of sound mind in every other respect, who having heard that many people had been bitten by a mad dog, and that though they had been bled, and had tried the most approved remedies, they had yet been seized with the hydrophobia; took the notion into his head, that, as the surgeons had probably used the same lancets in bleeding other persons, that dreadful poison might be spread, and diffused, through a number of people in whom the disorder had not yet made its appearance, and might by them be communicated to others. To avoid, therefore, this calamity, he would not suffer a single mortal to touch him. And notwithstanding his good sense in other respects, not even his affection for his wife, and children, could make him deviate from this severe resolution."

To this head may be referred the insanity of the carpenter, mentioned by ARETÆUS; and another similar instance related by BARTHOLINE; which seem both to have owed their existence to a whimsical and absurd fear,—the one of going from home, and appearing in public,—and the other of receiving the sacrament at church.—*Vide* ARETÆI CAPPAD. *Morb.. Diuturn.* lib. i. cap. vi. p. 32, A—*et* BARTHOLINI *Acta Medica et Philosophica Hafniensia*, vol. i. n. 50, p. 102.—BONET. *Med. Sept. Coll.* lib. i. § 19, cap. iv. tom. i. p. 185.—BOERHAAV. *de Morbis Nervor.* tom. ii. p. 408.

ᵐ Ὕποπτος—Suspicious.—ARETÆI CAPPAD. *Morb. Diuturn.* lib. i. cap. v. p. 29, F, et p. 32, C.

" Cum

of considerable, and even of vast extent, and magnitude, to account for the existence of things, circumstances, or events, comparatively mean, inconsiderable, and no way uncommon or extraordinary.

As whimsical and absurd fancies, 'fears, and suspicions, are the characteristic of this species of insanity; so such persons are more especially liable
to it, who are naturally of a whimsical turn of
mind, or of timid, irresolute, and suspicious tem-
pers, and of a weak judgment: they are often indeed exceedingly ingenious, and much admired
for quick parts, lively feelings, and brilliancy of
imagination; but their judgment may, on a strict
examination, always be discovered, from some
cause or other, chiefly perhaps from an aptitude to
form slight and hasty associations, to be considerably defective.

" Cum suspicionibus velut insidiarum sibi paratarum."—
CÆL. AUREL. Morb. Chronic. lib. i. cap. vi. p. 340, § 181.

" Some suspect—that treacherous designs are formed against
them."

" Suspicionesque falsas habeat [æger], quasi nonnulli velint
eum interimere, aut gladio arrepto, aut medicamento exhibito."
—ALEXAND. TRALLIAN. de Arte Medica. lib. i. cap. xvii.
inter HALLERI Art. Med. Princip. tom. vi. p. 90.

" The patient has groundless suspicions, as if people had a
design to take away his life, either by the sword, or by poison."
—Vide BONETI Med. Sept. Col. lib. i, § 19, cap. iv. tom. i.
p. 184.

We

- We need not therefore be surprized to find that the very ingenious, and, in many respects, amiable ROUSSEAU,—whose quickness of imagination, and delicacy, not to say irritability of feeling, were scarcely to be equalled,—was affected by the last variety of this species of insanity.

In a late publication, entitled *Rousseau Juge de Jean Jacques*, consisting of dialogues between himself and a Frenchman,—in which ROUSSEAU defends his own character, as that of a third person, under the appellation of JEAN JACQUES,—in order to account for the ill usage he had met with from mankind, he supposes, and endeavours to prove, that all the world had entered into a combination to humble his pride, and defame his character. The most natural way, he says, of explaining the mysterious, and inhuman conduct of mankind towards him, is,—" To suppose a league, the object of which is the defamation of JEAN JACQUES, whom it hath taken care to render an unconnected, and insulated being, for that very purpose. But why," he continues, "do I say suppose? Whatever were the motives which gave rise to this league, it actually exists: according to your own account it appears to be universal; it is at least great, powerful, and numerous; it acts in concert, with the most profound secresy with regard to all who are not concerned in it, and especially with regard to the unfortunate being who is the object of it. To defend himself

self against it, he has no succour, no friend, no support, no council, no light. He is surrounded with nothing but snares, falsehoods, treacheries, and darkness. He is absolutely alone, and has no resource but in himself. He has no prospect of aid, or assistance, from any one person upon earth. A situation so singular is an unique, and has had no parallel from the creation of the human race to this day[n]."

The prepossessions, and fancies, of the whimsically insane, being strong and lively, they are usually obstinate both in opinion and conduct; and sometimes, when their imaginations are deeply impressed with violent suspicion, or other erroneous notions, and the disorder is bordering upon ideal insanity, of the phrenitic kind, they

---

[n] " De supposer une ligue dont l'objet est la diffamation de J. J. qu'elle a pris soin d'isoler pour cet effet. Et que dis-je, supposer? Par quelque motif que cette ligue se soit formée, elle, existe: sur votre propre rapport elle sembleroit universelle, elle est du moins grande, puissante, nombreuse, elle agit de concert dans le plus profond secret pour tout ce qui n'y entre pas, et surtout pour l'infortune qui en est l'objet. Pour s'en defendre il n'a ni secours, ni, ami, ni appui, ni conseil, ni lumiere; tout n'est autour de lui que pieges, mensonges, trahisons, tenebres. Il est absolument seul, et n'a que lui seul pour ressource; il ne doit attendre ni aide ni assistance de qui que ce soit sur la terre. Un position si singuliere est un unique depuis l'existence du genre humain."—ROUSSEAU *Juge de* JEAN JACQUES, *Dialogues*, p. 307.—See a curious anecdote of ROUSSEAU's insanity in the European Magazine for October 1787, p. 295.

are

are disposed, when any convenient opportunity presents itself, to commit both whimsical, and horrid, acts of violence.

7. FANCIFUL INSANITY is a species of insane delirium, of the notional kind, in which there appears to be very great activity, and vivacity, of imagination; which displays itself in almost incessant talking, accompanied with frequent sallies of wit, quick repartee, acute observation, ready invention, lively, and even brilliant fancy, and, in a variety of respects, with much appearance of genius° ; and arises from a rapid succession of vivid and sprightly images; and a wonderful aptitude to catch at the slightest associations, and to run through all the relations, whether natural,

---

° " Vidi fœminam, quæ aliquot vicibus maniam passa fuit, dum insaniret, omnia ligato sermone pronunciasse, et mira facilitate rythmos invenisse, cum nihil tale unquam aliter perficere potuerat dum esset sana, imo nunquam tentaverat, a prima juventute manuum laboribus victum sibi comparare coacta, et satis hebetis ingenii.—VAN SWIETEN *Comment.* Aph. 1125, tom. iii. p. 530.

" I have seen a woman, who had been several times maniacal, who, when her fits of insanity were upon her, always spoke in metre, and had a wonderful facility at finding out rhymes: though, at other times, when in her right mind, she not only had no skill in this way, but had never so much as attempted any thing of the kind; having been used, from her youth, to get her living by the labour of her hands; and being no way remarkable for quickness of parts." — *Vide etiam* SCHENCKII *Obs. Medic. Rar.* lib i. p. 137, Obs. 10.

or accidental, of whatever objects may chance to present themselves.

This species admits of numerous varieties, which it might be more difficult, than useful, to distinguish. Its chief characteristic is an active fancy, which may display itself either in mere smartness and vivacity,—or in ready invention and ingenuity,—or in much appearance of fine imagination, and genius.

ARETÆUS seems to have had a view to this sort of insanity, when he observes, that—" Their fancies are innumerable; the ingenious, and acute, have become astronomers without instruction, philosophers of their own creating, and poets by the immediate inspiration of the muses'."

Without accurately marking the varieties, it may be proper to distinguish two degrees, or rather opposite extremes, of fanciful insanity.

In the one though there is a lively and active state of the imagination; yet there is more of sprightliness than of impetuosity; more of ingenuity than of volubility; and, to a superficial observer, more of acuteness than insanity; the patient attends to the ordinary calls of appetite, obeys the usual solicitations to the natural excretions, observes the seasonable returns of rest and

---

▸ Ἰδέαι δὲ μυρίαι, τοῖσι μὲν γε εὐφυέσι τὲ καὶ εὐμαθέσι, ἀϛρονομίη ἀδίδακτος, φιλοσοφίη αὐτομάτη, ποίησις ἥθεν ἀπὸ μουσέων.—De Causis et Sign. Morb. Diuturn. lib. i. cap. vi. p. 31, F.

sleep,

sleep, and the other common demands of nature and decency, with tolerable attention and regularity: his brain being more delicately, though often not less, and sometimes even much more, obstinately affected than in the other extreme; in which the active state of the imagination is more incessant, rapid, and ungovernable, and, if I may so express it, in a higher, and more vigorous state, of excitement; the vessels of the head, and brain, are more visibly affected; the patient is less attentive to the necessary calls of nature, or the decent ones of propriety, and is less disposed to sleep than he ought to be.

Most, if not all, the varieties of this species, but especially the higher degrees of it, have a great similarity to the fourth variety of impulsive insanity; with which they are sometimes combined; as they are, likewise, not unfrequently, with whimsical: and in the higher degrees, the mind is sometimes in so very active a state, as to indicate a near approach to phrenitic insanity; from which, this species, in such cases can alone be distinguished by its apparent freedom from erroneous images.

8. I call that IMPULSIVE INSANITY, in which the patient is impelled to do, or say, what is highly imprudent, improper, unreasonable, impertinent, ridiculous, or absurd, without sufficient, with very slight, or with no apparent cause.

M 2

Of

Of this species there are several varieties. Thus a man may be reckoned to be affected with impulsive insanity,—1. When impelled into imprudent, absurd, or otherwise incongruous conduct, by an irresistible propensity, uninfluenced by any passion, or any other apparent motive, and merely from an incapacity to restrain his wayward inclinations[q] :—2. When impelled by the passion

---

[q] Οἱ μὲν θέουσι ἀχέτως, ἔτι ὅπως εἰδότες ἐς ταυτὰ παλινδρομέουσι.—ARETÆI CAPPAD. de Causis et Sign. Morb. Chron. lib. i. cap. vi. p. 32, F.

" Some run without stopping, and, not knowing whither they are going, return back again to the same place."

" Grassata est etiamnum diu multumque patrum nostrorum memoria, stupenda insaniæ quædam species, tum alibi, tum præcipue in Germania. Qua cujuscunque conditionis homines, maxime vero sedentariæ operæ et plebes correptæ : subito sutores quidem et sartores atque rustici, calceis, vestibus, aratroque abjectis ; horrendo saltandi furore perciti ; certis per intervalla locis convenientes ; sine omni decubitu et ορθοςαδην, ut HIPPOCRATES appellat, saltantes, choreas ad extremum usque vitæ spiritum, nisi per vim ad tempus cohiberentur, ducebant. Sæpe etiam eousque furoris progressi sunt, ut sibi ipsis, ni caveretur, vim inferrent. Quibusdam horum in petras, nullo discrimine facto, impingentibus : nonnulli vero Rheno, aliisque fluviis saltando se præcipitantibus. Unde ab argumento D. Viti choreæ, amentiæ istæc species, nomen invenit," &c.— SCHENCKII Obs. Med. Rar. lib. i. p. 136, Obs. 8.

" So lately as in the memory of our fathers, there raged for a long time, and very generally, both elsewhere, and more especially in Germany, an amazing species of insanity: which seized upon all conditions of men, but especially upon the lower

passion of anger, or resentment, or impatience
of opposition or restraint, such passion being
liable

---

lower sorts of people, who were engaged in sedentary occu-
pations. On a sudden, shoemakers, tailors, and peasants,
leaving their shoes, their garments, and their ploughs, were
seized with a dreadful rage of dancing, and meeting at intervals
at certain places, would dance without going to bed, or sitting
down, and, as HIPPOCRATES terms it, ἀφόρμως, if not restrained for a while by compulsion, till they dropped down and
died. They often even proceeded so far as, if not prevented,
to lay violent hands on themselves. Some, running any where
indiscriminately, would bruise themselves among stones, and
against rocks. Some, in their dancing, would rush into the
Rhine, and other rivers, and drown themselves. From a kind
of analogy, this species of insanity was called St. Vitus's
dance."—See a great deal more on this subject, in SCHENCKII
Obs. Med. Rar. lib. i. p. 135, 136, Obs. 7, 8, 9.

A somewhat similar epidemic delirium, returning at inter-
tervals, is mentioned by Lord MONBODDO, who describes from
his own knowledge, a particular instance of it, in his Ancient
Metaphysics; or the Science of Universals, vol. i.—*See the
Monthly Review for Sept.* 1779, vol. lxi. p. 197.

Something not unlike this, so far as relates to the irresistible
impulse, is the following case extracted from VAN SWIE-
TEN:

" Vidi egregium virum, qui nimiis lucubrationibus sanitatem
perdiderat, ilico vertigine molestissima correptum, si attente
mente ausculteret alios narrantes etiam brevem historiolam.
Nihil autem molestius sibi accidere querebatur, quam, dum
aliquid in memoriam revocare vellet, tunc enim summopere
angebatur, imo quandoque in animi deliquium incidebat, cum
summæ lassitudinis sensu: nec poterat a scrutinio hoc semel
incepto desistere, licet omni modo obluctaretur : sed cogebatur

invitus

liable to be excited by the slightest and most
trifling cause :—3. When, by a kind of hysterical affection, he is impelled to laugh, cry, sing,
or the like :—4. When, by the quick, and vary-
　　　　　　　　　　　　　　　　　　ing,

---

invitus in so pergere, donec deficeret."—*Comment.* tom. iii.
Aph. 1075, p. 413.

‡ " I have seen a man of great worth, who by late and intense studies, had so ruined his health, that he was instantly
seized with a very troublesome giddiness, if he attentively listened but to the relation of a short story. He complained that
nothing was so painful to him as the attempt to recollect any
thing: that on such occasions he felt the most exquisite distress, and sometimes even fell into a swoon, accompanied with
a sensation of extreme weariness: and yet he could not desist
from the search, when he had once begun, though he strove
with all his might; but was obliged to proceed in it, even
against his inclination, till he fainted away."

¶ " In melancholicis affectuum varietas, et frequentissima
mutatio, ut nunc canant, furant, fleant, rideant, imo et unico
vultu diversissimorum affectuum signa appareant, per constric-
tionem et relaxationem villorum cordis, ex alternatim in-
gruentibus phantasiis, cum apprehensione boni vel mali."—
SCHENCKII *Obs. Med. Rar.* lib. i. p. 125, Obs. 2.

" The melancholic experience great variety, and frequent
changes of the passions. They by turns sing, rage, weep, and
laugh; and sometimes the expressions of different passions appear in the countenance at the same time; as the mind is variously affected with the apprehension of good or ill, by the
alternate existence of different fancies, producing, according to
their nature, sometimes constriction, and sometimes relaxa-
tion, of the fibres of the heart."

" Quidam Wildenbergius tribus diebus continuis ad risum
pronus erat, ut quicquid ageret vel ipse, vel alii, risum ipsi
　　　　　　　　　　　　　　　　　　　　　　　moveret.

ing, impulses of imagination, he is disposed to
be witty, waggish, mischievous, profane, inso-
lent, or obscene.

A mixture of the first, and fourth variety, of
this species of insanity, is excellently delineated
by the judicious Dr. MONRO, physician to Beth-
lem-hospital, in the following lines:—" High
spirits as they are generally termed, are the first
symptoms of this kind of disorder; these excite
a man to take a larger quantity of wine than
usual (for those who have fallen under my observation in this particular, have been naturally
very sober), and the person thus affected, from be-

moveret. Is, cum forte inter concionandum mulier dormiens
de subsellio caderet, et omnes reliqui, qui id viderant, ride-
rent, cœpit etiam ipse ridere, ita ut sibi temperare a risu amplius non posset tribus diebus continuis, et noctu, ex quo admodum debilitatus. Immoderatum istum risum subsecuta est
ingens melancholia, mœror, et tristitia."—*Ib.* Obs. 3.

" An inhabitant of Wildenburgh, was for three days together so disposed to laugh, that whatever he did himself, or
saw others do, became an object of laughter. The occasion of
this extraordinary risibility was as follows. It happened that a
woman, being overtaken with sleep during sermon time, fell
from her seat. The whole congregation, who saw it, laughed at the accident: and he joined so heartily in the laugh,
that from that time he could not refrain from laughing for three
days and nights successively; in consequence of which he was
greatly debilitated.—This immoderate laughter was succeeded
by deep melancholy, grief, and dejection.—See another case of
a similar nature: *Ib.* Obs. 4.

ing

ing abstemious, reserved, and modest, shall become
quite the contrary; drink freely, talk boldly, ob-
scenely, swear, sit up till midnight, sleep little,
rise suddenly from bed, go out a hunting, return again immediately, set all his servants to
work, and employ five times the number that is
necessary; in short, every thing he says or does,
betrays the most violent agitation of mind, which
it is not in his own power to correct, and yet in
the midst of all this hurry he will not misplace
one word, or give the least reason for any one
to think he imagines things to exist, that really
do not, or that they appear to him different from
what they do to other people: they who see him
but seldom, admire his vivacity, are pleased with
his sallies of wit, and the sagacity of his remarks;
nay, his own family are with difficulty persuaded
to take proper care of him, until it becomes absolutely necessary from the apparent ruin of his
health and fortune'."

In most of these cases it is difficult, and in
many perhaps impossible, to discover by what
notions the patient is influenced; or whether
there be any other cause for such irregular impulses, than merely an active state of the brain:
so that one would almost be inclined to make an
additional, or third article in the general division
of insanity, under this title of *impulsive insanity;*

---

* Monro's Remarks on Dr. Battie's Treatise on Madness,
p. 7.

and to consider the varieties just enumerated as
so many distinct species; since, however obscure
the prevailing notion, or notions, may be, it is obvious that such madmen are void of the restraint
of prudence, or propriety, and are irresistibly impelled to act, and talk, as they do.—The same
may be said of fanciful insanity.

, But as we cannot easily conceive of conduct
without motives; or of motives without notions;
and must therefore suppose notions, of some kind
or other, to be the immediately antecedent causes
of every voluntary action; we may safely, I
think, rest satisfied that the conduct of these sorts
of patients is regulated by notions, however they
may conceal themselves from our observation.—
Whatever these notions may be, there is reason
to believe that they are as often the consequence,
as the cause of the increased activity of the brain,
and imagination; and are as various and momentary, as the fancies, and absurdities, of such patients, are various, and momentary.

Madmen of this sort, and especially of the second variety, often see, and lament the absurdity, and folly, of their conduct. Though incapable of resisting the inclination they feel towards it, yet they, not unfrequently, severely
repent of it in their calmer moments[1]:—so that

---

[1] ARETÆI CAPPAD. de Causis et Sign. Morb. Diuturn. lib. i.
cap. v. p. 30, C.

they

they may justly apply to themselves the noted passage of the poet,—

* * * * * *
" Discretion this, affection that persuades:
" I see the right, and I approve it too,
" Condemn the wrong—and yet the wrong pursue";—

GARTH.

—and may with propriety say with ARASPAS in XENOPHON,—" I plainly perceive that I have two souls:—for if I had but one, it could not be, at the same time, both good and bad; it could not at once act both virtuously and viciously; or will, in the same moment, to pursue and to avoid the same conduct. But having two souls, when the good one prevails I act virtuously, and when the bad one prevails I disgrace myself by vice"."

9. In SCHEMING INSANITY the patient thinks himself either endowed with better natural talents, and with more penetration and sagacity,

---

" Sed trahit invitam nova vis : aliudque cupido,
" Mens aliud suadet. Video meliora, proboque ;
" Deteriora sequor :"—

OVIDII Metamorph. lib. vii. v. 19, &c.

' Δύο γὰρ ἔφη, ὦ Κῦρε, σαφῶς ἔχω ψυχάς.——Οὐ γὰρ
δὴ μία γε ἔσα, ἅμα ἀγαθή τέ ἐςι καὶ κακὴ, ἠδ ἅμα κα-
λῶν τε καὶ αἰχρῶν ἔργων ἐρᾷ, καὶ ταυτὰ ἅμα βάλεταί τε
καὶ ἐ βέλεται πράττειν· ἀλλὰ δῆλον ὅτι δύο ἐςὶν Ψυχὰ,
καὶ ὅταν μὲν ἡ ἀγαθὴ κρατῇ, τὰ καλὰ πράττεται· ὅταν δὲ
ἡ πονηρὰ, τὰ αἰχρὰ ἐπιχειρῖται.—ΧΕΝΟΦΩΝΤ. De Cyri
Institutione, lib. vi. p. 328.

or

or improved with greater acquisitions of knowledge and experience, or more enlightened by the
especial favour of Heaven, or more secure of success, by the happy concurrence of power, interest,
opportunity, or some other advantageous circumstance, than most other men; and, either by
his superior knowledge, or cunning, capable of
doing great things, which few, or none, but
himself, are able to accomplish:—or at least feels
an irresistible inclination to be engaged in some
scheme, or schemes, of traffic; and, as he thinks
himself, if not actually the most kno ing, at
least among the most knowing of mankind, so
he is secure of that success which the simple and
ignorant may wish for, but the wise and provident
alone can command.

This species of insanity has several varieties;
and manifests itself in literary, philosophical, al-
chemical, trading, political, ambitious, heroical,
or any other sort of scheming. Self-conceit is
one of its striking features; and it is nearly allied
to the next species:—

10. The VAIN, or SELF-IMPORTANT INSANITY;
with which they who are possessed, have a very
exalted opinion of their own imaginary dignity,
consequence, opulence, elegance and finery of
dress, charms of person or manners, sense, learning, or of some other valuable quality, with which
they suppose themselves dignified or adorned.

The

The characteristics of this species of insanity being either an excessive, and even childish, vanity; or a serious, and sometimes a solemnly ridiculous, self-importance: its appearances are as various as may be the objects, and forms, of absurd pride, or silly vanity; and display themselves in the exhibition of almost every conceivable variety of preposterous pomp, and puerile affectation.

Those, therefore, whose insanity is of this kind, discover it—in an excessive attention to dress, and ornament; and are either led by vanity to a solicitous neatness in their persons and attire, of the charms of which they appear sufficiently conscious; or what is not less common, render themselves completely ridiculous, by adorning themselves in the most trifling, tawdry, and fantastic taste, by the most childish self-admiration, and by every kind of gesture which can indicate the prevalence of consummate vanity:—in the most romantic talk of their own wealth, and possessions:—in stateliness of gait, voice, and manner:—in vast affectation of science, sagacity, and learning:—in perpetual effusions of nonsense for knowledge:—in an ostentatious display of scraps of Greek, Latin, French, or other languages, which they repeat upon every occasion, without much regard to sense, or propriety; and even in the uttering of an unmeaning jargon, which they wish to pass upon the hearers for specimens

cimens of their great attainment, and wonderful skill, in the languages.

The following is a case of self-important insanity, just becoming maniacal.

" A Russian merchant, whose name was ZACHARY PANKIEVIEZ, who was rich, and had a smattering of several languages besides the Russian, as the Hebrew, Greek, Latin, German, and Polish, and had some skill in the military art, imagined himself wiser than the rest of mankind;— not long ago he shewed us some papers, with this superscription; ZACHARY PANKIEVIEZ, by the grace of GOD King of Poland, Czar of Muscovy, great Duke of Lithuania, Russia, Prussia, Masovia, &c. At the same time he assured us, that, in imitation of DAVID, King of Israel, he would have seven hundred wives, of which, three hundred and fifty should be joined to him in matrimony, and the rest concubines. He lately told us that, if we would believe him, he could assure us that, though we were doctors, he knew more than both of us, and that there was not a more learned man than himself in the whole kingdom of Poland; tell me," said he, " the number of veins, and articulations in the human body, &c. &c*."

11. In

---

* " Russicus quidam mercator,—ZACHARIAS PANKIEVIEZ, dives, linguarum præter Russicam, Hebraicæ, Græcæ, Latinæ, Germanicæ, et Polonicæ ex parte gnarus, artisque militaris
peritus,

11. In HYPOCHONDRIACAL INSANITY the patient is for ever in distress about his own state of health, has a variety of disagreeable, and sometimes painful feelings, to which he is ever anxiously attentive, and from which he can rarely divert his thoughts, either to business, or amusement: and though the causes of these disagreeable, and painful feelings, are usually obstinate, and sometimes incurable, yet his fear, anxiety, and conceits, are such as at best indicate an irrational, and insane imbecility of mind; and often lead him to fancy himself threatened, or wasting, with dreadful diseases, which exist only in his distressed imagination[x].

Some, when the disease has gained ground, and become much exasperated; when unremitted brooding over their own unhappy state, and misera-

---

peritus, supra omnes sibi sapere videtur:—non ita pridem nobis monstravit chartas, cum hac inscriptione; ZACHARIAS PANKIRVIEZ, D. G. rex Poloniæ, imperator Moscoviæ, magnus dux Lithuaniæ, Russiæ, Prussiæ, Masoviæ, &c. Eo ipso tempore asseveravit, se ducturum septingentas uxores ad exemplum Israelitarum regis DAVIDIS, trecentas et quinquaginta vinculo matrimonii copulatas, et tot pellices. Idem nobis nuper dixit, credite mihi, quamvis vos sitis doctores, me plus intelligere, quam vos ambo, neque me in toto regno Poloniæ doctiorem esse: dicite mihi numerum venarum et articulorum in corpore humano, &c. &c."—BONETI *Medicin. Septentrional. Collatitiæ*, lib. i. § 19, cap. vi. tom. i. p. 186, col. 2;— where are several other examples of self-important insanity.

[x] Vide BONET, Med. Sept. Coll. lib. i. § 19, cap. iii. iv, tom. i. p. 184.

ble

the apprehensions, has produced an habitual gloom, and dejection of mind; are afflicted with a constant impression of melancholy, which neither business nor amusement can obliterate, which no efforts, of themselves, or their friends, can overcome; which yet they can ascribe to no particular cause, and which seems to have no fixed, or determinate object; and, while they scarcely can describe, or even distinguish, what it is that distresses them, experience a perpetual depression of spirits, a *tædium vitæ*, which destroys all power of enjoyment, and often, amidst a profusion of every earthly blessing, renders life an insupportable burden, from which death alone affords any prospect of relief.

In proportion as this gloom continues, and increases, life becomes daily more and more intolerable; and they complain of a frequent intrusion of momentary temptations to destroy themselves, and to quit a wretched state of being, in which they not only no longer have the smallest hope of happiness, but experience an hourly increase of the most grievous present misery, and still more grievous future apprehensions. — Such temptations recur with more frequency, and violence, as the disorder acquires strength; and too often end in actual suicide.

This species of insanity, like most of the others, assumes various forms; three of which are peculiarly striking, and prominent, and may be justly
considered

considered as constituting three distinct varieties.
—1. Some of its unhappy victims, and especially
in the beginning of the disease, at the same time
that they experience the most distressing nervous
feelings, for which they fear there is no remedy ;
and, being aware that their heads are a good deal
disordered, express frequent apprehensions lest
they should lose their senses; no otherwise appear
irrational than in the general gloom with which
they are affected, in viewing their affliction as
of vast and unparalleled magnitude, and in bearing
the present without patience, as they look to the
future without hope.—2. There are many, who,
besides this distress, impatience, and despondency,
fancy they have, or are threatened with, at one
time or other, almost every disorder which can
afflict, or destroy, the human frame.—3. Others
torment themselves with some one unconquerable disorder; and there is no one they more
frequently make choice of, for this cruel purpose,
than the venereal.—It is common to the three
varieties, except in the last stages, when they
are degenerating into some of the other species;
and especially into pathetic insanity; to be as
anxious and impatient about a cure, as they are
without hope of obtaining one. But, when the
insanity, from hypochondriacal, is become pathetic, the patient is apt to lose sight of the bodily
disorder ; and to consider the whole as a disease
of the mind, which medicine cannot reach ; or,

rather,

rather, as a well-grounded mental affection, originating from a just, and irremediable mental cause,—from some unpardonable transgression of the moral, or divine law, with which the skill of the physician has no concern; and of which the knowledge, and repentance, come too late.

Hypochondriacal insanity, in all its varieties, is, I cannot say universally, accompanied with flatulency, and such other symptoms of a disordered state of the stomach and bowels, as are commonly esteemed by medical writers, both ancient and modern, to be inseparable companions of what they call *melancholia hypochondriaca,* or *hypochondriac melancholy*[y]. I have indeed seen several

---

[y] " Tertia vero melancholiæ species est, quam flatulentam et a præcordiis hypochondriacam appellant, ob inflammata circa stomachum præcordia proveniens : quæ modo auram quandam maligniorem, modo substantiæ humoris partem ad cerebrum sursum transmittit.—Communia omnium [specierum] signa sunt, metus tristitia, &c.—At qui ex præcordiis hoc vitii conceperunt, eos testantur cruditates, accidi ructus, ardor, et ipsorum gravitas, &c.—Ad hæc quod tam incipientem morbum quam majorem jam effectum melancholica comitantur symptomata, quodque hæc leventur, concoctione, vel excretione, vel multis flatibus, vel vomitu, vel rectu. Cum autem nullum ex his, aut certe pauca eveniunt, melancholica quæ apparent signa cerebrum primario affici in totum succi contagione melancholici fatentur."—PAUL ÆGINET. *de Re Medica,* lib. iii. cap. xiv. p. 20.

" A third species of melancholy is what is called *flatulent,* and from the seat of the disease *hypochondriacal,* arising from

several cases of this species of insanity in which
there was not only no appearance of any remarkable flatulency, but I have thought I saw good
reason to doubt whether the cause of the disease
was in any degree seated in the viscera, and have
been strongly inclined to suspect that it had
taken up its habitation wholly in the head; because while there were none of the symptoms of

---

an inflammatory affection of the præcordia about the region of
the stomach; whence sometimes is transmitted to the brain a
kind of malignant vapour, sometimes a portion of the atra bilis
itself.—Fear, dejection, &c. are the common symptoms of all
the species.—But they whose disorder originates in the præcordia, are likewise troubled with indigestion, with acid eructations, with heat, and a sense of weight in those parts, &c.—
Moreover symptoms of melancholy attend the disease, as well
in the beginning, as in its advancement, and are relieved either
by digestion, or evacuation by stool, or the discharge of wind
downwards, or vomiting, or eructation. But when no such
symptoms, or very few of them, appear, the symptoms of melancholy which discover themselves, are owing to a primary
affection of the brain itself, in consequence of the melancholy
humour being in immediate contract with it, and affecting that
organ alone."—Vide etiam Cæl. Aurel. Morb. Chronic.
lib. i. cap. vi. § 182, p. 340.—Aretæi Cappad. De Causis
et Signis Morb. Diuturn. lib. i. c. v. p. 29, C.—Nic. Pison.
de cognos. et curand. Morb. lib. i. cap. xxiii. tom. i. p. 164.—
Sydenhami Oper. Univers. Loco supra citato.—Schenckii
Obs. Med. Rar. lib. 1, p. 129. Obs. 1. Melancholiæ Hypo-
chondriacæ Dilucidatio.—Zacut. Lusitan. Prax. Histor.
lib. i. Operum tom. ii. p. 208, et De Prax. Medic. Admirand.
p. 42. Obt. 9, 10.—Van Swisten Comment. Aph. 1108.
tom. iii. p. 504.

indigestion

indigestion universally attributed to this disorder, there were, very probable signs of an immediate affection of the brain; such as dullness of hearing, noise in the head, dizziness, sense of weight, numbness, and stupefaction, and often a kind of paralytic tremor of the hands, on extending them, and of the tongue, on putting it out.

Nor can I say that insanity attended with flatulency, and those other symptoms which are generally esteemed hypochondriacal, is universally accompanied with such symptoms as I have described to be essential to hypochondriacal insanity. Many instances might be produced to the contrary; and though it should be allowed that in its early stages, it usually exhibits such symptoms; yet must it be acknowledged, as I have already observed, that they commonly disappear when it degenerates into pathetic, and some other species of insanity.

I am satisfied, however, that the disease, as I have defined it, constitutes a complete and distinct species, agreeing in a great measure with the. *melancholia hypochondriaca* of the ancients; comprehending a few cases which they perhaps would have excluded, and excluding a few which they appear to have taken in, but which, on account of the nature of the delirium, my plan obliges me to refer to some of the other species.

It is common to all constitutions: and is most generally induced by a sedentary life; close appli-

cation

cation to study, or to whatever deeply engages the attention, or affections; habitual excesses in eating, drinking, or venery; or whatever else may occasion a disordered state of the nerves and viscera: and, while it lays a foundation for every species of insanity, is peculiarly apt to run into the sensitive, delusive, or pathetic.

SYDENHAM, in his *Dissertatio Epistolaris ad Gulielmum Cole*, when treating on the hysterical disease, has given us some good incidental observations on this disorder; but seems to have fallen into an error, in confounding it with the hysterical disease, from which it appears to be perfectly distinct, though it may sometimes arise out of it, and not unfrequently borrows a few of its symptoms.—After asserting that the hypochondriacal disorder, in men, is the same as the hysterical, in women; he adds—" All hysterical and hypochondriacal persons, are apt when the disease has taken deep root, to bring up offensive wind from the stomach, after eating, with the most perfect moderation, what their appetite seemed to require: they have sometimes, also, eructations of an acid matter, which, as it rises into the mouth, tastes like vinegar; the digestion being both ways impaired, and the juices consequently degenerated from their natural state.*

" Nor is it their only unhappiness, that the body is so disordered, and shattered, as,—like a house threatening to fall,—but just to hold up,
and

and keep together; but they are still more diseased in mind than in body: for as incurable despair is of the very nature of the disorder, they,
cannot bear that any one should suggest to them
the smallest hope of their recovery; readily be-
lieving that it is their lot to suffer whatever ills
man can undergo, or nature inflict; and therefore foreboding the worst of misfortunes that can
befall them.—Nor is this the case with what we
call maniacal, and furious madmen, only; but with
such also, who, excepting these agitations of
mind, are eminent for prudence and judgment;
and who for depth of thought, and wisdom of
discourse, far surpass other men, whose minds
have never been harassed with these tormenting
notions. So that it was not without reason that
ARISTOTLE observed, that the melancholy ex-
celled the rest of mankind in ingenuity.

" This very dreadful state of mind is, however, only experienced by those, who, after a
long and obstinate struggle with the disorder, are
at length totally subdued; and especially when
misfortunes, grief, anxiety, too close application to
study, and attention of mind, conspire with the
disordered constitution of body, to add oil to the
flame which was already kindled[a]."

To

---

[a] " Quin et omnibus, tam hystericis, quam hypochondriacis,
quibus scilicet jam malum inplevit, id accidit, ut flatus quandoque nidorosos e ventriculo emittant, quoties aliquid comede-

rint.

To the above general account of hypochondria‑
cal insanity, let me add the following more parti‑
cular one, taken from a few very similar cases
which fell under my own observation in a short
space of time, and in all of which it proceeded
nearly in the same course.—They were all men
rather of a robust habit of body, had used an

---

rint, licet moderate tantum et pro ratione appetitus, tum etiam
aliquando acidum eructent, acetum sapore referens, quoties in
os ascenderit : læsa nempe utrobique coctione, et succis pro‑
inde a naturali statu interversis.

" Neque hoc tantum nomine infelices sunt, quod corpus ita
male affectum et quasi conquassatum, ad instar ædium ruinas
undequaque minitantium, tantum non corruant et fatiscat, cum
magis adhuc animo ægrotent, quam corpore : cum enim des‑
peratio plane insanabilis de hujusce morbi natura sit, indignan‑
tur admodum quoties aliquis vel miminam de sanitate recupe‑
randa spem injecerit; facile interim credentes omnia se quæ‑
cunque in homines cadere possunt incommoda, quæque adeo
fert rerum natura, perpessuros, tristissima quæque sibi ominan‑
tes, &c. &c.—Neque hoc tantum maniacis accidit et furiosis,
quos dicimus, sed etiam illis, qui, si hos animi impetus exci‑
pias, prudentia ac judicio valent, quique et meditationum pro‑
funditate, et sapientia orationis longe eos superant, quorum
mentes his cogitationum aculeis nunquam fuerint excitatæ.
Ita ut non sine ratione observaverit ARISTOTELES, melancholi‑
cos cæteris ingenio præstare.

" At vero tam horrendus animi status—non aliis competit,
quam iis, qui diu multumque cum hoc morbo conflictati, tan‑
demque subjugati quasi victas manus dant: maxime si res ad‑
versæ, animi mœrores, sollicitudinesve, nimia in literarum
studio assiduitas, atque animi contentio, cum prava corporis
diathesi conspirantes, oleum camino adjecerint."—SYDENHAMI
Oper. Univers. p. 392, 3, 4.

active

active life, but had indulged in late hours, and
too much irregularity, dissipation, and drinking.
The pulse was generally full, and there was a
frequent tendency to fever, which had been often
.increased, together with an increase of all the
hypochondriacal symptoms, on catching, or seeming to catch, cold ; an accident to which the patients were exceedingly liable. The tongue was,
for the most part, covered with a kind of pellu-
cid, bluish white, film, an appearance not uncommon in several of the species of insanity, and
was generally moist. The blood was of a dark colour, and of a loose texture, but had a due proportion of serum. Such patients were always sensible of their disorder, complained of a hurry of
spirits, and confusion of the head, which were
exceedingly distressing to them ; and of an inability to keep the mind from dwelling upon certain thoughts, such as the hopeless and deplorable nature of their unhappy disorder, or the pains
in various parts of the body, which greatly harassed, and disturbed them ; and which they had
not the power to avoid thinking of; and attending
to, how much soever they might wish, and endeavour to divert their minds from these ceaseless
objects of their distress, and anxiety. In this situation they were usually laughed at, or chided, by
their friends and acquaintances, for complaining
when but little ailed them, and suffering themselves, as they termed it, to be hypped and va-

N 4   poured,

poured, with imaginary, or trifling evils, for
want of great and real ones.—As the disorder,
however, increased, it assumed a more alarming
appearance. The unhappy sufferer grew quite
melancholy; had strange, and terrifying, thoughts
of the dangerous state of his soul; which,
though unable to suppress, he was still sensible
were owing to the disordered state of his body.
This sense, however, of his disorder at length
went off; he then thought himself quite well, as
to bodily health; and, falling into a religious
melancholy, imagined he had committed some
unpardonable crime; and, despairing of ever re-
gaining the favour of God, was disposed to seize
the first opportunity of destroying himself; but if,
through the vigilance of his friends, no such opportunity could be obtained, he has usually become
maniacal, or phrenitic, and some patients of this
sort have died raving.

This disorder is sometimes rapid in its progress,
and soon ends fatally; but is for the most part,
slow, and tedious, and void of danger, though
most uncomfortable, and tormenting; and many
have recovered in every stage of it. They who
are afflicted with it are, in general, anxious to be
cured, and too fond of medicines, but have not
the resolution to adhere to any: for if they do
not speedily experience, as they rarely do, the
wished-for benefit; their impatience to be free
from their present misery, is perpetually urging
                                        them

them to change a medicine, in which they have no longer any confidence: whereas there is scarcely any species of insanity, in which a steady perseverance is more requisite; or the noted adage of the celebrated JUSTUS LIPSIUS more frequently verified—" Illos ab atra bile curat dies, et quies*."— " That—time and composure, are of much importance in the cure of atrabilious disorders."

12. PATHETIC INSANITY exhibits a striking and melancholy picture, of the empire of the passions. In this species of insanity some one passion is in full, and complete possession of the mind; triumphs in the slavery, or desolation, of reason; and even exercises a despotic authority over all the other affections, which are rarely permitted to exert themselves but in the aid, or to appear but in the train, of this master passion. It is distinguished from the other species of insanity in which the passions are concerned, or intermix themselves, partly by the striking features of a predominant passion, which is for ever present, and, though in some cases assiduously disguised, is, in most, for ever conspicuous; but chiefly, and more certainly, by the absence, at the same time, of the characteristic symptoms of all the other species. It may be farther observed, that all, or nearly all, the varieties of this species

---

* Vide Tυλριι Obs. Med. lib. i. cap. xix. p. 39.

of

of insanity, are accompanied with distress, dejection, anxiety, or restlessness of mind. For even love, when excessive, and inordinate, is all agitation, or distress; is scarcely a moment at ease; but forever, as its views of the object of affection vary, whether from real, or merely from imaginary causes, dejected, anxious, or restless:—pride is solicitous to support its imaginary dignity; jealous of its honour; and tormented by every real, or apparent failure of that respect which it thinks its due:—and enthusiasm itself, however intoxicated with religious elevation, and rapture, not only originates, for the most part, from religious distress; but is often interrupted by intervals of depression; is at best ardent and restless; and not unfrequently tumultuous, and turbulent; as might abundantly be shown, were it necessary, by taking but the slightest view of the history of fanatics, and fanaticism.

Pathetic insanity may arise from bodily disease; or it may grow out of some other species of insanity; or it may proceed from an habitual indulgence, or accidental excitement, of some immoderate passion, desire, or propensity of mind; and displays itself in their unreasonableness, and excess; in an unremitted, and intense attention to their object, in preference to, and sometimes almost to the exclusion of, every other; and is as various—as violent, and permanent passions,

passions,—as ungratified, or unconquerable desires,—may be various.

Insanity, therefore, of this sort, may exhibit itself under a great variety of forms; of which, however, the following seem to be the most common, and obvious;—inordinate love,—jealousy, —avarice,—misanthropy,—pride,—anger,—aversion,—suspicion,—bashfulness,—irresolution, timidity, fear, or terror,—grief,—distress,—nostalgia, — superstition,—enthusiasm,—despair;—to which, possibly, might be added several others.

Hence arise sixteen varieties of pathetic insanity, which, from the passion predominant in each, may be properly termed—1. Amorous,— 2. Jealous,—3. Avaricious,—4. Misanthropic,— 5. Arrogant, — 6. Irascible, — 7. Abhorrent,— 8. Suspicious,—9. Bashful,—10. Timid,—11. Sorrowful,—12. Distressful,—13. Nostalgic,—14. Superstitious,—15. Enthusiastic,—and 16. Desponding.

Most of these have a tendency to urge their unhappy victims to suicide; or to some other desperate act of violence to themselves, or to those about them; and they are all exceedingly prone to degenerate into some of the species of ideal insanity.

When pathetic insanity arises from sudden bodily disease, as a fever, some change produced in the animal system in consequence of lying-in, suppression of the menses, of the hæmorrhoids, healing

healing of old ulcers, or the like, it is usually violent, and rapid in its progress towards some of
the species of ideal insanity; and often, whether
it becomes maniacal, incoherent, or phrenitic, is
accompanied with great distress, the most horrid
despair, and an incessant and invincible propensity, in the unhappy sufferer, to put an end to a
being, the continuation of which appears to be
but the continuation of the most intolerable, and
hopeless misery.

1. *Amorous Insanity.*—Every instance of that
extravagance, and absurdity, in which the passion
of love is abundantly fruitful, may be considered
as a degree of insanity. Many writers have actually viewed it in that light[b]. PAULUS ÆGI-
NETA[c] reckons immoderate love among the species of insanity, describes its symptoms with accuracy, and makes some judicious observations on
its nature, and on the method of cure. But we

[b] See the references in ZACUTI LUSITANI de Medic. Princip. Histor. lib. i. Hist. 40. Operum tom. i. p. 79. Paraphrasis
in the beginning, and again at the conclusion.—See also his
Prax. Histor. lib. i. cap. viii. Oper. tom. ii. p. 211; 212, de
Amore insano, sive erotico, passim.—CICERONIS Tusculanar.
Disputat. lib. iv. cap. xxxv. where, speaking of love, he
says,—"nam ut illa praeteream, quae sunt furoris"—" for
to pass over those circumstances of love which partake of madness."—SENNERTI Oper. tom. ii. p. 522, col. 2.—TOZZI
Oper. tom. i. p. 115.

[c] De Re Medica, lib. iii. c. xiv. p. 22, l. 30.

ought

ought to distinguish between the ordinary symptoms of this unruly and intemperate passion; which a philosopher, perhaps, may think it right to place in a very eminent rank among the species of moral insanity; and such other less frequent, but, unfortunately, too common symptoms, as evidently indicate a disordered state of the brain, and which, all the world will allow, have a just title to take their station, among the other species of insanity. This is the disorder which I mean to distinguish by the appellation of *amorous insanity;* a disorder which is not ill described by AVICENNA, as I find him quoted by ZACUTUS LUSITANUS, in these words :—" The insanity of lovers is an anxious kind of melancholy, proceeding from immoderate love, and occasionally agitating the mind with a variety of passions[d]."

This variety of pathetic insanity may, I think, not improperly be defined as follows :

Amorous insanity is, every insanity arising from love, in which the character of that passion[e], and the effects[f] of its predominancy, are

---

[d] " Est ergo amantium insania, solicitudo melancholica, ex immoderato amore profecta, variisque subinde pathematibus animum exagitans."—*Prax. Historiar.* lib. i. *Oper.* tom. ii. p. 212, col. 2, A.

[e] SCHENCKII Obs. Med. Rar. lib. i. p. 137. Obs. 2, et p. 134. Obs. 5. In this last observation, the insanity was become phrenitic.—See the case quoted above, in the text, at p. 118.

either

either obviously visible, or, though cautiously
concealed, may be discovered by a skilful and attentive

' Instances of this are all the cases of insanity from concealed
love; several of which will be referred to in the next note :—
also all cases of suicide, and other violent acts, and effects,
which have proceeded from love; and have indicated an insanity, which did not plainly discover itself till those acts were
committed, or attempted, or those effects produced.—Vide
ZACUTI LUSITANI de Medic. Princip. Histor. lib. 1. Hist. 40,
p. 80, col. 2, A, B.—SCHENCKII Obs. Med. Rar. lib. i.
p. 133, Obs. 5.

" Juvenis Britannus, impensius (ut solet illa ætas) amori indulgens, perculsus fuit adeo vehementer ex inopinata matrimonii repulsa : ut obriguerit instar stipitis; sedens in sedili sua
κατοχος, sive detentus, sive congelatus, per integrum diem, re-
tinensque continenter eundem situm, et oculos non minus
apertos; atque olim simillimum adfectum delineavit GALENUS,
Comment. 2, in Prorrh. cap. lv."

" A qua figura, ne latum quidem cum recederet unguem :
jurasses certo, te statuam potius quam hominem videre. Adeo
quippe fuere omnia non modo rigida, sed plane immobilia.
Verum ubi exclamaretur, alta voce; rem ipsius meliori esse
loco, et cupitam habiturum amicam; modo ad se reverteretur;
prosiliit confestim ex sedili, et quasi excitatus ex profundiore
somno, rediit ad se, disruptis protinus illis vinculis, quibus
ipsum arcte ligaverat, tenacissima hæc catoche."—TULPII
Obs. Med. lib. i. cap. xxii. p. 43.

" A young man, a native of Britain, indulging in a violent
affection, as youth are apt to do, was so shocked at an unexpected refusal on his proposing marriage, that he became as
rigid as a log of wood; sitting in his chair quite cataleptic, or,
as it were, fixed, and congealed, for a whole day; always
continuing in the same posture, and keeping his eyes as wide
open,

tentive observer[s]; and which has not yet acquired ideal symptoms of any kind.

2. *Jealous Insanity.*—In jealous insanity the tormenting passion of jealousy is predominant;

---

open, as in the case related by GALEN, in his Commentary on the Predictions.

" Remaining thus rivetted, without the smallest change of position, you would have taken him rather for a statue, than for a man: so rigid was every part, and so perfectly immoveable. But when one called out to him, with a loud voice, that his affairs were now in a better situation, and that he might obtain the mistress he wished for, if he would but come to himself; he immediately sprung from his chair, and returned to himself again, as if just roused from a deep sleep: the bands being instantly broken with which he had been so firmly bound by this violent catalepsy."

[s] ARETÆI CAPPAD. de Causis et Signis Morb. Diuturn. lib. i. c. v. p. 30, E.—ZACUTI LUSITAN. de Medic. Princip. Histor. lib. i. Hist. 40. Operum tom. i. p. 79, 80, containing a case of insanity, related by GALEN, which, by attentive observation, he discovered to be owing to a concealed love for a person of the name of PYLADES: into the paraphrase on which is transcribed, from PLUTARCH, the story of ANTIOCHUS's attachment to STRATONICE, the wife of his father, King SELEUCUS, which he had concealed till he was supposed to be on his death-bed, when it was discovered by his physician ERASISTRATUS. We are also referred, for the same relation, to VALER. MAXIM. lib. v. cap. vii. and to APPIANUS in Syrio, and LUCIANUS in Lib. de Syria Dea.

The same stories are repeated by SCHENCKIUS. Vide Obs. Med. Rar. lib. i. p. 135, Obs. 6.—Vide etiam SAUVAGES. Nosol. Method. tom. iii. Part i. Class viii. Gen. 19, Spec. 2, Melancholia amatoriâ.

and

and discovers itself to proceed from a disordered
state of the brain, either by being totally, and
indisputably groundless; or by being accompanied, or succeeded, by other obvious symptoms
of insanity. It originates from natural temper;
from an acquired habit, occasioned by really suspicious circumstances, of indulging this distressing passion; from a bodily constitution tending
to insanity; or from an accidental excitement of
that disorder in a body no way peculiarly disposed
to it. Though not so common as several other
varieties of pathetic insanity; it has, neverthe-
less, been noticed by medical writers, who sometimes mention jealousy as a symptom of insanity[n].
SCHENCKIUS gives us a short narrative of a very
remarkable case of this kind[i] : and it is a disorder
which has fallen under my own observation.

3. *Avaricious Insanity.*—Of avaricious insanity
the instances are very common. I will not say
that every miser is medically insane; though the

---

[n] Tozzi Operum, tom. i. p. 114.

[i] Animi dolores ac morbi, si diu perseverent temporis pro-
cessu dementes reddunt, quales sunt zelotypi. Quod quidem
pistori accidisse, cum juramento etiam mihi asseverarunt com-
plures, mihi familiares. Pistor is, ut retulerunt, cum suspectam
de adulterio uxorem suam haberet, tametsi pudicam et probam,
nec eam in stupro deprehendere posset, testes sibi amputavit,
ratus, si illa forte uterum gereret, non ex se, ut qui ob adempta
genitalia generando ineptus esset, sed ex altero concepisse certo
sciret."—SCHENCKII *Observ. Med. Rar.* lib. i. p. 133, Obs. 5.

descrip-

descriptions of the poets, the authority of credible histories, and the testimony of living examples which must have occurred to almost every man, seem to vindicate the title of insanity to many an opulent pauper, to many a penurious, and self-tormenting oppressor. Of this, however, I am certain, that avarice has a natural tendency to induce, and often actually terminates in, this truly miserable disorder; which I do not consider as having yet taken place, till avarice be accompanied with such irrational, and absurd, fears and distresses, as plainly indicate a distempered brain. As when a man in opulence, and over-burdened with riches, has the most groundless apprehensions that he shall come to want; when a man who is really the owner of no contemptible possessions, imagines himself poor, and destitute, and in need of being supported by charity. This sort of insanity, which is a very frequent one, was not unknown to Celsus, who tells us, of " a man of great wealth, who was afraid lest he should perish for want; and whose friends found it necessary to quiet his fears, by the news of pretended legacies¹ :" an innocent deceit, which he recommends to the imitation of others on similar occasions.

ʲ " Quorandam enim vani metus levandi sunt: sicut in homine prædivite famem timente incidit: cui subinde falsæ hereditates nunciabantur."—Celsi *de Medicina*, lib. iii. cap. xviii. p. 151, l. 14.

This,

This, like most of the other varieties of pathetic insanity, is sometimes the offspring of an habitual, and growing passion; and sometimes it is the produce of disease, and, when so, even seizes upon people, who, while in their right minds, were naturally of a benevolent, and generous, temper. Like the other varieties, it is very apt to degenerate into the most violent degrees of ideal insanity. I have known several cases of each sort. SCHENCKIUS relates one which seems to be of the latter.

"A young man, the son of a wealthy merchant, having had occasion to go to a fair, and having spent ten days on the journey, fell, upon his return, into a deep melancholy; fancied he had been robbed of all the money he had received at the fair; and in the end grew so highly delirious, that he imagined he was no longer a human being[k]."

4. *Misanthropic Insanity.*—Misanthropic insanity shows itself in a violent dislike to mankind in general: a disposition of mind so perfectly re-

---

[k] " Juvenis ditissimi mercatoris filius, cum ante annum ad nundinas Nordlingenses proficisceretur, ac per decem dies integros, in eadem profectione insumeret, in reditu gravem melancholiam incurrit qua sibi persuadebat, omnem pecuniam quam eo mercatu conquisierat furto sibi ablatam; quin eo usque delirabat ut sese hominem esse haud agnosceret."—SCHENCKII *Obs. Med. Rar.* lib. i. p. 127, Obs. 7.

pugnant

pugnant to the natural feelings of the human
heart ; and to the production of which any injury
received from individuals, from a body of men, or
even from the society at large with which it is
our lot to be connected, is, in the eye of reason,
a cause so totally disproportioned, and inadequate,
that wherever me meet with it, we ought in charity to suppose, that bodily disease, or intemperate passions, or grievous wrongs, have injured
the brain, and depraved the intellectual faculties,
rather than grant that a character so absurd, and
so unnatural, can possibly exist, without some
degree of actual insanity.

Insane persons of this sort—avoid the conversation, and hate the society, and the very sight
of the human species : if spoken to, they answer, if they vouchsafe to answer, with surliness,
acrimony, and impatience ; or turn away with
silent scorn, or but muttering malice and dislike :
and their countenances are clouded with a gloomy
and unfriendly frown ; or flash with malevolence,
hatred, and indignation.—ARETÆUS observes of
them, that " they fly into deserts to shun mankind, whom they hate ;"—ἐς ἐρημίην φεύγεσι μισανθρωπίην[1].

Not a few, it is possible, may have been possessed by this kind of insanity, who have passed

---

[1] ARETÆI CAPPAD. De Causis et Signis Morb. Diuturn.
lib. i. cap. v. p. 29, F.

with

with the world for saints, or philosophers. I cannot say that I have met with any who have actually fled to deserts, but I have seen several—" qui odio habent homines"[m]—" who hate mankind;" a symptom mentioned by GALEN, and some other of the ancient medical writers, and by many of the moderns.—Such as have fallen under my observation, whose cases I would refer to this variety of pathetic insanity, have discovered it, by railing at all who approached them; by seldom speaking but with surliness and ill-nature; by suspecting all mankind of sinister views, and villanous intentions; and by wearing in their countenances the malevolent frown of suspicion, moroseness, and rancour.—It sometimes rises out of other species of insanity, and is not owing to any depravity in the habitual constitution of the mind; sometimes it grows out of an habitual indulgence of pride, and malevolence;—and on other occasions it is derived from the unhappy experience of unexpected ingratitude, and unmerited disappointment. I have seen striking instances of it, owing to the second cause; and symptoms of this sort accompanying other species of insanity, though I do not now recollect any case of pure misanthropic insanity, owing to the first cause; as to the third, I know of no instance which I could fairly deduce from it; it is, how-

---

[m] GALENI de Locis Affect. lib. iii. c. iv. LACUNÆ Epitom. p. 744, l. 4.

ever,

ever, beautifully exemplified, in the story of Timon of Athens, by Lucian among the ancients;
and by our own inimitable Shakespeare among
the moderns, who to satisfy us that he considered
him as insane, makes Alcibiades observe of
him, that—

———————" his wits
" Are lost and drown'd in his calamities[n]."

5. *Arrogant Insanity.*—In arrogant insanity
the characteristic feature is sober, formal, stately,
reserved, and excessive pride; by the uniform
predominancy of which it is distinguished from
vain, or self-important insanity; which has more
of the versatility of fancy, of the pertness of conceit, of the levity of vanity, and of the silliness
of a ridiculous and childish ostentation, than of
the dignity of pride; which displays itself, in this
variety of pathetic insanity, in its genuine perfection of gloom, and insolence, uninterrupted by
the intrusion of any rival passion, and accompanied only with its dependent ones, jealousy of
disrespect, or insult, and resentment of every appearance of slight, or inattention.

The insanity of Nebuchadnezzar, King of Babylon, seems to have been originally of this kind;
and afterwards, as it increased, to have become
sensitive. " Is not this great city Babylon," says

[n] Timon of Athens, act iv. scene 4. See Shakespeare's
Works, vol. vii. p. 166.

he,

he, " which I have built for the house of the
kingdom; by the might of my power, and for
the honour of my majesty°?"

6. *Irascible Insanity.*—When the prevailing
symptom is anger, such insanity merits the appellation of *irascible;* whether this passion exhibits
itself in violent and groundless rage; or in as
groundless, though, less violent, anger, from
peevishness, and discontent; or in a contentious
and irritable disposition, which is forever engaging
in quarrels, and flaming with resentment.   It is a
symptom of insanity much noted by medical writers: and is very apt to exist, especially in the last-
mentioned form, when the disorder is either occasioned by, or accompanied with, immoderate
drinking.   It disposes the patient to every kind
of mischief, and not unfrequently to mischief of
the most violent and desperate nature; especially
when it rises into rage, which is usually a symptom of approaching phrenitic, or incoherent insanity.

Aretæus mentions anger as both a cause, and
a symptom of insanity:—" Some there are whose
disorder is neither accompanied with wind, nor
with black bile, but with violent anger, &c°."

---

* Daniel, chap. iv. verse 30.

ᵖ Μετεξετέροισι δὲ ἐδέ φύσα, ἔτε μέλαινα χολὴ ἐγγίγ-
νεται· ὀργὴ δὲ ἄκρητος, κ. τ. λ.—*De Causis et Signis Morb.
Diuturn.* lib. i. c. v. p. 29, D.

Trallian

TRALLIAN relates a case of insanity, occasioned by grief, in which the patient replied with anger to all who spoke to her[a]; which affords a speci‑ men of the peevish sort of irascible insanity.

7. *Abhorrent Insanity.*—Abhorrent insanity, which consists in a violent aversion to, and ab‑ horrence of, certain persons, or things, so nearly resembles one of the varieties of whimsical insa‑ nity, that in some instances it may be difficult to determine to which of the two the insanity ought to be referred: but it may be observed, that while in the latter the aversions are various, changing, and fantastical, in abhorrent insanity they are less numerous, more permanent, formed upon some real, or plausible grounds, violent, and not with‑ out evident marks of disgust, hatred, or terror.

Certain aversions which are generally supposed to be natural; but which are, most probably, by some means or other acquired; such as the being in great agitation, or even fainting away, at the sight of a cat, or, as we are told of some, when a cat is but in the room without being seen or known to be so but by these effects; and some other very troublesome aversions of a similar nature, as the abhorrence of a rat, a mouse, an eel, or the like, border upon, and arise from a cause per‑

---

[a] De Arte Medica. lib. i. cap. xvii. HALLERI Artis Med. Princip. tom. vi. p. 92.

fectly

fectly similar to that of, this variety of pathetic insanity; both being the consequence of some strong impression made at some time or other upon the mind, and nerves, which they have not been able to recover. But when aversion merits to be considered as insane, it is not only violent, and absurd, either in kind or degree, but is accompanied with other symptoms of a disordered brain; whereas the persons who experience the aversions I have just mentioned, not only know them to be groundless, and ridiculous, but are often people in other respects, of a sound and manly understanding.

8. *Suspicious Insanity.*—Suspicion is also a symptom of whimsical insanity, when slight, or transient, and accompanied with other symptoms of that species; but when violent, permanent, and predominant, deserves to be considered as a variety of pathetic, under the title of *suspicious insanity.*

9. *Bashful Insanity.*—In bashful insanity shyness is the prevailing, and most conspicuous symptom. Such persons as suffer its distressing embarrassments, say but little, love retirement, anxiously avoid the sight of all who approach them; appear uneasy, dejected, and timid; and, though less disturbed by those who are constantly about them, observe even towards them a remark-

a remarkable shyness, reserve, and taciturnity.
Though they avoid, all society, and are fond of
privacy and retirement ; yet it cannot with propriety be said that—" odio habent homines"—
" they hate mankind ;"—but rather that they are
afraid of them. They seem to experience that sort
of fear, which is felt by the modest, and bashful,
on going into the company of strangers, or of their
superiors: they appear distressed, embarrassed,
timid, afraid to look up; in short, in the words
of Aretæus, to be affected with a most painful
and dejected bashfulness—κατηφείη δεινή.

Bashfulness is sometimes a striking symptom,
where the insanity is owing to concealed love:
and seems to be no very uncommon, or unnatural prelude to that dreadful kind of insanity the
furor uterinus.

10. *Timid Insanity.*—In whatever instance of
notional insanity, fear, or terror, in any degree, is a
constant and prevailing symptom, such delirious
fear, or terror, I would denominate *timid insanity.*

This is a frequent variety of pathetic insanity,
and puts on every conceivable form of the passion from which it derives its name. Some are
afraid of they know not what, are filled with terror every moment, and have the most dreadful

Vide De Blegny Zodiaci Medico-Gallici, Anni quarti,
Mens. Martii, p. 60.

apprehensions from every occurrence, however common and insignificant: others are afraid they shall be brought to trial and condemned to die, or shall otherwise undergo some extraordinary punishment, for the commission of some imaginary crime[*]: and yet, so intolerable is their suffering from these groundless fears, that they are very apt to put an end to their own lives, and thus— " while they experience the most cruel tortures from the mere apprehension of death, rashly to rush upon the very death they fear:"—" mortem timent, quam sibi tamen consciscunt[t]."

I have often known this disorder take its rise from a fright: and VAN SWIETEN relates a remarkable case of it, proceeding from the same cause:

" A great and sudden emotion of mind arising from terror, may often so strongly impress the idea of its object on the common sensory, that it may afterwards be impossible, by any means whatever, to efface it. Unhappy persons thus affected, however they may strive against it, can think of nothing but the single object of their terror; and by degrees sink into the most deplorable melancholy. I have seen an instance of this in a woman, who, being terrified

---

[*] " Plerique se criminis reos imaginantur, &c."—WIERI de Præstig. Demon. lib. iii. De Lamiis, cap. vii. § 1, p. 180. " Many think that they are to be tried for some crime."

[t] GALENI de Loc. Affect. lib. iii. c. iv. Epitom. p. 743, l. 60.—WIERI de Præstig. ib.

in

in the night by a sudden alarm of thieves attempting to get in at her chamber window, was, ever after, in every place, in fear of some design upon her, and whenever she was dropping to sleep, used to awake in a fright, though she knew that the servants sat up to guard the house every night. This terror could never be overcome; and was particularly strong towards the evening, when she began to tremble, grow pale, and to look fearfully about, as if she suspected some ill design. In a short time she fell into a fixed melancholy*."

11. *Sorrowful Insanity.*—Sorrowful insanity, is that which is attended with continual, and wasting grief; owing to some real, and natural cause;—as the loss of an object held in great esteem, such as a husband, wife, child, friend,

---

ᵃ " Verum ingens et subita turbatio mentis per terrorem summum imprimit sensorio communi tam fortiter novam ideam, ut sæpe nullo modo postea deleri possit ; tunc miseri tales nil cogitant nisi hoc unicum, etiam inviti et obluctantes, atque in pessimam melancholiam incidunt. Vidi hoc in muliere, quæ subito de nocte perterrita, dum fures fenestram cubiculi effringere moliebantur, semper ac ubique metuebat insidias, et in primo somni limine cum summo terrore evigilabat, licet novisset domesticos excubias agere singulis noctibus : nunquam potuit deleri ille terror, imprimis circa vesperam; tunc enim incipiebat tremere, pallescere, undique circumspicere, insidias metuens, sicque brevi in pertinacissimam melancholiam incidit."—*Comment.* Aph. 1108, tom. iii. p. 503.

repu-

reputation, possessions, or the like;—or some important error in conduct, which it is likely, may be productive of great, and of what will probably be irretrievable mischief; — it is so far from being uncommon, that we find grief, its characteristic, usually enumerated among the ordinary symptoms of melancholy. · ARETÆUS tells us there are three kinds of melancholy, the *first* accompanied with black bile, the *second* with wind, and the *third* with the passions of violent anger, or grief, and of dreadful depression and bashfulness*. This variety is often mixed with fear, and distress, which might lead us to place it under timid or distressful insanity; were it not sufficiently distinguished from the former by the obvious predominancy of grief; and from the latter, or

12. *Distressful Insanity.*—Distressful insanity, by the cause of the distress; for this symptom is not in distressful, as in sorrowful insanity, the consequence of any great loss, or capital error in conduct; but arises from smaller misfortunes, habits of anxiety, vexation, disgust, a disrelish of the world, and its enjoyments; and sometimes merely from disease. Indolence, luxury, and a sedentary life, whether passed in application to study, or to any other employment, are principal

---

* De Causis et Signis Morb. Diuturn. lib. i. cap. v. p. 29, D.

sources

sources of this disorder; and produce such an uncomfortable state of the bodily feelings, as while it renders every trifling occurrence an object of inquietude, is itself aggravated by the petty anxieties and vexations it produces, till the mind becomes totally sunk and depressed into a constant distressful dejection and melancholy, which, without any apparently extraordinary, or adequate cause, is often so excessive, as to destroy all comfort, and to render life itself an intolerable burden.

An insanity resembling this has frequently been described by foreigners, under the title of *melancholia Anglica,* or *morbus Anglicus,*—*English melancholy,* or the *English disease.*—And the Aphorism of HIPPOCRATES,—" If fear or distress continue for a long time, this is a symptom of melancholy"*,"—seems to have had a particular view to this and the milder degrees of timid insanity.

Dr. LORRY pays this island the compliment, of attributing this its constitutional insanity to the philosophical turn of its inhabitants:—

" Nor ought I here," says that ingenious writer, " to omit a kind of disorder, which is not unfrequent, and which leads innocent mortals to

---

* Ἐν φόβος ἢ δυσθυμίη πολὺν χρόνον διάτελίη, μελαγχολικὸν τὸ τοιᾶτον.—*Aphorism.* § vi. Aph. 23. *Oper. Omn.* p. 1257.

procure

procure their own death, without any reason to induce them to wish for it, but what their insanity
suggests. For it is undoubtedly a species of melancholy insanity, which urges them to this fatal
madness. It is silent, morose, inatentive to every
thing external, and common to such as have acquired a disordered habit of body by too much
thinking; and is said to be familiar to our neighbours of Britain, a nation which seems to have received its existence for the advancement of the
sciences. So true is the observation of PLINY,
that to shorten our days even by the study of
wisdom, is to die of a disease[x]."

SAUVAGES[y] gives a similar account of what he
calls *melancholia Anglica;* and very judiciously remarks that the insanity of the Milesian virgins,
mentioned by PLUTARCH, which produced a kind of
epidemic suicide, which they committed by hang-

---

[x] " Nec infrequens annumeranda hic morbi species quæ sibi
mortem insontes consciscunt, sine ulla legitima mortis optan-
dæ, nisi quam suggerit insania, ratione. Et est sane aliquod
insaniæ genus melancholicum vere, quód miseros in hunc furorem præcipites agit. Taciturnum est illud atque morosum,
circa omnia externa inattentum, iisque familiare qui nimia me-
ditatione morbum hunc contraxerint, diciturque vicinis nostris
Britannis, gentj ad scientias promovendas natæ, familiare; ita
verum est, quod ait PLINIUS, quod aliquis sit morbus per sa-
pientiam mori."—*De Melancholia,* Part ii. cap. vi. tom. i.
p. 380.

[y] Nosolog. Method. Class viii. Gen. 19. Spec. 11. tom. iii.
Part i. p. 390.

ing

ing themselves, and to which nothing could put
a stop, till the magistrates wisely ordered, that
all such young women as should for the future
be guilty of self-murder, should be exposed
naked to the public view ;—and a similar insanity
of certain Frenchwomen, as related by PRIMROSE,
according to SAUVAGES, but according to SCHENC-
KIUS, by CRINITUS in his book *de Honesta Dis-
ciplina*[a], who drowned themselves in great numbers,—were all probably of this kind.

13. *Nostalgic Insanity.*—The attachment to
their kindred, to their friends, to their acquaintances, to the scenes in which they have passed
the happy period of youthful innocence, and
simplicity, in which whatever is dear to them
is contained, and whatever has most nearly in-
terested them has been transacted,—an attachment which all mankind, in some degree or other,
experience,—is as amiable, when not immoderate
and illiberal, as it is grateful and natural to the
human heart. But like the other passions, and
especially grief and love, both of which in some
respects it much resembles,—the latter in its
general nature, and the former in some of its
effects,—when it becomes violent and unreasonable, not only leads to, but, under certain circumstances, actually is a variety of, pathetic

---

[a] SCHENCKII Obs. Med. Rar. lib. i. p. 137, Obs. 1.

insanity,

insanity, to which, from nostalgia its most usual appellation, I have given the epithet *nostalgic*.

This unreasonable fondness for the place of our birth, and for whatever is connected with our native soil, is the offspring of an unpolished state of society, and not uncommonly the inhabitant of dreary and inhospitable climates, where the chief, and almost only blessings, are ignorance and liberty.

It shuns the populous, wealthy, commercial city, where a free intercourse with the rest of mankind, and especially the daily resort and frequent society of foreigners, render the views and connexions more extensive, familiarize distant nations with each other, rub off the partiality of private and confined attachments, and while they diminish the warmth, vastly increase the extent of affection; making, of rude and zealous patriots, benevolent, though less ardent, citizens of the world; and, of bigots in their attachment to some insignificant state, or petty district, the friends, and often the benefactors of human nature:—from these scenes of civilization, and refinement, it flies to pastoral life, and rural retirement; and loves to roam at large, with the peasant, or manufacturer, in his forests, and plains—

" Where ev'ry good his native wilds impart,
" Imprints the patriot passion on his heart;
" And e'en those ills, that round his mansion rise,
" Enhance the bliss his scanty fund supplies.
                              " Dear

" Dear is that shed to which his soul conforms,
" And dear that hill which lifts him to the storms ;
" And as a child, when scaring sounds molest,
" Clings close and closer to the mother's breast,
" So the loud torrent, and the whirlwind's roar,
" But bind him to his native mountains more*."

While, in England, whatever may be our partiality to our native land of plenty, opulence,
and liberty, we know nothing of that passionate
attachment that leads to this sort of insanity,—
an immoderate affection for the country which
gave them birth, is often productive of this
disorder, as we are assured upon the best authority, among the inhabitants of the ice and snow
of Lapland[b], of the bleak mountains of Switzerland, and of the remote and less civilized districts
of Germany[c], when torn by force, or detained

---

* GOLDSMITH's Traveller.

[b] " The Laplanders are proud of their country and constitution,
and have so high a notion of it and of themselves, that, when
removed from the place of their nativity, they actually die of the
nostalgia, or longing to return."—*Critical Review for March*,
1780, vol. xlix. p. 175, from a publication entitled " Russia ;
or a complete Historical Account of all the Nations which com-
pose that Empire," in 2 vols. 8vo.

[c] " New recruits often fall into very obstinate disorders, if they
be not dismissed from the army. Some are seized with an
acute fever, which proves mortal ; whilst others are either affected with madness, or become scorbutic."—See the account
of—" A Chirurgical Treatise on the Phlegmone and its Termi-
nations, by JOH. ALEXANDER BRAMBILLA, first surgeon to
the Emperor of Germany,"—in the Foreign Medical Review,
vol. i. Part ii. p. 117.

by necessity, or misfortune, from the scenes, the manners, and the connexions, which nature and habit had bound about their hearts.

This inordinate attachment to their native soil, as it is sometimes termed, not only frequently produces nostalgic, which is a purely notional insanity; but is often so violent in its effects, as to terminate in such insane symptoms as are commonly denominated maniacal.

HOFFMAN[d] mentions nostalgic insanity as a very familiar disorder among the Swiss when residing in foreign regions.

HALLER, who was himself a Swiss, acknowledges its frequency among his countrymen, says it is a kind of grief on account of absence from their friends, and that it affects even the citizens;—compares it to what indeed it greatly resembles, the pining of certain animals on being deprived of their associates, and to the inconsolable grief of disappointed love, which gradually consumes the vital flame, preys upon it unceasingly till it be extinguished, and is termed by the English a broken heart;—and informs us that it sometimes assumes maniacal symptoms[e].

SAUVAGES

---

[d] Medicinæ Rationalis Systematicæ, tom. iii. sect. 1, cap. v. § 22. Operum tom. i. p. 313.

[e] Nostalgia," says he, "genus est mœroris subditis reipublicæ meæ familiaris, etiam civibus, a desiderio nati suorum. Is sensim consumit ægros, et destruit, nonnunquam in rigorem,

SAUVAGES gives a similar account of this disorder; he defines it to be a kind of morosity, or idiotism, which affects persons in foreign countries
with so vehement a desire of returning to their
parents and to their native land, that, if unable
to gratify their longing, they pine with grief,
watching, loss of appetite, and other violent
symptoms of great disorder. He adds, that it
is either simple or complicated, that both kinds
frequently attack young people, who have been
tenderly educated in their father's house, and happening on their first arrival abroad, to be either
sick, or unfortunate, revolve in their minds the
delights of their native country, and their own
unhappy lot in being deprived of the aid and con-
solation of their friends:—that the simple nostalgia is unconnected with any violent disease;
is attended with dejection, love of retirement,
taciturnity, aversion to food and drink, prostration
of strength, and a low fever in the evening:—that
he had seen it often in the infirmary at Mont-
pellier, and had sometimes observed livid spots
on the bodies of those affected by it:—that he
had ·known it to exist, after the loss of his pa-

---

rem, et maniam abit, alias in febres lentas. Eum spes sanat.
Etiam animalia consueta societate privata nonnunquam depe-
reunt, et ex pullis amissis etiam lutræ maris Kamtschadalensis.
Sic ex amore frustrato lenta et insanabalis consumtio sequitur,
quod Angli cor ruptum vocant."—*Element. Physiolog. Corporis
Humani*, lib. xvii. sect. 2, § 5, tom. v. p. 583.

rents,

212 DEFINITION AND ARRANGEMENT.

rents, in the son of a common beggar, who could
scarcely be said to have any country but the
streets, and public roads:—that the students of
physic who resorted to that place, were too agree-
ably situated in the midst of a multitude of young
acquaintances, and surrounded with too abundant opportunities of pleasing enjoyment, to re-
gret very severely the absence of their friends,
and to experience this disorder:—but that it was
frequent among the soldiers of Switzerland,
when at a distance from home; and had been so
much promoted by singing a common Swiss song
which celebrated the delights of their country,
that they were at length forbid to sing it under
pain of death:—that the complicated nostalgia
is accompanied with considerable fever, and great
debility; and that it is necessary, in the course of
the cure, to be particularly attentive in supporting
the strength of the patient[f].

14, 15, 16.—Reason abused, uncultivated, or
despised, has been the source of the greatest
corruptions which have crept into, and contaminated, the christian profession; and of the most
horrid enormities which, in consequence of such
corruptions, have, in almost every age of the
church, been the scourge of society, and the disgrace of human nature.

[f] Notolog. Method. Class viii. Gen. 11. tom. iii. Part i.
p. 334, &c.

Early

Early in the annals of our divine religion, we find the abuse of reason, in the acrimony of disputation, and the contention for victory, laying those foundations of degeneracy and error, which were afterwards raised to a stupendous pile of folly and superstition. Reason once abused, and misled, the farther it proceeded, the more it was bewildered; and had little chance of returning back into the paths of truth, while interest, ambition, and all the passions which usually, though undeservedly, have the most powerful influence on human conduct, too often united their efforts to retain, to encourage, and to advance it in error.

The next step to the abuse of reason, was the neglect of its cultivation. The same passions, and the same interests, which inspired the one, of course led to the other. That the good christian people might be retained in that ignorance and darkness, into which they had been so happily conducted by ambition, craft, and bigotry, it became the interest of their guides that they should, if possible, be totally deprived of sight; or, what would amount to the same thing, no longer dare to trust their own eyes, but submit their sense of things to the regulation of their superiors, who pretended to see better than they. For there was danger, if they should presume to see for themselves, that some distant and imperfect glimmerings of truth, which yet remained,

might

might chance to excite their curiosity to search
for the source from whence they proceeded ; that
they might be conducted in the search, into the
broad and perfect day-light of that glorious lumi-
nary which enlightens the empire of reason;
which would at once dispel the illusions of error
which had so long misled them ; and would put
an end to that slavery of the mind on which the
greatness of the priesthood was founded ; a greatness which was, in the course of time, to grow
into an immense, and astonishing fabric, of ec-
clesiastical tyranny and despotism.—To obviate
an event so unfavourable to their designs, the
eye of the mind was to be enfeebled ; reason was
to be obscured ; it was to be suspected and mistrusted, that it might go uncultivated ; and, being obscured, suspected, mistrusted, and uncultivated, it was to be rendered useless, and, if possible, to be annihilated.

The Goths and Vandals contributed to pro-
mote these illiberal views, and to complete the
mischief which the degenerate leaders, and pas-
tors, of the christian church had so successfully
begun ; and, while their arms spread devastation
and terror over the western empire, reason, neglected, and uncultivated, sunk under the depressing influence of the ignorance and barbarism
of the conquerors, into the lowest state of degeneracy, till, continuing to proceed in depravity,
and scarcely any thing being too absurd to be believed,

lieved, it was at length almost lost, and forgotten, in those dark ages of the church, when popish usurpation tyrannized, with little control,
over the minds, persons, and properties, of almost every individual in christendom.

That in this twilight, or rather perfect night,
of the mind, we should see human reason despised, discouraged, and decried, as an insuffi-
cient and dangerous guide in matters of religion;
and made to submit, with the Scriptures themselves, to the decrees of councils, and the
decisions of the church ; is but small cause of wonder: but to every man of rational views, and
a cultivated understanding, it must appear as extraordinary, as it is real, that in this enlightened
age, after reason has long been emerged from
this dismal night of mental darkness, there are
men to be found of no mean learning, and, in
other matters, of good understanding, who suffer themselves to be so blinded by false reasoning,
as to be perfectly insensible to the true; to
slight, and despise its divine illumination; to shun
it, as a dangerous, and delusive light, where the
revelation of the gospel is concerned; and with
an unaccountable inconsistency, to reason with
much earnestness, and a specious plausibility,
against the use of reason in matters which, as
they inform us, rather require the exercise of faith ;
and to trust to an inward light, for the reality
of whose presence, and illumination, no better

evidence

evidence can be produced, or pretended to, than
the very doubtful one of every man's own imagination; than which nothing can be more uncertain, or unsatisfactory, or a more inexhaustible fountain of every conceivable variety of superstition, fanaticism, or desperation.

Indeed every man who is acquainted with human nature, and who understands the Scriptures,
must be sensible how dangerous it is to abuse
the most valuable gift of Heaven, at the instiga-
tion of fancy, passion, interest, or ambition;—
to despise the guidance of a divine light, to which
the Scriptures themselves appeal, and on whose decision the belief of their truth or falsehood must
ultimately depend;—or to neglect the culture,
and improvement of a faculty, which, if rightly
considered, it is perhaps our chief duty, and our
best interest, in this life, and possibly in the
next, to cherish, exercise, and follow; and is
probably that talent which we are commanded
to employ to the best advantage, and are severely
forbidden indolently to hide in a napkin.—But nothing can afford so instructive a lesson of the
danger of such a conduct, and of the happy influence of an opposite mode of proceeding, as a
minute detail of the history of the church, and
of all those nations which were called christian,
from the conversion of CONSTANTINE, and even
earlier,—while, reason thus imperceptibly sink-
ing under the influence of ambition and barbarism,

rism, not only religious, but almost every other species of knowledge, gradually declined, expired, and was forgotten,—to the time when LUTHER, aided by a favourable, and providential, contingency of circumstances, by breaking the chains of human authority which had so long enslaved the mind, roused it from its lethargy; made it feel its own native and independent strength and dignity; and infused a spirit of inquiry,—which has since extended itself to every object about which the mind can employ its faculties, and, though it may have been productive of a few partial, temporary, and perhaps necessary evils, has had the happy effect of promoting civilization, increasing human happiness, improving reason, and advancing pure and genuine christianity, to a degree, which,—if we consider the vastness of the effect, the apparent imbecility of the causes which put it in motion, the immense resistance of a multiplicity of powerful obstacles, the short space of about two hundred and sixty years, in which so total a revolution in the minds and manners of the European nations has been accomplished, —seems to have no parallel in history, since the first propagation of christianity; and appears no less wonderful, than pleasing, to every friend of reason, religion, and humanity.

From the abuse, diminution, and rejection, of reason, in various degrees and combinations, have proceeded three kinds of deviation from the spirit,

and

and wisdom, of true religion; superstition, enthusiasm, and despondency.

Superstition considers the Deity as an unreasonable, fantastical, and capricious being, whose favour is to be obtained, or anger averted, by idle ceremonies, ridiculous observances, or painful mortifications[s].

Enthusiasm views GOD as the friend, and his spirit as the guide, of the happy individual, who experiences his favour, and is sensible of his influence; and acting by the impulse of internal feeling, conviction, and illumination, and of an ardent zeal for the cause, and honour, of GOD, and the advancement of his kingdom, is prepared to believe every suggestion of a wild imagination to be the suggestion of the Holy Spirit, and every impulse of a foolish, or frantic zeal, to be an intimation of the will of Heaven, which ought to be attended to, and obeyed.

Despondency represents the Deity in the same ignoble light in which he is exhibited by superstition; and is as little governed by reason, and as much by feeling, as enthusiasm; but paints him at the same time, not only as capricious, but inexorable; not merely as void of friendship, but as an enemy, and a tyrant.

---

s In quâ [scil. superstitione] inest timor inanis deorum.—Cicero. De Nat. Deor. lib. i. cap. xlii. edit. Davisii.

" Which [i. e. superstition], consists in a vain fear of the gods."

Though,

Though, perhaps, every degree of superstition, enthusiasm, and despondency, may, in the eye of a philosopher, appear so nearly to resemble in- sanity as scarcely to merit a distinction; yet great allowance must be made for that common imbecility of the human intellect, which renders the less cultivated part of mankind extremely lia- ble to contract, in some degree, one or other of these unworthy apprehensions of the Deity: it is only when they become so conspicuous, so ab- surd, and so excessive, as greatly to exceed the common deviations of human belief and conduct in these respects, and to appear plainly to pro- ceed from a disordered brain, that they are to be considered as having an undoubted claim to the titles of superstitious, enthusiastic or fana- tical, and desponding insanity; titles which, however they may seem doubtful in many cases, are sometimes obviously applicable even in the early stages of the disorder; will usually be al- lowed in its advancement to the height; and are often irrefragably confirmed by its progress from notional, to some of the species of ideal insanity.

14. *Superstitious Insanity.*—Superstitious insa- nity may, therefore, be defined to be such an excess and extravagance of superstitious notions and conduct, as bear evident marks of a distem- pered brain, and are not unfrequently observed

to

to terminate in maniacal, or some other species of ideal insanity.

Superstition, which was noticed by Aretæus[*] as being sometimes a symptom of insanity, was the principal instrument, as it has always been the most prominent feature, of the Roman Catholic Church. It is no wonder, then, that that church should be of all others, the most prolific parent of superstitious insanity. Ascetics, anchorets, and monks, of every age, have afforded abundant examples of this sort of madmen; of which a more striking one is no where to be found than that of the noted Simeon Stylites, whose extraordinay methods of securing the favour of the Deity, exhibit a painful specimen of superstitious insanity which cannot be better delineated than by the elegant pen of Mr. Gibbon, in his History of the Decline and Fall of the Roman Empire.

" At the age of thirteen," says that celebrated historian, " the young Syrian deserted the profession of a shepherd, and threw himself into an austere monastery. After a long and painful novitiate, in which Simeon was repeatedly saved from pious suicide, he established his residence in a

---

[*] "Η ἐς δισιδαιμονίην τρέπονται.—*De Causis et Signis Morb. Diuturn.* lib. i. cap. v. p. 30, A.

" Some take a turn to superstition."

mountain,

mountain, about thirty or forty miles to the east of Antioch. Within the space of a mandra, or circle of stones, to which he had attached himself by a ponderous chain, he ascended a column, which was successively raised from the height of nine, to that of sixty, feet, from the ground. —In this last, and lofty, station, the Syrian anchoret resisted the heat of thirty summers, and the cold of as many winters. Habit and exercise instructed him to maintain his dangerous situation without fear or giddiness, and successively to assume the different postures of devotion. He sometimes prayed in an erect attitude, with his outstretched arms, in the figure of a cross; but his most familiar practice was that of bending his meagre skeleton from the forehead to the feet: and a curious spectator, after numbering twelve hundred and forty-four repetitions, at length desisted from the endless account. The progress of an ulcer in his thigh might shorten, but it could not disturb, this celestial life; and the patient hermit expired, without decsending from his column."

This variety of pathetic has some relation to whimsical insanity; from which it differs in having religion for its sole, or for its chief, object.

15. *Fanatical Insanity.*—Enthusiastic, or fanatical insanity, is an ill-founded notion of the uncommon favour, and communications of the Deity;

Deity; sometimes accompanied with unremitting fervors of zeal, gratitude, or devotion; sometimes with absurd, extravagant, or violent conduct; and sometimes with extraordinary, and incredible, expectations, of divine manifestation, and interference: and, though in many cases purely notional, is exceedingly disposed to acquire ideal symptoms.

We cannot read the history of the irregular and turbulent conduct, or of the groundless and absurd expectations, of most fanatics, without concluding, that while some were merely designing, and wicked, others, who were more honest, and serious, were actually influenced either by a temporary, or by a permanent insanity[1]: and it will appear the less wonderful that so many should become insane, at the same time, by a kind of epidemical contagion, when we reflect on the influence of example, and of any favourite and popular notion, in exciting the wildest, and most outrageous, extravagances, of a misguided mob; when we consider, how apt the brain is to be affected by a constant attention of the mind to one object; how liable such attention is to be excited when the object is of a religious nature; and how much the propensity, and danger, is increased, if

---

[1] Vide SAUVAGESII Nosolog. Method. Class viii. Gen. 19, Spec. 13. Melancholia Enthusiastica, tom. iii. Part i. p. 392, et Spec. 6. Dæmonomania fanatica, tom. iii. Part i. p. 397.— LORRY De Melancholia, Part i. cap. vi. tom. i. p. 135.

it

it be contemplated, as religious objects, when they have gained the ascendant of the mind, are extremely apt to be, with emotion and ardor.

This variety of pathetic insanity, as has already been observed, is peculiarly disposed to become maniacal; and is productive of every form of enthusiastic raptures, extatic reveries, glorious visions, and divine revelations.——Passing over the history of the first Anabaptists[j], who in the time of LUTHER made wild work in Germany; and of the first Quakers, whose fanaticism made no small stir in England[k]; and of many other instances of epidemic enthusiasm, which were probably fruitful in this sort of insanity; I shall relate a few single examples, and some cases of a more private nature, as specimens of this variety.

JOHN KELSEY went to Constantinople upon no less a design than that of converting the Grand

---

[j] Some account of whose excesses may be seen in Dr. ROBERTSON's History of the Reign of the Emperor CHARLES V, vol. iii. p. 76—90.

[k] See a minute, and possibly somewhat exaggerated, detail of their fanaticism, in " LESLIE's Snake in the Grass," which, together with several pieces in its defence, is published in the second volume of his works.

I ought to add, that the Anabaptists and Quakers of the present day, are the very reverse of their predecessors whose history I have here referred to; and are as remarkable for coolness of reason, and sobriety of passion, as were their namesakes of former times for warmth of fancy, and the intoxication of enthusiasm.

Signior.

Signior. He preached at the corner of one of the
streets of that city, with all the vehemence of a
fanatic : but unfortunately preaching in his native
English, which was probably the only language
of which he had any knowledge, he was disappointed in his expectation of being understood ;
but was treated with that humanity which his
state of mind obviously demanded, and safely
lodged in an hospital for lunatics[1].

DANIEL, OLIVER CROMWELL's porter, whose
brain was supposed to be turned by plodding in
mystical books of divinity, was treated with the
same humanity, and confined for many years in
Bedlam; from one of the windows of which he
used frequently to preach, chiefly to female au-
diences, who would often sit for many hours under his window, very busy with their bibles, and
turning to the quotations, with great signs of devotion[m].

ARTHINGTON, COPPINGER, and HACKET, three
enthusiasts, in Queen ELIZABETH's time, met
with less gentle treatment; the latter of them
was hanged, drawn, and quartered, the second
died raving mad, and the third, recovering from
his fanaticism, and insanity, was pardoned. They
had been accused of being guilty of a conspiracy
against the Queen.—" On Friday the 15th of

---

[1] GRANGER'S Biographical History of England, vol. iv.
p. 208.

[m] Idem. ib. p. 210.

July,

July, COPPINGER having sent for ARTHINGTON out of his bed, declared to him that he had had a revelation, which assured him that he was prophet of mercy, and ARTHINGTON prophet of judgment; that HACKET was king of Europe, and that they were to go before him, and separate the sheep from the goats. ARTHINGTON the more readily credited this because he found a mighty burning in himself, which he interpreted a commencement of the angelic nature."—" COPPINGER magnified HACKET as the holiest man that had ever lived, except CHRIST:—a little after he was apprehended, he ran absolutely distracted, and never recovered his senses, but obstinately refusing all nourishment, died of hunger the day after HACKET was executed[n]."

THOMAS VENNER, and his associates, were treated with no less severity.—" VENNER was reputed a man of sense and religion, before his understanding was bewildered with enthusiasm. He was so strongly possessed with the notions of the millenarians, or the fifth monarchy men, that he strongly expected that CHRIST was coming to reign upon earth, and that all human government, except that of the saints, was presently to cease. He looked upon CROMWELL, and CHARLES II. as usurpers upon CHRIST's dominion, and persuaded his weak brethren, that it was their duty to rise

---

[n] Biograph. Britan. ed. 2d, vol. i. art. ARTHINGTON.

and seize upon the kingdom in his name. Accordingly a rabble of them, with VENNER at their head, assembled in the streets, and proclaimed King JESUS. They were attacked by a party of the militia, whom they resolutely engaged; as many of them believed themselves to be invulnerable. They were at length overpowered by numbers, and their leader, with twelve of his followers, was executed in January, 1660-1. They affirmed to the last, that if they had been deceived, the LORD himself was their deceiver°."

" Mr. JOHN MASON, minister of Water-Stratford, near Buckingham, was a man of great simplicity of behaviour, of the most unaffected piety, and of learning and abilities far above the common level, till he was bewildered by the mysteries of Calvinism, and infatuated with millenary notions. This calm and grave enthusiast was as firmly persuaded as he was of his own existence, and as strongly persuaded others, that he was the ELIAS appointed to proclaim the approach of CHRIST, who was speedily to begin the millennium, and fix his throne at Water-Stratford. Crowds of people assembled at this place, who were fully convinced that this great æra would presently commence; and especially after MASON had in the most solemn manner, affirmed to his sister and several other persons, that, as

---

° GRANGER's Biograph. Hist. of England, vol. iv. p. 206.'

.·.· he

he lay on his bed, he saw CHRIST in all his majesty. Never was there a scene of more frantic
joy, expressed by singing, fiddling, dancing,
and all the wildness of enthusiastic gestures and
rapturous vociferation, than was, for some time,
seen at Stratford; where a mixed multitude assembled to hail the approach of King JESUS.
Every vagabond and village-fiddler that could be
procured, bore a part in the rude concert at this
tumultuous jubilee. MASON was observed to
speak rationally on every subject that had no relation to his wild notions of religion. He died in
1695, soon after he fancied that he had seen his
Saviour, fully convinced of the reality of the
vision and of his own divine mission[p]."

We have an instance of this sort of insanity in
the singular and tragical history of the family
of the DUTARTRES, who were all so infatuated
as to fancy that they were the only family upon
earth who had the knowledge of the true GOD,
and whom he vouchsafed to instruct, either by
the immediate impulses of his spirit, or by signs
and tokens from heaven;—and that GOD had
revealed to them in the plainest manner, that
the wickedness of man was again so great in
the world, that, as in the days of NOAH, he was

---

[p] GRANGER's Biographical History of England, vol. iv.
p. 207, note.—See a particular account of his life and character by H. MAURICE, rector of Tyringham, Bucks, 1695, 4to.
pamphlet.

determined

determined to destroy all men from the face of
it, except this one family, whom he would save
for raising up a godly seed upon earth. This in-
fatuation led some of them, with the approbation
and aid of the rest, to commit incest and mur-
der; and to suffer that death which was the consequence, by the hand of justice,—if there could
be justice in so punishing poor deluded madmen,
—with the utmost cheerfulness, and even exulta-
tion, in the firm belief of their own divine inspiration, and that they should prove to the world the
truth of their pretensions, by actually rising again
on the third day[q]."

The very extraordinary visionary Count EMA-
NUEL SWEDENBORG, affords a striking example
of fanatical insanity with maniacal symptoms.
He imagined he had the singular happiness of
enjoying frequent interviews with the world of
spirits; and has favoured mankind with exact
descriptions of the scenes he visited, and the
conversations he heard and partook of, in those
wonderful excursions of a deluded fancy. " The
Lord himself," says he, in a letter prefixed to his
Theosophic Lucubrations, " was graciously pleased
to manifest himself to me his unworthy servant,
in a personal appearance in the year 1743, to

---

[q] This remarkable history is related at length in the Monthly
Review for December 1779, from " An Historical Account of
the Rise and Progress of the Colonies of South Carolina and
Georgia," 2 vols. 8vo.

open

open to me a sight of the spiritual world, and to enable me to converse with spirits and angels; and this privilege has continued with me to this day'."

Very similar to this, were the visions of John Engelbrecht, who, after passing many years in a state of the most gloomy and agonizing desperation, in which he had frequently been tempted to commit suicide, appeared at length, to his friends, and to himself, to die, and to be restored again to life; and fancied he had visited, during the short space from his supposed death to his resuscitation, first hell, and afterwards heaven; and was from that time freed from his despondency, which he had exchanged for the opposite emotions of religious joy.

Now this pretended death seems to have been in reality no other than what Sauvages', and other nosological, and pathological writers, term an asphyxia, or a total privation of external sense, and of all the vital motions; and was of an exceedingly short duration; for he himself tells us, that the whole process was but of a moment's con-

---

* See the Monthly Review for June 1770, vol. xlii, p. 445—and for November 1778, vol. lix., p. 365.

' Nosol. Method. Class vi. Gen. 28, tom. ii. Part ii. p. 401.

† Boerhaavii Institut. Medicinæ, § 829, p. 388.—Gaubii Institut. Pathologiæ, § 783, p. 288.—See something similar in the account of Monboddo's Antient Metaphysics, vol. ii.—Critical Review for December 1782, p. 422, &c.

tinuance,

tinuance, that it was much about twelve o'clock, at midnight, when his bodily hearing failed and left him, and that when the watchman cried twelve o'clock, the extatic rapture had fully passed upon him.

But a short view of the symptoms of this curious disorder, as described by himself, in their gradual advancement, and decline, will sufficiently explain its nature.

" It was on Thursday noon, about twelve o'clock, when I distinctly perceived that death was making his approaches upon me from the lower parts upwards;—insomuch that my whole body becoming stiff, I had no more feeling left in my hands and feet, neither in any other part of my whole body: nor was I at last able to speak or see; for my mouth now becoming very stiff, I was no longer able to open it, nor did I feel it any longer. My eyes also broke in my head in such a manner, that I distinctly felt it. But, for all that, I understood what was said when they were praying by me;—and I heard distinctly that they said one to another, pray feel his legs, how stiff and cold they are become; it will now be soon over with him. This I heard distinctly; but had no perception of their touch. And when the watchman cried eleven o'clock, at midnight, I heard that too distinctly; and much about twelve o'clock, at midnight, the bodily hearing failed and left me too. Then was I (as it seemed

to

to me), taken up with my whole body; and it was transported and carried away with far more swiftness than any arrow can fly, when discharged from a cross-bow."—He then, after some observations, relates what he saw, and heard, in the other world; and afterwards describing his return to life, and telling us that he was twelve hours in dying, and the same space in recovering, he thus proceeds :—" Remarkable it is, that as I died from beneath upwards, so I revived again the countrary way, from above to beneath, or from top to toe.—Being now conveyed back again out of the splendorous glory, it seemed to me as if I had been replaced with my whole body upon the same spot; and then I first began to hear again corporally something of what they were praying in the same room with me. Thus was my hearing the first of all the senses I recovered again. After this I began to have a perception of my eyes, so that by little and little my whole body became gradually strong and sprightly. And no sooner did I get a feeling of my legs and feet again, but I rose and stood up upon them with a strength and firmness I never had enjoyed before, through the whole course of my life. The heavenly joy invigorated me to such a degree, that the people were greatly terrified at it; seeing that, in so rapid and almost instantaneous a manner, I had recovered my strength again to such great advantage."

During

During this supposed, and apparent, death, he had been carried in imagination, or, as he terms it, in a trance or vision, and set down before hell; where he had perceived a dismal darkness, a thick nasty fog, smoke, and vapour, and a horrible bitter stench, and had heard dreadful howlings and lamentations: had from thence been conveyed by the Holy Ghost, in a chariot of gold, into the radiant and splendorous light of the divine glory, where he had seen the choir of holy angels, prophets, and apostles, singing and playing round the throne of God, the angels in the form of flames of fire, and the souls of believers in the shape of luminous sparks, and God's throne under the appearance of a great splendor; had received a charge or message from God by means of an holy angel; had had such assurances of divine favour, and felt such delight from this momentary glimpse of the glory of God, that he was ever after a happy enthusiast, and the joy he retained from this splendid spectacle was so very great and unspeakable in his heart, as to surpass all kind of description.

After this he had, for several years, frequent visions, and revelations, sometimes in the day-time, and with his eyes open, and always without any of those symptoms of disorder which had preceded his first vision: lived sometimes, as he assures us, for eight, twelve, and thirteen days,

days, and even for three weeks together, without eating and drinking; for the space of three
quarters of a year without the least wink of sleep;
and once heard with his bodily ears, for one and
forty nights together, the holy angels singing
and playing on the heavenly music, so that he
could not help joining them; and the people
who were with him were so much affected with
joy, as to be unable to sleep likewise, and often
continued singing along with him almost the
whole night through.

' I have been the more minute in this account
of JOHN ENGELBRECHT, and other enthusiasts,
because an attempt is now making by an apparently
serious and well-meaning christian, to give credit to his almost forgotten revelations, and the
reveries of some other Dutch and German mys-
tics and visionaries, by publishing them in an
English dress, and in a cheap form, at a time
when enthusiastic, and mystical notions are gaining but too much ground in this kingdom, among
the weak, the ignorant, and the credulous: for
though it be allowed that they may possibly do
some good among the populace, by rousing
men's attention to religious matters, and exciting them to sobriety, and seriousness; yet it
seems not improbable that they may, in the
end, do more harm, by giving too much scope,
and consequence, to feeling and imagination,
                                             and

and by impairing and blinding the understanding".

. The next and only instance, more, of fanatical insanity, which I shall here relate, exhibits a specimen of the more common effects of an indulgence in enthusiastic notions, and feelings.

"I knew a woman," says Tissot, "several years ago, who, after conducting herself for 25 years together as a woman of sound sense and understanding, happening, in an evil hour, to associate with the sect of Herneuters, experienced the most ardent emotions of love to our Saviour, and to him alone, and dwelling entirely on this idea day and night, so destroyed the tone of the brain, that in a few months she became an idiot; and yet retained such a recollection of the Lamb of God, on whom she had thus wholly fixed her thoughts, and affections, that though I visited her and talked to her in a variety of ways, every day for half a year together, I could never get a single word from her, but my sweet lamb; and this she

---

* For a more particular history of this extraordinary man, and his wonderful visions, I refer the reader to a recent publication, called—"The divine Visions of John Engelbrecht, a Lutheran Protestant, whom God sent from the dead to be a preacher of repentance and faith to the christian world: translated from the original German by Francis Okely, formerly of St. John's College, Cambridge, in 2 vols. 12mo."—from which I have extracted the above account.—See vol. i. p. 2, 56, 57, 58, 60, 68, 73, 75, 78.

would

would repeat about every half-hour, always sitting with downcast eyes, and never uttering a single syllable besides, for the space of a year and half, at the expiration of which term she died perfectly wasted to a skeleton[v]."

The ancients esteemed enthusiasm to be a peculiar sort of insanity, sometimes occasioned by disease of body, sometimes by erroneous notions, and sometimes by the immediate influence of APOLLO. In all these cases it was supposed, as the very term implies, that the enthusiast was actuated, either in imagination, or in reality, by the inspiration of a divinity; and that while in the two former he mistakingly pretended to, in the latter he really possessed, the gift of foretelling future events. It is no wonder, then, that the ideas of enthusiasm, madness, and divination, were considered on many occasions, as almost inseparable ideas; and that the terms were frequently used as sy-

---

[v] " Novi ante plures annos fœminam, vere per viginti quinque annos sapientem, quæ, malo fato, Herneutarum sectæ addicta, tota et unice sacro amore servatoris nostri flagrans, tota huic ideæ noctu diuque dedita, sic cerebri tonum fregit, ut intra aliquot menses fatua fieret ; agni tamen sui adeo memor, ut illam per semiannum quotidie visitans, variisque alloquens sermonibus, nullam unquam aliam vocem obtinere potuerim quam mi suavis agne (mon doux agneau) ; et hanc omni semihora, demissis semper oculis, edebat, et nullam aliam per sesquiannum edidit, quo lapso tempore penitus tabida periit."— TISSOT *de Valetud. Literator.* p. 22.

nonymous;

nonymous; as may be seen by consulting; among
others", the writings of PLATO*, ARETÆUS CAP-
PADOX*, CŒLIUS AURELIANUS*, and PAULUS
ÆGINETA*: But as a rational christian can
allow of no such inspiration, but what was given
to CHRIST, and to the prophets, and apostles'; we
must of course conclude that the pretenders to
divine illumination, and the gift of prophecy,
were among the ancient heathens, as they have
since been among modern christians, of two
sorts; and were either no better than insane,
or were downright cheats and impostors. The
latter became such, either from private views of
ambition, reputation, and emolument, a zeal
for the public good, or an attachment to the
interest of a party; as seems to have been the
case with NUMA, APOLLONIUS TYANÆUS, SER-
TORIUS, and many others: or like the priestes-
ses of APOLLO, they were such from the very
nature, and necessity of their office.

Wild gesticulations, incoherent ravings, foam-
ing at the mouth, and convulsive motions, being
looked upon as symptoms of the workings of the
divinity within, these were always assumed by

---

* SCHENCKII Obs. Med. Rar. lib. i. p. 135, Obs. 7.
* In PHÆDRO.
* De Causis et Signis Morb. Diuturn. lib. i. cap. vi. p. 33, B.
* Morb. Chron. lib. i. cap. v. § 144, p. 325, and §.150,
p. 327.
* De Re Medica, lib. iii, cap. xiv. p. 20, l. 8.

the

the Pythoness, and have in all ages had a principal
share in the artifices of such kind of impostures.
But as the body cannot be thus agitated without
much exertion of mind, and enthusiasm cannot
be well, and frequently, imitated, as interesting
characters on the stage cannot well be represented till the mimic forgets himself, and feels
the emotions, and imagines himself in the very
situation of the character he is exhibiting; so
many of these impostors, either through the
violence of their exertions, the long habit of
personating madness, and the really enthusiastic feelings which a zeal for the honour of their
God had excited, or with which natural constitution had endowed them, might possibly, in the
end, actually experience the insanity they had so
often feigned; and such insanity, it may naturally be supposed, might sometimes terminate in
idiotism. Granting the probability of this representation, we may hence possibly account for the
veneration, which in some countries, and especially in the more eastern, is paid to madmen,
and idiots; and for the belief that they are the
peculiar favourites, and are often honoured with
the inspiration, of Heaven.

16. *Desponding Insanity.*—Desponding insanity is a groundless apprehension of having lost
the favour, and irretrievably incurred the resentment of the Deity; and of being destined, in
conse-

consequence of some supposed unpardonable of-
fence, which, if real, is usually at the worst but
trifling, and is not uncommonly merely imaginary, to the most unrelenting severities of ever-
lasting torment: and is frequently accompanied
with the dread of immediate, and temporal,
while it anticipates the horrors of future, and eternal, condemnation and punishment.

This variety may be connected with superstition, or with enthusiasm, or with a mixture of
them both; and may therefore either precede, or
follow both superstitious, and fanatical insanity:
but while it is capable of uniting itself with the
former, it can only alternate, as it often does, but
can never exist in immediate combination, with the
latter.

To refuse all kinds of nourishment, and to
have the most invincible, and unremitting propensity to suicide, are symptoms familiar to this
deplorable variety of pathetic insanity; and can
no way be accounted for, but by the intolerable
horror of those dreadful feelings, and that frantic
distress, which, though in part arising from views
of futurity, make the unhappy sufferers under this
shocking calamity sensible only to their present
agonies, which at any rate they are eager to ex-
change: and by that self-detestation, on account
of the supposed enormity of their guilt, and that
full conviction of its atrocious and unpardonable nature, which render them impatient to meet

an

an evil which they know to be inevitable, which at best cannot long be delayed, and of which the actual suffering can scarcely be more painful than the anticipated apprehension ; and ready, and eager to inflict on themselves the merited punishment of their hardened, aggravated, and unexampled crimes. I have known patients of this sort express the most violent resentment and indignation against themselves ; and, though firmly persuaded that they were destined to eternal damnation, yet so bent upon quitting the present load of misery, as to expostulate with their friends on the cruelty of their care—in preventing them from executing this desperate purpose,—in detaining them in a state of such exquisite anguish, as could not easily be exchanged for a worse,— or in preventing the execution of vengeance on a wretch for whose unprecedented wickedness and impiety no punishment could be too severe. Such motives, and such reasoning, may appear too irrational and inconsistent, to be real ; but it must be remembered that they are the motives, and the reasoning, of madmen, with whom nothing can be so incredible as not, on some occasion or other, to gain belief; or so absurd, as not to become a motive of conduct. Of this I am certain, that I have endeavoured to exhibit a true picture, though I am sensible it is a very imperfect one, of what I have repeatedly seen, and carefully attended to.

This

This truly pitiable disorder is not ill delineated by Wierus[b]. And Zacutus Lusitanus relates a curious instance of it, which had acquired, as it is apt to do, ideal symptoms; and was cured by an extraordinary stratagem[c]. Indeed cases of this kind are so common, that few can have lived long in the world, and been at all attentive to such occurrences, but must, at one time or other, have had an opportunity of observing it. It is finely painted by the picturesque pencil of our inimitable Spenser, in the ninth canto of the first book of his Fairy Queen; from which my reader will pardon me, if I transcribe, in this place, the three following beautiful stanzas:—

> The knight was much enmoved with his speech,
> That as a sword's point through his heart did pierce,
> And in his conscience made a secret breach,
> Well knowing true all, that he did rehearse,
> And to his fresh remembrance did reverse
> The ugly view of his deformed crimes,
> That all his manly powers it did disperse,
> As he were charmed with inchaunted rimes,
> That oftentimes he quak'd, and fainted oftentimes.
>
> In which amazement, when the miscreant
> Perceived him to waver weak and frail,

---

[b] Wieri de Præstig. Dæmon. lib. iii. De Lamiis, cap. vii. § v. p. 182.

[c] Zacuti Lusitani de Prax. Med. Admirand. lib. i. Obs. 49, p. 11. Operum, tom. ii. ad calcem, et de Med. Princ. Hist. lib. i. Obs. 39. Operum, tom. i. p. 75.

While

. While trembling horror did his conscience dant,
; And hellish anguish did his soul assail ;
To drive him to despair, and quite to quail,
He shew'd him painted in a table plain,
The damned ghosts, that do in torment wail,
And thousand fiends that do them endless pain
With fire and brimstone which for ever shall remain.

The sight whereof so throughly him dismay'd,
That nought but death before his eyes he saw,
And ever burning wrath before him laid,
By righteous sentence of th' Almighty's law :
Then 'gan the villain him to overcraw,
And brought unto him swords, ropes, poison, fire,
And all that might him to perdition draw ;
And bade him chuse what death he would desire :
For death was due to him, that had provok'd God's ire[d].

13. In *Appetitive Insanity* there is an immoderate, and ungovernable, desire, of gratifying an
appetite, without that regard to modesty, and
decency, which is commonly observed even by
the most dissolute, when in their right minds:
and as the disorder advances, it usually, sooner
or later, discovers such other symptoms as evidently indicate a distempered brain.

This species of insanity is, in some cases, very
slow, and gradual, in its progress, free from
impetuosity and violence, and assumes, as circumstances determine, without relinquishing its
own peculiar symptoms, an appearance of im-

---

[d] Stanza xlviii. xlix. and L. vol. i. p. 140.

pulsive, or of distressful pathetic, and sometimes of mildly maniacal insanity: in others it is as rapid and violent, as it is indecent, disgusting, and shocking ; and readily acquires turbulently maniacal, and not very rarely phrenitic symptoms.

It usually attacks those, who, though in a single state, and under the outward restraint of an artificial modesty, have imprudently indulged in the wantonness of lascivious thoughts, and amorous desires, of which they had neither the sanction of law, nor of custom, nor of religion, to pursue without guilt, or blame, the irregular gratification. But though it most commonly attacks such as have thus secretly cherished a forbidden flame; yet the purest, and most immaculate, in thought, and conduct, are not perfectly secure from its invasion. Certain conditions of body may sometimes induce the disorder, without the previous existence of any mental turpitude. But whatever may be the exciting cause, it rarely discovers itself till it has risen to a considerable height, and has acquired such vigour as to overcome, and break through, the very strong barriers, and powerful restraints, of modesty, and decorum.

As it exists, with some necessary difference of symptoms, in the different sexes, it may be divided into two varieties: to which there will be no difficulty in appropriating names; since a disorder of this sort in men, has already acquired the
appellation

appellation of *satyriasis*[e]; and, in the other
sex,

---

[e] Vide ARETÆI CAPPAD. de Causis et Signis Morb. Acut.
lib. i. cap. xii. p. 25.—PAUL. ÆGINET. de Re Medica, lib. iii.
cap. lvi. p. 96.—GALENI de Tumorib. præter Naturam; in
LACUNÆ Epitom. p. 708, l. 66.—BONETI Polyalth. lib. iv.
cap. lxxv. tom. ii. p. 1195.—SAUVAGESII Nosol. Method.
Class viii. Gen. 13, tom. iii. Part i. p. 339.

A very curious case of this kind is circumstantially related
by WIERUS, which I shall here transcribe, as exhibiting a
pretty exact specimen of the insanity which I mean to discriminate under the name of *satyriasis*. His words are these:—

" Scribit PAULUS GRILLANDUS, quendam hispanum cleri-
cum et decretorum doctorem anno ætatis suæ quadragesimo
quinto Romæ quarundam juvenum monialium amore captum,
quas et forma venusta sæpius in monasterio visitans, verbisque
et muneribus abblandiens, usque adeo deperiit, ut nocte die-
que, tam somnietis quam vigil, nihil aliud, nisi earundem am-
plexus concubitusque meditaretur corde, verbo, gestis, et signis : paulatim et eo venit amentiæ, quum clericus esset, ut se
ecclesiæ sponsum, et moniales ejusdem sponsas esse palam as-
sereret ; hoc usus argumento, quod dicerentur sponsæ christi,
qui representatur per ecclesiam : hinc concludebat, sponsum
et sponsas spirituales, hoc est sacerdotes et moniales, posse
simul carnaliter congredi sine peccato, et Deum ita præordi-
nasse, ac se putare summum bonum in ejusmodi congressu
esse positum. Eadem insuper juvenculis sæpius prædicabat.
Tandem quoque orationes et preces nefarias componebat, quibus apud Deum et alios instabat sanctos, ut maximas vires in
renibus posset consequi, in lumbis vero talem calorem, ut
abundanter et sæpenumero suam posset explere libidinem : deinde ut diva Cecilia, Ursula, Magdalena et Clara ex dono
specialis gratiæ mentibus monialium iisdem nominibus nuncu-
patarum infunderent, nullum fieri posse opus magis Deo me-

ritorium,

sex, that of *nymphomania*[f]. But it may be
proper to observe, that I use the term *satyriasis*
in a more limited sense than most medical writers, who extend it to disorders, which I, who
confine it to insanity, am obliged to exclude, and
who reckon symptoms, as essential, which, however frequently they may occur in this variety of appetitive insanity, are merely concomitant, do not necessarily enter into the idea of the

---

·ritorium, quam carnaliter commisceri, cresqere et multipiicare,
citra ullam personarum distinctionem, et voti castitatis læsio-
·nem, idque Deo placere magis quam holocaustum sive saerifi-
·cium : ut item illarum corda inflammarent amore ardenti erga
sacerdotem ecclesiæ sponsum, ne ejus vota carnalia maxima
cum humilitate adimplere, mandatisque ut veri patris parere
·gravarentur," &c.—*De Præstig. Dæmon.* lib. iii. *de Lamiis,*
·cap. vii. p. 181.

[f] SAUVAGESII Class. viii. Gen. 14, tom. iii. Part i. p. 345.
—SAUVAGES, and others, reckon both nymphomania and
satyriasis distinct genuses from insania; because they are not
always accompanied with what they call *delirium*, that is, with
ideal delirium. Nor do I here mean to comprehend every disorder to which others have given this appellation; but such
only as shall be found, on strict examination, to be included
in my definitions. The case of satyriasis in the preceding note,
is plainly so; and all the instances of nymphomania, which
have fallen under my observation, have been accompanied
with other indisputable symptoms of insanity.—See also—
BARTHOLINI Hist. Anat. Rar. Cent. 2. Hist. 69, p. 258.—
SCHENCKII Obs. Med. Rar. p. 134, Obs. 4.—ZACUTI LUSI-
TAN. Prax. Med. Admir. lib. ii. Oper. tom. ii. ad calcem,
p. 64, Obs. 93.—SENNERTI Medicinæ Pract. lib. iv. Part ii.
§ iii. cap. v. Operum omnium, tom. iv. p. 688.

disorder,

disorder, and, I have reason to believe, do not always exist. What these symptoms are will readily be seen, by comparing the passages, referred to in the notes, with the definition which I have given above.

———

I have already mentioned that all these species, of insanity may be variously combined, and frequently interchange, one with another. It may be proper farther to remark, that the same patient sometimes goes through several kinds of insanity, —which may be reckoned in such cases, as so many degrees, or stages,—during the course of the same illness. Of these combinations, and changes, there is almost an endless variety. One remarkable, and not uncommon transition of insanity, is from great dejection, and distress, to ease and cheerfulness, and sometimes to an uncommon flow of spirits. But most frequently it retains its character of liveliness, or anxiety, elevation, or depression. In general, all kinds of insanity, so far as they arise from mental constitution, and are not the sudden effect of any accidental bodily disease, may be considered as proceeding from two different, and opposite constitutional sources;—in one of which the characteristic temperament of mind may properly enough be called *fanciful*,—and in the other, *thoughtful*. The first degree of insanity in the former case

R 3   may

may be called *flighty*; and the first in the latter *melancholy*. The following scheme will show the natural progression of these constitutional temperaments of mind from their sound state, if they can ever strictly be said to be in a sound state, to the height of disorder, and insanity; and from thence again to their ordinary state of sanity.

I. 1. Fanciful—2. flighty—
$\left\{\begin{array}{l} 3.\ \text{maniacal} \\ 4.\ \text{phrenitic} \\ 5.\ \text{maniacal} \end{array}\right\}$
$\begin{array}{l} 6.\ \text{flighty.} \\ 7.\ \text{fanciful.} \end{array}$

II. 1. Thoughtful —2. me-
lancholy—
$\left\{\begin{array}{l} 3.\ \text{maniacal} \\ 4.\ \text{phrenitic} \\ 5.\ \text{maniacal} \end{array}\right\}$
$\begin{array}{l} 6.\ \text{melancholy.} \\ 7.\ \text{thoughtful.} \end{array}$

From the first of these constitutional classes it appears obvious why—" great wits to madness nearly are allied."—Both of them, where the disorder was not brought on by some disease of body; or other very powerful exciting cause, as intense study, the violent passion of love, sudden terror, or the like, which spare neither weak nor strong faculties,—are usually the attendants of a weak judgment:—but with this difference, that in the first case the imagination is chiefly in fault; and in the second the affections: the insanity in the one arising from too slight and hasty combinations of fancy, and an increased activity of that lively faculty; and in the other, from violent, and unreasonable, attachments and aversions;—both of which originate from, or tend to produce,

duce, weakness of judgment. Persons, therefore,
who are thus constitutionally disposed to one, or
other, of the above-mentioned classes of insanity,
have active imaginations, strong and permanent
affections, and weak judgments; though ingenious, witty, and acute, they are usually conspicuous for the want of that sober investigation
in matters of reasoning, and of that prudent moderation in the conduct of life, which characte-
rise men of cool heads, and sound understandings:—with regard to *religion*, they are apt to run
into superstition, or enthusiasm, on the one hand,
or into infidelity on the other, overleaping that
temperate mean within which a better judgment would have restrained them;—with regard
to *morals*, to deviate either into austerity, or licen-
tiousness;—and with regard to their *health*,
are either incautious, and intemperate free livers,
or anxious, and scrupulous valetudinarians.

It may also be noticed, that insanity appears
sometimes to be *epidemic*; and either to derive
its origin from some accidental, and temporary,
state, and constitution, of the atmosphere, which
fits it to produce such bodily disorder as has a
tendency to affect the brain, in a certain, and
determinate manner; or to take its peculiar turn
from the prevailing notions, and fashionable prejudices, of the times, or places, in which it occurs. Of the first sort of epidemic insanity we
have instances in the cases—of the Milesian vir-

R 4   gins,

gins, and of the French women of Lyonnois, who hanged and drowned themselves in great numbers, as has already been mentioned, without any obvious cause[g];—and of those who formerly, in Germany, were affected with what was called, by the medical writers of those days, who saw and described the disorder, *St. Vitus's dance*[h]; as well as of those in Holland, who, in the year 1373, were in like manner affected with an epidemic propensity to dance, which so readily communicated itself to such as looked on with too much attention, that it was attributed by the populace to the possession of the devil, and was called *St. John's dance*[i].—Examples of the second have been numerous, both in ancient and modern times; and have grown out of the superstition, and enthusiasm, of almost every country. Such was the insanity which took its character from the fanaticism of the crusades; from the romantic notions of chivalry; from the absurd belief of possessions[j], and witchcraft[k], which have led

---

[g] SCHENCKII Obs. Med. Rar. lib. i. p. 137, Obs. 1.—See above, p. 206.

[h] SCHENCKII Obs. Med. Rar. lib. i. p. 136, Obs. 9.—See above, p. 164.

[i] SAUVAGESII Nosol. Method. Class viii. Gen. 19, tom. iii. Part i. p. 389.

[j] SAUVAGESII Nosolog. Method. Class viii. Gen. 19. Dæmonomania, tom. iii. Part i. p. 393.—SCHENCKII Obs. Med. Rar. lib. i. p. 138, 1, 139, 2.—BARTHOLINI de Morbis Biblicis, cap. xix. p. 82.

many

many to confess, on their trials, this imaginary crime, though they knew that death was the inevitable consequence,—not a few to believe that they were bewitched, or possessed,—and some to persuade themselves that they had actually been tempted to enter into a compact with the devil[l]. In short, as all these absurdities abounded in the dark ages of ignorance and credulity[m], so the several sorts of epidemic insanity, which have been stamped with a similar character, have been the peculiar production of those ages; and if now, at any time, a solitary instance of a like nature discovers itself, it is always found to take possession of the weak, the ignorant, and the credulous. Nor can we exclude from this second division in the catalogue of epidemic insanity,

---

[k] SAUVAGESII Nosolog. Method. Class viii. Gen. 19. Dæmonomania Sagarum, ib.—WIERI de Præstig. Dæmon. lib. iii. De Lamiis, cap. v. p. 177, cap. xiv. p. 206. n. 8. DE HAEN de Magia, part ii. cap. i. p. 64, n. 14.—JOANNIS CLERICI Logica, Ontologia, et Pneumatologia, p. 348. Pneumatolog. § 2, cap. v.—BARTHOLINI de Morb. Biblicis, p. 82.

[l] SCHENCKII Obs. Med. Rar. lib. i. p. 138, Obs. 1.

[m] "Our forefathers," says ADDISON, "looked upon nature with more reverence and horror, before the world was enlightened by learning and philosophy, and loved to astonish themselves with the apprehensions of witchcraft, prodigies, charms, and enchantments. There was not a village in England that had not a ghost in it, the church-yards were all haunted, every large common had a circle of fairies belonging to it, and there was scarce a shepherd to be met with who had not seen a spirit."—SPECTATOR, vol. vi. No. 419, p. 106.

the

the pretended astrologers, conjurers, alchemists, and rosicrucians, who flourished about two centuries, or more, ago ; among whom, in England, were the celebrated JOHN DEE, with his prophet, or seer, EDWARD KELLY, who, as HUDIBRAS informs us,

> ————did all his feats upon
> The devil's looking-glass, a stone ;
> Were playing with him at bo-peep,
> He solv'd all problems ne'er so deep*—

the no less remarkable Dr. SIMON FORMAN, and many others ; who, though usually esteemed impostors, appear to have been as much cheated themselves, as they were disposed to cheat others; and, if they were in some degree rogues, were also, in no small degree, silly fools, and madmen ; and as much misled by a deluded imagination, as their more respectable brethren, the superstitious devotees, and fanatical enthusiasts, who abounded in the declining state of christianity, and at the dawn of the Reformation, while the mists of ignorance, which are now disappearing before the mild illumination of reason and truth, overclouded and darkened those divine lights of the mind, and involved in gloom, and obscurity, the engaging beauties of pure and rational religion.

Such insane persons as do not recover, remain

---

* Part ii. cant. 3, v. 31, &c.

gloomy,

gloomy, or fanciful, or become idiots; and sometimes have returns of maniacal insanity, at uncertain, and irregular intervals.—As for regular intervals, they are seldom met with:—and though
many are thought by their friends to be affected
by the full and change of the moon, I could never clearly, and certainly, perceive any such lu-
nar influence, I do not assert that these relative
positions of the moon have no influence in producing fits of insanity: there is some plausibility
in the opinion that they have; and many instances are related by medical writers in its support; but written histories are often inaccurate,
and fallacious: if such cases really exist, I think
I have reason to believe that they are exceedingly
rare.

SECT. IV.

OF THE APPEARANCES ON DISSECTION.

———

DISSECTIONS of bodies after death, with a
view to discover the real seats, immediate causes,
and internal effects of diseases, although they too
often throw much less light on these matters than
is wished for by the curious investigator, or the
humane physician, are yet of no inconsiderable
assistance towards the improvement of our knowledge of the nature, and the cure, of the many
dreadful maladies which afflict our feelings, and
destroy our frame: and it is much to be lamented
that the necessary, and inherent imperfections,
of this mode of investigating the causes of diseases, should be not a little increased by the frequent inattention, and inaccuracy, of those who
have dissected, and described the appearances of,
morbid bodies:—for not only are we liable to err
in many cases, even where we carefully examine
the appearances after death, with our own eyes,
or have a full, and distinct, relation of them from
other capable, and accurate observers; and to
mistake causes for effects, and effects for causes;
but, to increase our difficulties, and multiply the
sources of error, of the histories of diseases which
we meet with in the writings of physicians, very

few

few are pure, and complete in all their parts; and too many are miserably inaccurate, redundant, or deficient, in a variety of respects. And in scarcely any instance are they less decisive, either in consequence of the obscurity of the subject, or of the prejudices, and inattention, of the writers, than in those which relate to the disorder which is the object of our present consideration. Even the histories of the great, and accurate, Morgagni, are, on this head, exceedingly loose, and imper- fect: for, however exact the description of the appearances of the brain, that of the contents of the abdomen, as well as the history of the disease, is, in almost every instance, either greatly de- fective, or entirely wanting:—what then could be expected from the indiscriminate collections of the laborious, but less judicious, Bonetus?— For want, however, of better materials, I must content myself with giving little more than a sy- noptic view of the more important facts contained in their relations.

I. ACCORDING TO BONETUS.

The appearances on dissection of the bodies of such persons as, in the common acceptation of the term, had been esteemed mamacal, were, according to Bonetus*, as follows:—

* Vide Boneti Sepulchret, lib. i. § 8, de Mania et Rabie seu Hydrophobia.—Et § 9, de Melancholia et Affectione Hy- pochondriaca : cum additamentis, tom. i. p. 205—253.

The

The *contents* of the *skull* were sometimes found so turgid, on taking off the upper part of it, as immediately to expand, and not to admit of being again compressed into their former dimensions, and contained as before, within the limits of the skull (1).

The *sutures* were found obliterated; the *dura mater* adhering to the skull in several places (2); insinuating itself into the sutures, and retaining the traces of them when the upper hemisphere of the skull was torn away (1).

The

---

(1) This was the appearance on opening the skull of a boy of five years of age, who, with a moderate fever, and a pain in the head, was quite phrenitic, and died after four days illness. *Obs.* 2, p. 208—9.

(2) This was observed in dissecting the body of a gentleman, who in his youth had been conspicuous for his excellent endowments, both of body and mind; but becoming insane, from some unknown cause, was at length so violently maniacal, that he was kept chained in prison for thirty years; and would eat straw, lime, his own dung, or any kind of nastiness. For the last six years, however, of his life, his fury was so much abated, in the intervals of the full moon, that he was no way disposed to hurt any body, and was suffered to go at large within the area of the prison; and, though he still ate whatever came in his way, he had so much remaining sense, that he could sometimes recollect past events, would answer to questions which were put to him, and could read very well the French or Italian, as well as his native language. For two years before his death he was excessively costive, having a stool, at first, only once in about a week; and the interval, by degrees, increasing to four, five, ten, twelve, and even fifteen weeks;

The *vessels* which run along the *dura mater* were found turgid with black blood(1), and sometimes so dilated as to appear varicous (3). This membrane has also been observed to be marked with black spots (4);—and has sometimes appeared, by places, quite corrupted, or purulent (5).—The *sinuses* have, also, been found vastly distended with blood (1).

---

weeks; so that his belly became extended to an enormous size : yet during all this time he had a large appetite. He had once a spontaneous discharge of so vast a quantity of excrement, which had been long collecting, that his belly became quite flabby, and wrinkled. In short, having, at last, been without a stool for sixteen weeks, he grew thirsty, lost his appetite, drank great quantities of cold water, the size of his belly daily increased, the rest of his body fell away, his strength failed, he languished, and expired.

Among other appearances, there was water in the cellular membrane, and in the cavity of the abdomen; the rectum and colon almost entirely filled the remaining space, the latter being greatly distended, and the former to the immense size of more than an ell in circumference. The stomach, when opened, saluted the noses of all present with an excessively acid stench. The mesentery was sprinkled with innumerable glands of about the size of peas. The spleen was small, and when cut open, and pressed with the finger, was readily broken down into a red sanies. The pancreas was very large. The left kidney was surrounded by six hydatids ; one of the size of a pigeon's egg, of a livid colour, and resembling a venous sack; the others all transparent, and filled with serum, some of them about the size of large, and some of small walnuts.—The remaining appearances, of more immediate consequence, are related in the text,—*Obs. 1, of the Additamenta*, p. 245—7.

(3) In

The *pia mater* has likewise had its blood-vessels more or less enlarged, and dilated with
black blood (1); and has sometimes closely adhered to the dura mater, and forgot to insinuate
itself, as it ought to do, into the numerous
convolutions of the brain (2).

Water has also been met with, and even in a
large quantity, in the ventricles (1), and other
parts of the brain (2).

The *plexus choroides* has been found very large,
spreading quite over the inside of each ventricle,
composed of many very considerable branches
of blood-vessels from the carotids; and covered
all over with livid vesicles, or hydatids, like peas,
which, when broken, poured out a gelatinous
livid serum: from the plexus four large veins,
filled with fluid blood, have been observed to
proceed from the base of the pineal gland; but, in
this case, none of those vessels from the medullary substance of the brain, which are usually
said to be inserted in that gland, could any where
be found (2).

(3) In the dissection of many bodies of maniacs, who had
been originally melancholy; as observed by BALLONIUS.—
Obs. 6, p. 209.

(4) An observation of PLATERUS, who says, that such a spot
has been found on dissection to have been the cause of mania.—
Obs. 3, p. 209.

(5) An observation of the same writer, and to the same purpose.—*Obs.* 4, p. 209.

The

The *pituitary gland*, in one instance, dissolved into water on being touched (2).

The *pineal gland* was in the same subject found more solid than usual; and so besprinkled with innumerable minute blood-vessels, as to appear perfectly red (2).

And the *rete mirabile* was quite obliterated (2).

The *septum lucidum* appeared, in the same dissection, besprinkled with bloody spots (2): and, in another, the *corpus calosum*, particularly when pressed with the fingers, had a similar appearance (1).

The substance of the *brain* has been found marked with a black spot (4):—sometimes with an infinite number of bloody spots; and especially on pressing it (1):—and, in one case, it was observed to be very dry, hard, friable on the surface, and every were tinged with a yellow colour, to about the breadth of a finger below the surface (6).

It

(6) This patient was at first affected with deep melancholy, in consequence of misfortune; was in a few days after seized with an acute fever, without delirium, which left him in a state of idiotism; at length he became quite furious; and about the end of the fourth year, died an idiot.—*Obs.* 1, p. 205.— See the case at large in lib. i. § 4, *Obs.* 5, tom. i. p. 179.

(7) *Obs.* 5, § 1, 2, 3.—The case mentioned in the second section is borrowed from FERNELIUS; and as the patient, who was a soldier, is said to have long had a foul discharge from the nostrils, the worms were probably introduced that

It has, likewise, been said that *worms* have been found *in the brain*(7); and there seems to be no reason to doubt that they have been evacuated from the *nostrils*(8) of maniacal patients.

In

---

way, and found in the frontal sinuses; or if they were actually met with in the cavity of the cranium, they can only be supposed to have penetrated so far, in consequence of the bone being carious. FERNELIUS says the patient died in about 20 days.—Patholog. lib. v. cap. vii. Medicin. Univers. tom. ii. p. 96.—See some valuable observations on the subject of worms, idly supposed to be generated in the brain, in the accurate and judicious MORGAGNI's first epistle de Sedibus et causis Morborum, n. 8, 9, Operum, tom. iii. p. 67.—SAUVAGES has a species of maniacal insanity which he terms *mania ob hemicrania*; and mentions two instances in which it had been produced by worms in the frontal sinuses; one from SCHNEIDER de osse cribriformi, p. 440, of a peasant who was cured by the evacuation of a hairy caterpillar by the nostrils; and the other from the Ephemerides Naturæ Curiosorum, Decad. I, Anno 4, Obs. 37, where ANTONIUS DE POZZIS relates the history of another peasant who was maniacal for six months after sleeping under a tree, and was at length cured by the use of snuff as a sternutatory, which brought away, in like manner, a long, hairy, caterpillar. He adds the case of another maniac, of this sort, who threw himself out of a window, and fractured his skull; and was happily freed from his disorder by the discharge of a large quantity of purulent matter, which flowed as he supposes, from the frontal sinuses.—Nosolog. Method. Class viii. Gen. 20, Spec. 3, tom. iii. Part. i. p. 405.

(8, This, as I have just observed in the preceding note, was probably the case of the soldier whose history is extracted from the Pathology of FERNELIUS. Several histories of this sort might be quoted. I shall only mention one, extracted by

DULÆUS

In the bodies of such as have been afflicted with *melancholy*, the following appearances have been observed after death :—

The *blood-vessels* have been unusually large, and distended with florid, with black, and sometimes with concreted blood, in the *dura mater*(1) (5), in the pia mater(1) (5), and on the surface of the brain(1) (7):—the *pia mater*, on the right side, has not only had its veins turgid with black concreted blood, but has itself been quite black(6): —this membrane has also been much thickened, and has neglected to insinuate itself, as usual, between the convolutions of the brain(5):— sanious matter, and water, have floated on the surface of the brain(5), and the brain itself has been eroded(7).—Also, sanious, mucous, and purulent matter(7) (8), and large quantities of water(1) (5), have been found in the *lateral ventricles:*—the surface of the lateral ventricles has been lined with a yellow, or rather rusty mu-

---

DOLÆUS from the German Ephemerides, Ann. III. of a pea-sant, who, after sleeping under a tree, was maniacal for half a year; when, on taking an ounce of snuff, which excited a violent sneezing, he discharged from the nose a long, black, hairy, maggot, and perfectly recovered his senses.— *Vide* DOLÆI *Encyclopæd. Medicin. Theoret. Pract.* lib. i, cap. iv. § 11, p. 44.

(1) In a man who had an obscure fever, was silent, thirsty, comatous, somewhat lethargic, had a violent pain in his head, and at length died.—*Sect.* 9, *Obs.* 1, p. 221.

cus,

cus, resembling, in appearance, the sediment
which lines the reservoirs of chalybeate waters;
the plexus choroides, and the *third ventricle*, covered with the same rusty mucus; but the *fourth
ventricle* quite free from it (5).

The *heart* has been perfectly dry (16) (2),
shrivelled, and resembling a roasted pear (3):
the blood so dried up that a very expert surgeon,
who opened the body, was unable to dissect the
heart properly, or to trace any of its vessels (41):
it has been immensely large, and of a pale lead

(2) In a man who died melancholy.—*Obs. 41*, p. 241.

(3) As in the case of CASIMIR, Marquis of Brandenburgh,
in consequence of much grief, and watching.—*Obs.* 5, § 1,
p. 223.—

And, also, in that of a lady who, being in a deep melancholy,
hanged herself; and whose heart, on dissection, was found
to be dry, and without a drop of blood in its ventricles.—
Obs. 5, § 2, p. 223.

(4) In a woman, who had been afflicted with hypochondriacal melancholy.—*Obs.* 4, p. 222; and *Obs.* 12, p. 226.

(5) It appears to have been florid in the case of a woman,
who, after having long been subject to a violent head-ach,
had an apoplectic fit, which left a palsy of the right side, and
an imbecility of the understanding, which terminated, about
five months afterwards, in so violent a degree of timid insanity as urged her three times to make an attempt upon her
own life. The delirium usually began at day-break, and
continued till evening, when it abated. Between two and
three years afterward, she died of a pleurisy.—*Obs.* 2, p. 221.
—See the same case, at large, and the appearances on dissection more fully, and perfectly, related, in the Section on the
Apoplexy, p. 111, Obs. 40.

colour:

colour (21): and it has been surrounded with a
great quantity of fat (33).

The heart, on being opened, has been observed
to pour out a large quantity of black gore (7):—
there has been found in the right ventricle (8),
and likewise in the left (4), a concreted substance
supposed to be a portion of the atrabilious humour:
—a large vesicle has been found adhering to the
right ventricle, containing black blood (9):—two
pounds of a black, glandular, flesh, has been observed in the left ventricle; the heart, like the gra-
vid uterus, being distended, to adapt itself to the
magnitude of its contents (10):—a thin, red, and
fetid fluid has been found in the left ventricle (11);
—black blood in the cavity of the heart (13):—the
ventricles, instead of blood, full of a vitreous pi-

---

(6) In the dissection of a young man, who was melancholy,
and epileptic.—*Obs.* 3, p. 222.

(7) In a man of thirty years of age, who was seized, in the
spring, with melancholy; became inactive, dejected, was continually sighing, and wished for nothing but death. In the beginning of the disorder, his head was unusually inclined to the
left side; and he had a little before been troubled with the
night-mare, and with terrors in the night. He died con-
vulsed in the beginning of July following.—*Obs.* 31, p. 232.

(8) This was observed in a man, of forty years of age, of
a melancholy habit, who had been exceedingly tormented with
the hypochondriacal disorder for some years, and had especially complained of a pain in the left hypochondre.—*Obs.* 19,
p. 227, and *Obs.* 25, p. 230.—See the case at length, lib. ii.
§ 5, Obs. 23, p. 660.

S 3   tuita :

tuita(12) :—both the ventricles full of thick blood,
intensely black like ink;—an abscess, of the
size of an egg, near the left auricle(13):—nothing
but black bile in the ventricles of the heart, in
the spleen, and in the whole vascular sys-
tem(14):—a large *aneurism* of the *aorta*(15).

On opening the *pericardium*, it has been observed to contain serum(13) ;—plenty of citron-
coloured water(16):—its moisture, on the other
hand, has been found dried up(3) ;—and con-
sumed(2) :—and the pericardium every where
adhering to the heart(17).

The *spleen* has been so large(8),—as to weigh
four pounds (18) ; — and so small (19) (20) (40),

---

(9) In a silent melancholy man, who shunned society, and
died of an inflammation of the liver.—*Obs.* 9, p. 226.

(10) In a gentleman who became very melancholy before his
death.—*Obs.* 13, p, 226.

(11) In a man, who had been troubled for three years with
hypochondriacal melancholy.—*Obs.* 14, p. 226.—Also book ii,
§ 10, *Obs.* 5, p. 864.

(12) In a youth, who had been long afflicted with melancholy.—*Obs.* 10, p. 226.

(13) In a boy of three years of age, who had passed his
short life in much pain, distress, and groaning; and at length
died suddenly.—*Obs.* 6, p. 223, and *Obs.* 11, p. 226.

(14) In a gentleman, who had long been troubled with an
hypochondriacal affection, from a supposed disease of the
spleen; and who, though he had the singular firmness of
mind to disguise his melancholy, and to be quite lively, and
jocose, among his companions, was obliged to give it vent
in private, and among his intimate friends.—*Obs.* 7, § 2,
p. 223.

as

as scarcely to weigh an ounce (21); and it has
likewise been wanting (22) :—the colour of its
surface has been either wholly livid (8) (21), or
of the colour of lead; or it has only been
partially livid (7), or black (23) :—it has been
hard (18); scirrhous (24) (25); with an unnatural scirrhous appendage of about the size of a
pigeon's egg (25); and it has, on the other hand,
been uncommonly soft, tender, and flabby (8) ;—
the internal substance, or parenchyma, has, on taking off its membranous integument, been in so
dissolved, and fluid, a state, as to run out, under
the appearance of a thick, black, putrid jelly (26);
and has sometimes been thought to be nothing
but black bile (14) :—on its convex surface have
been varicous veins, likewise distended with black
blood (23); as have been also the veins of the

(15) In a man, of an atrabilious temperament, who had been
much distressed in mind, and had experienced a variety of
symptoms of hypochondriacal melancholy —*Obs.* 38, p. 138.

(16) In one who had been melancholy, had been variously
tempted, had ineffectually stabbed himself, was afterward seized
with violent vomiting, and expired.—*Obs.* 8, p. 224.

(17) In a woman, who had passed the last years of her life
in a state of the most distressful melancholy.—*Obs.* 15, p. 226.
—*Obs.* 6, p. 880.

(18) In a man, who had long been hypochondriacal—
Obs. 23, p. 229.—See a similar case of a man who died of the
morbus niger, and whose spleen, which was soft, weighed four
pounds, &c.—BARTHOLINI *Hist. Anat. Rar.* Cent. 1, Hist. 80,
p. 115.

neighbour-

neighbouring parts (8).—It is, however, very com♦
monly found free from disease (27).

The *liver* has been found both unusually
large (21) (25), and unusually small (28):—it
has been either florid (24) (25), livid (7), black
in various degrees (28) (29), or of a pale lead co♦
lour (21) :—it has been either wholly, or in part
scirrhous (19) (28), œdematous (29), and full of
fissures (29) ; and its convex part has been covered with hydatids (21).

The *omentum* has, on several occasions, been
found diseased.—It has been remarkably thick,
large, and scirrhous (30) :—it has not only been
scirrhous, but so large as to occupy the whole
epigastric region, has been four fingers breadth
in thickness, and, in colour, has resembled the
spleen (31) :—it has been loaded with three large
excrescences, supposed by the patient, when alive,

---

(19) In the Emperor FERDINAND III. who had a variety of
hypochondriacal symptoms; and seems to have died of what
is termed by HIPPOCRATES the *morbus niger.* — *Obs.* 34,
p. 236.—See the case related at length, lib. iii. § 8, Obs. 47,
tom. ii. p. 111.—See a case of the morbus niger, with observations upon it, in SIMSONI de Re Medica Dissertat. quatuor,
p. 140.—See the morbus niger described in HIPPOCRATES'
Treatise de Morbis, lib. ii. Oper. tom. i. p. 486. 50.

(20) In a family subject to hypochondriacal melancholy,
several of whom died suddenly ; but, on dissection, no cause
could be discovered of their sudden death, unless it might be
attributed to the smallness of their spleens.—*Obs.* 28, § 2,
p. 231.

to

to have been the heads of three living frogs, which she imagined she had swallowed, but which were found upon examination to be indurated, and scirrhous, glands of the omentum; and a scirrhous tumor of the omentum itself, which weighed two pounds and a half(32).—Its colour has been sometimes red(30), sometimes livid, and sometimes black(42).—The vessels have been turgid with black blood(42),—it has adhered in several places to the peritoneum(42):—and has been found tender(42), lacerated (42), destitute of fat(42), and exceedingly fetid, and putrid(28) (42).

(21) In a gentleman of an atrabilious temperament, who had been troubled from his youth with hypochondriacal melancholy, with which, when he died, he had struggled for more than twenty years; and had been perpetually distressed with fear, dejection, and pusillanimity: though in his youth he had been of a hot constitution, as he advanced in life he became of a cold one, as appeared from the serous state of his blood, from the pale, and lead colour complexion of his liver, the size of his gall-bladder, and the watery state of the gall, with which it was distended. He had been guilty of great excesses in diet, had indulged in hard drinking, to relieve the dejection of his spirits: for more than a year he slept very little; and was obliged to court sleep by reading in the night till he became drowsy: for some weeks before his death he was troubled with a violent defluxion from his head, which, falling upon his breast, produced such a difficulty of breathing, that he was frequently in danger of suffocation. As his face, and blood taken from his arm, when he was alive, were of a livid, and lead colour; so were his viscera after death.—Obs. 28, p. 230.

The

The *mesentery* has been scirrhous, and, as it were, stony, and its vessels turgid with black serous blood (33):—it has been every where replete with a black fluid (25):—a collection of fetid, purulent, matter, has been met with between its two coats, which has occupied the greatest part of the lower belly, and has even contaminated the liver(34):—it has been every where overspread with black varices(28):—it has appeared as if sphacelated(35):—and its glands have been enlarged, indurated, and scirrhous(35).

---

(22) In a married woman, whose skin was tinged of a black colour; who had a perpetual melancholy, without fever; and whose disorder had been attributed by her physicians to an obstinate obstruction of the spleen, and mesentery.—*Obs.* 22, p. 229.—See the case at large, lib. iii. § 18, Obs. 30, tom. ii. p. 332.

(23) In a gentleman, who had been affected with symptoms of melancholy.—*Obs.* 27, p. 230.

(24) In a gentleman, who had been frequently troubled with hypochondriacal, and nephritic symptoms.—*Obs.* 24, p. 229.

(25) In a lady who had been usually troubled with hypochondriacal complaints, and a tension in the region of the spleen, every year about the time of the solstices, and equinoxes.—*Obs.* 26, p. 230.

(26) In a man who was melancholy, and hanged himself.— *Obs.* 29, p. 231.

(27) Obs. 21, § 1, 2, 3, p. 227.

(28) In a prince, of a very diseased habit of body, of a melancholy disposition, and of remarkable taciturnity.—*Obs.* 46, p. 242.

The

The mesenteric vessels have been turgid with black foul blood(25);—with black blood, and the veins varicous 36 :—the gastro-epiploic vessels(8), and the confines of the vena portarum, have been in like manner affected :—the parts to which the coeliac, and mesenteric, arteries, and veins, are distributed, have been in an inflammatory state(37):—and the vas breve has been obstructed(19).

The *intestines* have been inflated with wind (7) (33), have been livid, black, and sphacelated(38):—in some parts full of concreted, feculent, and very black blood, like pitch, exactly

---

(29) A nobleman, having experienced great losses, and being overcome with grief, and distress, became melancholy, was perpetually sorrowful, pensive, and sighing, contracted an excessive parsimony, and a dread of spirits, and apparitions. He continued in this unhappy state for about twenty years; declined, and died.—*Obs.* 32, p. 234.

(30) In a gentleman of an adust, and melancholy temperament, who had been troubled with obstinate vomiting, and frequent eructations.—*Obs.* 17, p. 227.

(31) In a man of a very melancholy temperament.—*Obs.* 39, p. 239.

(32) In a woman, who, after drinking water from the spout of a running spring, saw, after she had finished drinking, the foot of a frog sticking in the pipe, was persuaded that she had swallowed some living frogs, could perceive them move about, and hear them croak within her.—*Obs.* 40, p. 240.—A similar case is related, a few pages before, in which an imaginary frog was found, on dissection, to be a scirrhous tumor, of the size of a hen's egg, near the pylorus.—*Obs* 35, p. 236.

resembling

resembling what the patient had vomited when alive(19) (38):—their veins have been replete with thick, black blood, and have appeared distended, and varicous(30) (38):—and sometimes they have been almost destitute of moisture(25).

The *stomach* has likewise been much distended with wind(33):—it has been in some parts livid(30):—its coats have been either wholly, or in part, exceedingly thin, like paper(19) (30) (33):—it has contained a large quantity of dark coloured(19), or of black matter(28); in one case as black as ink(33), and, as was evident from

---

(33) In a case of hypochondriacal insanity, in a gentleman, minutely related, of several years standing, accompanied with heat, distension, lancinating pains in the hypochondres, anxiety about his disorder, and at length a silent melancholy, from a scirrhous of the pylorus and omentum.—*Obs.* 33, p. 234.

(34) In a gentleman, who had been exceedingly intemperate, was seized with a nausea, vomiting, dejection, and other hypochondriacal symptoms; with a pain, and tumor, in the lower belly, which gradually increased; and died quite emaciated in about seven months.—*Obs.* 37, p. 237.

(35) In hypochondriacs.—*Obs.* 16, p. 226.

(36) In flatulent melancholy.—*Obs.* 42, p. 241.—See *Obs.* 44, 45, p. 242.

(37) According to the observations of SPIGELIUS; who supposes the cause of melancholy to be an inflammation seated in those parts, from the heat and pulsation frequently felt there by the patient, and the inflammatory state in which he often observed them on dissection.—*Obs.* 31, p. 231.

(38) In a case of the morbus niger.—*Obs.* 43, p. 241.—See another of a somewhat similar nature in *Obs.* 47, p. 242.

its

its fetid smell, quite in a putrid state(33).—The stomach, as well as the intestines, has sometimes been found almost destitute of moisture(25).

The *pylorus* has been discovered to have been inflamed(35);—scirrhous(39); and in one case, not only scirrhous, but its passage so closely contracted, as scarcely to admit a quill to be thrust through it(33).

The *pancreas* has been large, black, and hard (19) (28).—The *kidneys* have been very large; as big as a child's head(28,; full of stones; gangrenous; and otherwise affected.—The *capsulæ atrabiliariæ* have been large, and of an unusual structure(40).—A large abscess has been observed near the *psoas muscle*(28).—The lungs, and neighbouring parts, have been variously diseased(7) (8) (21) (28) (29).

(39) In an hypochondriacal nobleman, who always vomited up his food, and with it a certain black matter.—*Obs.* 18, p. 227.

(40) In a man who had been melancholy.—*Obs.* 36, p. 237.

(41) In a certain subject, the blood of which is said to have been exsiccated by the melancholy humour.—*Obs.* 7, p. 623, § 1.

(42) In the body of a man, who had been hypochondriacal and scorbutic.—*Obs.* 20, p. 227.

II. ACCORDING TO MORGAGNI[a].

MORGAGNI does not always mention whether the persons, on whose bodies his dissections were made, had died maniacal, or melancholy. And were not this omission generally accompanied, as might be expected, with an imperfect history of the disease in other respects, it would not, perhaps, in itself, have been of much importance; since an exact description of the symptoms, as they occurred, would have conveyed much better information, than a distinction so exceedingly imperfect, inaccurate, and uncertain, as that of mania and melancholy; as has already been abundantly shown: and as MORGAGNI himself was well aware :—for he very justly observes, from the ingenious Dr. WILLIS that—" Mania has so near a relation to melancholy, that these disorders often mutually change sides, and pass one into the other[b];"—adding, " so that you may often see physicians in doubt, while on the one hand they observe taciturnity and fear, and on the other loquacity and boldness, not unfre-

---

[a] De Sedibus et Causis Morborum. Operum tom. iii. et iv.— Epist. 1, Spectat ad Dolorem Capitis.—Epist. 8, De Mania Melancholia, et Hydrophobia.—Epist. 59, De Morbis a Veneno inductis.—Epist. 61, Partinet ad Deliria quæ sine febre contingunt.

[b] " Melancholiæ—mania in tantum affinis est, ut hi affectus sæpe vices commutent, et alteruter in alterum transerat."

quently

quently alternating in the same patient, whether they should pronounce him melancholy or maniacal. And for this reason, I have been the less disappointed, when, on asking with what sort of delirium the insane persons, whose heads I was about to dissect, had been affected, I have often received very ambiguous, and sometimes quite opposite answers; which yet, I was sensible, might all be true, in consequence of the changes which might happen in the course of a long continued delirium^e."

The above passage, at the same time that it affords the best, and only proper apology, for his imperfect histories of the disorder, will serve, in conjunction with several others which occur in the course of the epistles, to show the very lax sense in which he uses the terms *stultus* and *fatuus*, which so frequently occur in the concise memorandums of the cases we are now considering; which he appears sometimes to confound as synonymous terms; while for the most part he seems to use the former as applicable, in general, like the *fou* and *folie*, of the French, to the

---

^e " Quin saepius dubitantes medicos videas, hinc taciturnitate et metu, hinc loquacitate et audacia, in eodem aegro subinde alternatis, melancholicum, an maniacum pronuncient. Quo facilius tuli cum stultorum capita dissecarem, atque utro laborassent delirio, quaererem, responsiones persaepe ambiguas, nonnunquam inter se pugnantes, veras tamen fortasse in longo delirii cursu."—*Epist.* 8. 1. tom. iii. p. 47.

insane

insane of every denomination; and the latter to express idiotism: and in one place, to reverse these meanings, and to transpose each into the place of the other.—In the dissections which he describes, we meet with the following appearances:—

The *dura mater* firmly adhering to the os frontis for a considerable space on the left side, and in that part so nearly ossified, as to be in a kind of intermediate state between that of a bone and a ligament (1):—the vessels of both the meninges distended with black fluid blood (2) :—a polypous concretion extending through the whole length of the longitudinal sinus (3):—the dura mater

---

(1) In a beggar, who had always been insane [*fatuus*]; and at length became so silly [*stultus*] as to throw away the bread which he had acquired by begging. He had also been subject to a head-ach.—*Epist.* 1, n. 10.

(2) In a robust young maniac, who, in about an hour after having had a pound of blood taken from the temporal artery, was found dead, with his tongue hanging out of his mouth. This sudden death was discovered to have been occasioned by the cruelty of his inhuman keeper; who, because he had removed the bandage from his head, and renewed the bleeding of the artery, though without any dangerous hæmorrhage, as it had been immediately replaced, struck him violently with his fist over the belly, and forehead, and then left him bound so strait round the neck, that he was presently strangled.—*Epist.* 8, n. 4.

(3) This was observed in a young woman, of about twenty years of age, who, on being refused admission into a nunnery,

mater thicker than usual(4):—water between the
pia mater and the brain(5) (6),—sometimes in
considerable quantity(7) ; — and sometimes but
just enough to make the pia mater slip with ease,
on the slightest attempt to separate it from between the convolutions of the brain(8) (9):—
sometimes air-bubbles were observed in the water, and were likewise seen in such great plenty
in some of the vessels, as entirely to fill them(7).

Out of the thirteen dissections described by

---

nery, immediately became insane, rambled in her talk, and
as the disorder increased, frequently refused to take food : she
continued in this state for some months, and, besides being several times indisposed by paroxysms of an irregular fever, was
at length attacked by a violent insanity without fever ; the
delirium, as MORGAGNI observes, which was at first melancholy, becoming maniacal ; so that she attempted to injure
those about her ; and, her strength gradually declining, she expired.—It was observed, in this dissection, that along the
outside of the longitudinal sinus, on the dura mater, were certain small white substances, some round, some oblong, some of
an irregular figure, but all soft; which VALSALVA supposed to be
concretions of the coagulable lymph, because he had before
observed such concretions, in persons who had died of wounds
of the head, arising from the stagnation of purulent matter
upon the dura mater :—but MORGAGNI reckons these white
tubercles to be natural.—*Epist.* 8, n. 2.

(4) In a man, dissected by one of his pupils, who was delirious without fever, and through the inattention of his keepers,
who had carefully watched him for three days, leaped out of his
chamber window in the night-time, fell upon his head, and
died.—*Epist.* 8, n. 15.

MORGAGNI, one of which was made by VAL-
SALVA(3) eleven by himself(1) (2) (5) (6) (7)
(8) (9) (10) (11) 12) (13), and one by one of his
pupils(4),—in that made by VALSALVA it is
mentioned—that the brain was moist, which
seems to imply that it was soft; or, at least, as
no such thing is noticed, we may, I think, safely
conclude that it was by no means remarkably
hard(3):—and in one of those performed by MOR-
GAGNI himself, the brain and cerebellum were
both found uncommonly soft; but it should be
noticed that in this case the patient had been free
from insanity for some little time before his death,
and was, apparently, killed by taking a concluding
dose of black hellebore, before his intended
dismission, as cured, from confinement(10).—In

---

(5) In a butcher who had been insane [*stultus*] for fourteen
months, in consequence, as was supposed, of a love potion;
and, being incapable of taking proper care of himself, was
starved to death by the severity of the weather.—*Epist.* 8,
n. 6.

(6) In a man who had long been insane [*stultus*], and died of
a lingering fever.—*Epist.* 8, n. 11.

(7) In a woman, who had been delivered of a child the year
before, without any relief to her insanity. She usually ran
about the streets; but hurt nobody. Her disorder commenced
about nine years before, on her lover having been killed on the
day preceding that which had been fixed upon for their marriage.—She died of an inflammation of the breast.—*Epist.* 8,
n. 9.

all

all the other eleven dissections(1) (2)—(4) (5)
(6) (7) (8) (9)—(11) (12) (13) the brain was
found more or less hard; generally very much
so; especially in its medullary substance: and
the cerebellum in seven of these universally
soft, in two very generally soft, but with partial hardness in small portions of the medullary substance, (4) (7) and in two universally firmer than ordinary (9) (13).—It may
also be worthy of notice, that in one case,
where the cortical substance of the brain was
pretty firm, and the medullary substance every
where

---

(8) In a man who had been insane [*stultus*].—*Epist.* 8,
n. 12.

(9) In a woman who had been insane [*stulta*], and died at
about a middle age.—*Epist.* 61, n. 2.

(10) To a man about fifty years of age, of a good habit of
body, who had been cured in an infirmary of a melancholy delirium, was given a dose of the extract of black hellebore before his intended dismission: it purged him smartly, and all
was supposed to be well: but in the evening, about seven or
eight hours after he had taken it, he was seized with vomiting,
and pains in his belly, which, by taking some warm broth,
seemed to be appeased in about an hour: in about four
hours after they returned again, and again seemed to be so
much abated in less than an hour, that he went to bed.
With all his straining, and vomiting, he had brought up nothing but about two or three table spoonfuls of blackish green
matter. On going to bed, he seemed to rest, as they who lay
in the beds near him heard not the smallest groaning, or sign

of

where exceedingly hard, the latter was found not so white as usual; which was supposed to be owing to its blood-vessels being uncommonly full, as the discoloration decreased in proportion as the dissection receded from the cortical substance (7). In this subject, also, the nerves, within the skull, were observed, on being cut, to be firmer, and less moist than common (7). The

---

of pain. In about an hour some kind of noise was heard to come from him by the attendants; they ran to him, and found him dead.—On dissection, the stomach, and œsophagus, were observed to be pretty generally, but slightly, inflamed; the intestines were inflamed in many parts, but less so than the stomach; and the large intestines were less inflamed than the small ones, excepting the rectum, some portions of which were as conspicuously inflamed as the stomach.—But there was no were any violent inflammation. The spleen was something larger than ordinary, of a rosy colour on the part adjoining to the stomach, and of so loose a texture, that, on dissecting it, the internal contents were found nearly approaching to a fluid state. The gall, as seen through the coats of the gall-bladder, appeared of a pale green colour.—A small quantity of bloody serum flowed out on taking off the skull; and a little blood was found in the sinusses of the dura mater, and in the larger vessels of the pia mater; and the brain, though the dissection was performed earlier than the sixth day after death, and it was taken out with the greatest care, was so exceedingly soft, that when placed upon a table, it had not sufficient firmness, excepting a small portion just at the entrance into the third ventricle, to retain its proper form. The same laxity was observed in the *cerebellum*; *medulla oblongata*; and in the pineal gland, which was somewhat larger and rounder than usual.—*Epist.* 59, n. 15.

hardness,

hardness, in another case, was found to extend to the beginning of the spinal marrow (10.).

In the *corpus callosum*, instead of those two protuberant lines, or chords, or as LANCISIUS calls them, *longitudinal nerves*, which usually run along its upper and posterior surface, in one subject were observed, in their place, two rather deeply indented furrows (5) :—in another, the protuberance consisted, for the most part, of a single line, which, however, in one place divided, and became a double one (12) :—in a third, it was one simple line (13):—in a fourth, it is said to have been in its perfectly natural state(10):—and in the other dissections it is not mentioned at all.

The *pineal gland* was, in some subjects, enlarged (9)(10)(13),more globular than usual(10), of a soft texture(10), and of a mucous appearance(9) (10):—in one, quite flabby and withered(8):—in another, fixed to its place by rather long medullary roots (4):—in some it was of a yellowish brown colour (8) (13):—and it had sometimes, adhering to its anterior part, a quantity of a pale yellow, granulated, matter (4) (5) ; resembling, in appearance, a congeries of small stones (7) ; which, when rubbed between the fingers, was found, in one case, to contain something like grains of sand (1);

---

(11) In a woman who had been insane [*stulta*], of about forty years of age, and who had died of a quinsy.—*Epist.* 8, p. 8.

in

in another the granulations were moderately
hard; and in a third, they were so far from approaching to the nature of sand, that they had
scarcely any perceptible hardness(7).

Water(1) (2) (4) (6) (7) (9*), or serum(3),
was frequently found in the *ventricles* (1) (2) (4)
(6) (9*), especially in the lateral ones (1) (2)
(3) (4) (6), and between the two lamellæ which
form the septum that divides them (6), sometimes in a large (2) (4), and sometimes only
in a small (1) (3) (6) (9*) quantity: which
was either limpid (1), or turbid (2); resembling
serum (1) (3), or of a reddish yellow (4).—But
sometimes the ventricles were quite free from
water, and their vessels red (7).—Water, of various appearances, was also observed in other
parts of the brain, and its connexions.

The *plexus choroides* was sometimes red (2)
(4); and sometimes discoloured (1) (9):—in one
case it adhered to the mouth of the opening
which leads into the third ventricle, as it passed
over it, and stopped it up (9):—it was in two instances (1) (2) beset with hydatids; in one of
which, one hydatid was as big as a moderate-

----

(12) In a man, of about forty years of age, who had been
ing made a galley-slave, became at first hypochondriacal, and
afterwards insane [*stultus*], but, was cheerfully so, and continued in that state about ten years, when he grew cachectic,
his whole body œdematous, had a difficulty of breathing, and
died in the hospital.—*Epist.* 61, n. 5.

sized

sized grape, with vessels running along its coats as large as those of the adjoining membrane of the plexus ; and in one instance it exhibited four large, yellow, almost spherical, and indurated, glands (3).

The *vessels of the brain* were in some cases distended with black (4) (8) (10), and fluid blood (2), both in its substance, on the sides of the septum lucidum, and all round the rest of the sides of the great lateral ventricles (2):—and in others with florid blood (7).—The arteries were in one subject observed to have firmer coats than usual (4).

In one case, the *carotid arteries*, and the *internal jugular veins*, in the neck, were larger than ordinary (6):—in another, the *pericardium* every where adhered to the heart (5) :—in another the *spleen* was obstructed (1) :—and in him who died by taking hellebore, after his insanity had left him, it was larger than usual, of a rosy colour on its flat part, which lies contiguous to the stomach ; and the whole was of so loose a texture, that, when cut into, its contents appeared to be in a state nearly approaching to that of a fluid (10).

From a view of the above enumeration of ap-

---

(13) In a woman, upwards of thirty years of age, who was born an idiot [*stulta*], and at last died in consequence of refusing all nourishment.—*Epist.* 61, n. 7.

(9*) In this case a good deal of water had flowed from the cavity of the vertebræ, on separating the head from the body, for dissection.—*Epist.* 61, n. 2.

T 4   pearances

pearances on dissection, as exhibited by MOR-
GAGNI, and I am not conscious that any thing
material has been omitted, it may be observed,
that he confines his attention almost entirely
to the contents of the head, and takes very little
notice of the abdominal viscera, some or other
of which have been so universally esteemed to
be the seat, and fountain of the atrabilis, and
melancholy humour, the supposed causes of hypochondriacal, and of most other sorts of insanity. Of these he has taken even less notice
than, in the dissections collected by BONETUS,
of patients who died melancholy, is taken of
the state of the brain. It is true, it was not
always in his power to examine the contents of
the abdomen; and he laments the misfortune;
which he could no more avoid, or remedy, than
the defective account which his imperfect information usually obliges him to give of the disorder; or than BONETUS could help the loose and
slovenly descriptions, and imperfect memorandums, which he often met with in the writers
from whom he collected.—These omissions, however, must be considered as capital defects in
both.

If the appearances on dissection, observed in
the contents of the skull of such as had been insane, of which I have just given a synoptic view
from these two eminent writers, be compared
with those which have been met with after other
diseases

diseases which principally affect, or at least derive
their origin from the head, but have not been
accompanied with the smallest symptom of insanity ; it will be perceived that scarcely a single appearance has occurred in the one case, which has
not likewise been found in the other : as may
be seen by consulting, in BONETUS, the sections
which treat—on the head-ach (1)—on the apoplexy (2),—on the various kinds of sleepy affections (3),—on the catalepsy (4), — on terrifying
dreams, and the night-mare (5),—on preternatural watchings (6),—on the phrenitis and para-
phrenitis (7),—on the depravation, and abolition,
of the imagination, reason, and memory (8),—
on the vertigo (9),—on the epilepsy (10),—on convulsions (11), — on stupidity, torpor, trembling,
&c. (12),—on the palsy (13),—and some others :—
by consulting the corresponding epistles of Mor-

---

(1) Lib. i. § 1, tom. i. p. 1.
(2) Lib. i. § 2, tom. i p. 77.
(3) Lib. i. § 3, tom. i. p. 148.
(4) Lib. i. § 4, tom. i. p. 176.
(5) Lib. i. § 5, tom. i. p. 180.
(6) Lib. i. § 6, tom. i. p. 183.
(7) Lib. i. § 7, tom. i. p. 187.
(8) Lib. i. § 10, tom. i. p. 253.
(9) Lib. i. § 11, tom. i. p. 262.
(10) Lib. i. § 12, tom. i. p. 271.
(11) Lib. i. § 13, tom. i. p. 305.
(12) Lib. i. § 14, tom. i. p. 344.
(13) Lib. i. § 15, tom. i. p. 354.

GAGNI :

GAGNI[d]:—and by comparing the whole with the appearances, just exhibited from them both, on the dissection of insane subjects.

No one was more sensible of the uncertainty arising from this similarity of appearances in the brain, and its appendages, after so many different disorders, than MORGAGNI himself; who, though much inclined to believe that the uncommon hardness of the brain, which so frequently occurred to him, was more than accidental, and had no inconsiderable share in the production of insanity; had yet too much accuracy, and candour, not to perceive, and to acknowledge, that this disorder had sometimes existed where no such hardness could be discovered; and that there were many examples of this unusual hardness of the brain without any preceding insanity[e]. But that his opinion relative to the comparative importance of the several appearances on dissection, as they may seem to have some agency in the production of insanity, may be better understood, I shall here give a concise abridgment of his observations on his own, and some other dissections, of insane subjects; in which it will be perceived that the illustrious writer, on some occasions, still uses the terms *fatuus, fatui-*

---

[d] De Sedibus et Causis Morbor. Epist. 1, 2, 3, 4, 5, 6, 7, 8, 9, 10, 11, &c. Operum tom. iii. p. 1—84.

[e] Epist. 8, n. 18.

tas,

tas, stultus, and *stultitia,* with a degree of latitude, but that he seems commonly to employ the latter as generally expressive of insanity, and the former to signify a state of idiotism.

(1) He remarks that if his own dissections be compared with those of others, it will be found that, of the appearances which they have described, some he had never seen, others rarely, others often, and some always.

That he had never seen the pia mater forget to insinuate itself between the convolutions of the brain;—that he had never seen, nor indeed did he ever expect to see, worms in the brain;—and that he had never seen an induration of the dura mater, though BAGLIVI[f] asserts that in two maniacs whom he had dissected at Naples, he had found the dura mater as hard as a board, and almost as dry; though M. LITTRE[g], and M. GEOFFROY[h], had each observed both the membranes of the brain, the former of these gentlemen in one case, harder and more compact, and the latter, in another, thicker and firmer, than was natural; not to mention that GEOFFROY found the falx at the same time, almost covered

---

(1) Epist. 8, n. 13, and 14.

[f] Specim. Libri primi de Fibra Motrice, cap. v. Coroll. 10, Operum, p. 287.

[g] Memoires de l'Acad. Royale de Sciences, Ann. 1705, p. 40—47.

[h] Ibid. Ann. 1706, p. 662.

with

with bony laminæ: — though ALEXANDER CA-
MERARIUS[i], and the celebrated VAN SWIETEN[j],
had also noticed this firmness, and unusual thickness of one, or both, meninges: the origin of
which, he tells us, he should be inclined to attri-
bute to the violence, or long continuance of the
delirium, did not he know that it had been observed by WEPFER[k] after melancholy deliriums;
—by KING[l] after idiotism [*fatuitas*];—by others[m],
—and by himself[n],—in the dissection of such
as had been of a sound mind.—That, however,
he found it less unfrequent in maniacs than those
large glands observed by VALSALVA[o] in the ventricles of the brain; though something similar
had been remarked in the ventricles of some who
had died melancholy[p].—Nor did he ever chance
to discover those cavities replete with water, or
any yellow corpuscle, in the medullary substance
of the brain, observed by SANTORINUS[q] in two

[i] Disput. de Apospasm. Piæ Matris.

[j] Comment. § 1121.

[k] Auct. Hist. Apoplect. Hist. 15, p. 375.

[l] Act. Lipsiens. Ann. 1688. Mens. Maii, p. 234, from the
Philosophical Transactions for December 1686, Numb. 185,
p. 228.

[m] Sepulchret. lib. i. § 1, Obs. 1. tom. i. p. 1.

[n] Epist. 5, n. 6, and Epist. 49, n. 16.

[o] Epist. 8, n. 2.

[p] WEPFER. loco citato, et Histoir. de l'Acad. R. des Sciences, Ann. 1700, p. 49.

[q] Obs. Anatom. c. ii. § 5.

old

old men, one of whom was an idiot[*fatuus*], and the other rather insane [*leviter stultus*].—Much less did he meet with the brain of a smaller size than it should be, as was observed in several idiots [*fatui*] by WILLIS[r], KERCKRINGIUS[s], and KING[t].

That he had rarely, and indeed only once, seen, in the body of an insane person [*stultus*], those deep furrows in the corpus callosum[u],—air-bubbles in the blood-vessels of the brain,—or the medullary substance rather of a brown colour, —appearances which were probably merely accidental: since LANCISIUS[v] had observed quite the reverse of the last-mentioned, having found the substance of the brain in an idiot [*fatuus*] whiter than ordinary.

[r] Sepulchret. lib. i. § 10, Obs. 3, 9, 10, tom. i. p. 256, 258.

[s] Ibid. Obs. 5, p. 257.—KERCKRINGII Obs. Anat. Rar. Obs. 35, p. 76.

[t] Act. Lips. loco citato.

[u] See farther observations on the appearances of the *corpus callosum*, in Epist. 61, n. 6.—SAUVAGES has a species of amentia, which he calls, after PLATERUS, *amentia a tumore*, and which he illustrates by the case of a soldier, who, in three years after receiving a violent blow on the head, became affected with this kind of insanity. On opening his skull, a large, globular, tumor, of an intermediate texture between that of a scirrhus, and a fungus, of about the size of a small onion, was found upon the corpus callosum; and there was water in the ventricles.—*Nosolog. Method.* Class viii. Gen. xviii. Spec. 4, tom. iii. Part i. p. 376.—See SIMPSON on Vital and Animal Actions, p. 222.

[v] Dissert. Var. vii.

But

But that he had often seen the vessels of the
brain distended with blood; water under the
membranes, or in the ventricles ;—and probably
might not unfrequently have met with a large,
or scirrhous, spleen, if, besides opening the heads
of the insane, he had always had leisure to in-
spect the other viscera.—That all these appearances were observed in one maniac by Hoyerus";
—that Van Swieten* found the vessels of the
brain distended with pitchy, and exceedingly
black blood, in a woman who had been melancholy ;—that Fabricius' often observed in maniacs the plexus choroides turgid and inflated ;—
that not only King*, and others, have observed
plenty of water in the brains of idiots [*fatui*] ; but
Wepfer* in that of a woman who had been troubled with melancholy; and others referred to by
Van Swieten, in maniacs^b ;—and Hoyerus^c,
when mentioning that he had found scirrhous
spleens in several who had died of intermittent
fevers, observes that he generally learned upon
inquiry, that such persons had formerly been subject to violent melancholy deliriums.—That he

---

" Act. N. C: vol. iv. Obs. 39.
* Comment. § 1010. 2. vers. fin.
ʸ Ideæ Anat. Pract. § 4.
ᶻ Loco citato.
ᵃ Loco citato.
ᵇ Comment. § 1124.
ᶜ Act. Nat. Curios. vol. v. Obs. 68.

was not, however, ignorant, that in three instances where the melancholy delirium had been
so violent as to occasion suicide, the spleen was
neither hard, nor large, was in one of them even
much less than usual[d], and that HEISTER[e], who
dissected two out of the three, found the pancreas, and the bile, and not the spleen, in a state
of disease.—That he had very often, to wit, four
times, met with a diseased pineal gland[f]:

And seven times, that is always, with a hardness of the brain[g].

(2) He farther observes that stony concretions
are in no part of the brain so frequently met with,
as in the pineal gland: and that he had more frequently seen them in those who had been insane

---

[d] Ephem. Nat. Curios. Cent. 7. Obs. 60.

[e] Earund. Cent. 6. Obs. 28.

[f] Vide etiam Epist. 1. n. 10. See more relative to the diseased state of the pineal gland, in Epist. 61, n. 3.

[g] He met with several other cases of insanity, or idiotism,
after this; which are inserted in Epist. 8, n. 15, 59, n. 15,
61, n. 2, 5, 7, which with that of VALSALVA, Epist. 8, n. 2,
make in all thirteen; in eleven of which the brain was found
more or less hard, at least in the medullary substance. See
above, p. 31, in the text.

SAUVAGES mentions an instance of what he calls, after BEL-
LINI, *melancholia attonita,* in which, on dissection, he found
every part of the body remarkably destitute of moisture, the
blood viscid, and the brain exceedingly firm and compact.—
Nosolog. Method. Class viii. Gen. 19, Spec. 6, tom. iii. Part i.
p. 387.

(2) Epist. 8, n. 16.—See also note [f] in this page.

[*stulti*],

[*stulti*], than in others:—and that KING[b], in an idiot [*fatuus*], and BERLINGERIUS GIPSEUS[i], in one who had become quite stupid through an extraordinary defect of memory, had found it entirely changed into stone.—That it was liable to other diseases, which had, likewise, sometimes been observed in the dissection of such as had been insane [*stulti*];—that LANCISIUS[j] had remarked it, in the idiot [*fatuus*] already mentioned, who was thirty-six years of age, so small as scarcely to be equal in size to a hemp-seed;—that himself[k] had seen it in one who had been insane [*stultus*], quite flabby and emaciated;—and that it was found, on the contrary, to be more solid than usual, and perfectly red, in the case of a maniac related by ZWINGERUS[l].

(3) That though in the Sepulchretum there is only one instance of that hardness of the brain which had always occurred to him in dissections of the insane [*stulti*]; yet there are not wanting similar observations which deserve to be produced. —That M. LITTRE, and M. GEOFFROY, had observed the substance of the brain, in the two maniacs already mentioned, much firmer than

---

[b] Loco supra citato.

[i] Apud CONTULUM de Lapid. Podagr. &c. c. v.

[j] Loco supra citato.

[k] Epist. 8, n. 12.

[l] Sepulchret. § 9, Addit. Obs. 1, tom. i. p. 247.

(3) Epist. viii. n. 17, 18.

usual,

usual, while the cerebellum had nearly its natural
softness:—that LANCISIUS had found the whole
substance of the brain more compact than ordinary, and the corpus callosum rather hard, in the
idiot [*fatuus*] repeatedly referred ,to ; — that
SANTORINUS, in the case of the idiot [*fatuus*]
already quoted, had found the brain so much
firmer than common, as enabled him to distinguish, and examine, some of its parts with greater
accuracy than he could otherwise have done:—and
that BOERHAAVE probably alluded to some other
observations, besides the one mentioned in the
Sepulchretum, when he asserted that the brain of
maniacs had been found, on dissection, to be
dry, hard, and friable, and its cortical substance
of a yellow colour[m].—That it may farther be remarked, that though the brain be observed to
be hard, as it was in a very eminent degree in
the case described by GEOFFROY, as well as in the
single one related by BONETUS, yet some parts,
and especially those about the ventricles, and the
basis of the brain, are usually found softer, and
moister, than natural.

He then mentions several instances of uncommon hardness of the brain, in young, as well

---

[m] Aphorism. 1121.—See two more instances of this hardness of the brain in insane subjects, from GUNZIUS's Prolusio
de Lapillis Glandulæ Pinealis in quinque mente alienatis inven-
tis; with some observations relative to the cause of madness, in
Epist. 61, n. 8.

as old people; in the latter of whom, as he observes, Haller[a] tells us the brain is always hard, and thence accounts for their imbecility of mind, and defect of memory; who, notwithstanding this preternatural state of that organ, so common in insane persons, had not the smallest degree of insanity : and adds, that, on the contrary, insanity [stultitia] may even exist without this hardness of the brain, and that it has been found even remarkably soft and flabby, not only in those dissections of idiots related by Tulpius[o], Kerckringius[p], King[q], and Scheidius[r]; but very commonly, as the latter asserts, in insane subjects, as he had not unfrequently observed in the dissection of maniacs.

The great Dr. Haller[s] was fully sensible of the uncertainty arising from this similarity of appearances after such different, and sometimes opposite diseases. Being persuaded that much useful information, relative to the destination and offices of the several parts of the brain, might be derived from a knowledge of the corporeal

---

[a] Ad Prælection. Boerhaavii, § 475, not. g.

[o] Sepulchret. lib. i. § 10, Obs. 16, tom. i. p. 259.—Tulpii Obs. Med. lib. i. cap. xxvii. p. 51.

[p] Sepulchret. ib. Obs. 5. tom. i. p. 257.—Kerckringii Obs. Anat. Obs. 35, p. 76.

[q] Loco citato.

[r] De duobus Ossiculis, &c. qu. 4.

[s] Halleri Element. Physiolog. lib. xvii. § 1, tom. v. p. 571—574.

causes

causes found to exist in that organ on the dissection of maniacs, and idiots, he took some
pains to collect, with that view, the histories of
all dissections of this sort which fell in his way.
But his success, he informs us, was not equal to
his expectations: the number of such histories,
besides those for which we have lately been indebted to MORGAGNI, being very few; and having had no opportunity of dissecting insane subjects himself.—He ventures, however, from these
scanty sources, to give the following general
view of the appearances on dissection in the several
kinds of delirium.

" In febrile delirium the vessels of the pia mater have been found full of blood (1),—a coagulated jelly has been observed under the dura
mater (2),—the brain has been hard (3),—an ery-
sipelas, which had left some other part, has been
discovered upon the brain, and dura mater, and
the cortical substance of the brain appeared red
and inflamed (4),—and scales, or fragments of
bones have been found pressing upon the brain (5).
In drunkenness, which is a species of delirium,
the blood-vessels of the optic nerve, and of the
retina, have been visible to the naked eye (6).

---

(1) MORGAGNI de Sed. et Caus. Morb. I. p. 53, 54, 49.
(2) MORGAGN. p. 49.
(3) Idem. p. 80, 59, cum cerebellum mollius esset.
(4) STORK ann. I. p. 101.
(5) MANNE Obs. p. 122.
(6) COWPER ad f. 28, append.

"In

" In the hydrophobia, a disorder of a similar nature, the brain has been observed to be drier than usual (7),—the blood rather concreted ; and vessels of the membranes of the brain distended with blood (8).

" The phrenitis has often appeared to arise from an inflammation of the pia mater (9),—of the brain (10),—and of the cerebellum (11), — from water in the brain (12),—from an unusual quantity of blood in the brain, and its membranes(13), —and from an abscess in the brain (14).

" In mania the brain has been dry (15),— hard (16),—and friable ;—there has been a congestion of blood in the brain or its membranes (17) —part of the brain has been consumed, and the

---

(7) Morgagni p. 61, 63.

(8) Idem. p. 62, 63.

(9) Bonet. Obs. 4, 5, 9, 17, 18, 19, 30. Sanguine plenæ meninges Morgagni I. p. 51, 52.

(10) Bonet. Obs. 7, 11, 12, 17, 21, 24, 25, 32, 33, 36. Mead of Poisons, p. 139, in hydrophobo G. v. Swieten Conf. L. X. p. 218.

(11) Bonet. Obs. 5.

(12) Idem. Obs. 16, 27, 28. Richa Const. Epid. III. p. 114. 34, &c. Willis Anim. brut. p. 307. Gelatinosa concrementa secundum vasa piæ membranæ Morg. I. p. 49, 51.

(13) Bonet. Conf. L. X. l. c.

(14) L. X. l. c.

(15) Bonet. Obs. 1.

(16) Morgagni I. p. 55, 56, non cerebelli.

(17) Idem. Obs. 26. Mekel. l. c. In meninges Barrere Obs. p. 52, seqq.

rest

rest soft and macerated (18—there have been
glandular substances in the plexus choroides (19),
—the carotid arteries have been ossified (20),—
and worms have been found in the brain (21).

" In hypochondriacs the brain has been harder (22)—and drier than natural ;—the blood has
been coagulated in the longitudinal sinus ; in the
pia mater, it. has been of a pitchy blackness (23) ;
—the vessels of the brain have been distended (24) ;—and there has been water in the ventricles (25).—In the nostalgia, which is a kind
of melancholy, the vessels of the brain and cerebellum have been surprisingly distended (26).

" In idiotism the head has been observed to
have an unnatural form (27),—as when the skull
has been compressed (28) ;—the dura mater has
been livid, putrid, and inflamed (29) ; the brain

---

(18) INGRAM Cases, p. 101.

(19) MORGAGNI I. p. 54.

(20) HARMES cas. mania.

(21) BONET. Obs. 7.

(22) SCHMIEDEL de pericard. &c.

(23) G. v. SWIETEN III. p. 264.

(24) BARRERE in nostalgia ed II. Obs. 5, p. 20, Ob. 6,
p. 24. LOTICH C. IV L. III. Obs. 3.

(25) BARRERE ibid.

(26) Idem. L c. Obs. 6, p. 24.

(27) Addit. ad Obs. 4.

(28) HILD. Cent. III. Obs. 21.

(29) LIEUTAUD precis, p. 209. FANTON Obs. 25. Bo-
NET. Obs. 8, 17, compactum. LANCIS. de sede cogitant.
p. 158, 159.

U 3   exceed-

exceedingly dry; mishaped (30);—replete with
blood (31);—remarkably soft (32),—or, on the
contrary, remarkably hard (33);—a scirrhous tumor has been observed upon the corpus callosum (34),—or in other parts, compressing the
brain (35);—vesicles in the corpus callosum (36);
—scirrhous tumors in the plexus choroides (37);
—the brain less than natural (38),—inflamed,
and corroded (39),—a good deal of water in the
brain (40);—a dropsy in the brain (41)—a stone

(30) Pozzi, p. 88.

(31) Bonet. Obs. 11. Forst. de sensib. intern. p. 56.
Barrere ed. nov. ex hyoscyami radice, p. 54, seqq.

(32) Bonet. Obs. 2, 5, 16, L. X. p. 318. Histoir. de
l'Acad. 1705. Obs. 17, 1704. Obs. 12. Cum glandula pitui-
taria magna, memoria deleta et judicium destructum Vieus-
sens nov. syst. vas. fin.

(33) Morgag. I. p. 55.

(34) Bonet. Obs. 4. Plater, Obs. 51. Wepfer de
Apoplex. p. 277. Bauhin. Theatr. p. 305.

(35) Duverney de l'ouie, p. 100. Flamerding de Apoplex.

(36) Obs. 12, aut in cerebro. Opusc. scientif. III. p. 162.

(37) Boehmer, l. c.

(38) Bonet. Obs. 9, 10. Ad tertiam partem consumtum
cum aqua inter meninges, King Phil. Coll. 1686.

(39) Rumler, l. c. Coiter, p. 111.

(40) Santorin. p. 54. Boehmer, præf. fascic. I. p. xvi.
xvii. Bonet. Obs. 1, 4, 7, 13, 14, 15, 20. Chifflet Obs.
Huc historia surdi et muti, qui auditum recuperavit, cum
aqua de aure effluxisset.—Histoire de l'Academie des Sciences,
1703, p. 18.

(41) L. X. p. 319.

in

in one of the ventricles (42),—and in the falx (43) ;
—the pineal gland beset with stones (44),—become scirrhous (45),—or assuming a bony appearance (46) ;—and various disorders of the brain,
as tumors of the glands, &c. (47)"

He adds that—" from these few observations,
for which we are chiefly indebted to MORGAGNI,
but little certainty can be derived : since it not only
frequently happens that we can discover no disorder
in the bodies of maniacs (48), or even of such as
have been totally insensible (49) ; but where we
do, we are so far from being able to perceive a
uniform connexion between any one disorder of
the mind, and some corresponding preternatural
state of the contents of the skull, that the
very same appearances are exhibited after the most
opposite disorders, idiotism, and phrenzy : which
last seeming inconsistency may possibly appear
less extraordinary, if we consider the symptoms

---

(42) BONET. Obs. 5. MEKEL, ib. p. 94.

(43) VATER propr. ad disp. ZIEGENHORN.

(44) MEKEL, Mem. de Berlin. T. X. p. 93. KING, l. c.
GUNZ. lap. gland. pinealis, in quinque hominibus. In ventriculo cerebri MEKEL.

(45) L. X. p. 319.

(46) DUVERNEY, ibid.

(47) Idem Mem. avant 1699, II. p. 25. FANTON. ad
PACCH. p. 112. Opusc. III. p. 182.

(48) Frank. Anmerk. T. V. p. 281. WILLIS de cerebro,
p. 188. ed. 8. MEKEL, l. c.

(49) HOME Med. Facts, p. 53.

of

of drunkenness, and phrenzy, in which we may observe that the very same cause produces at first delirium, and afterwards, as the disorder advances, drowsiness, and insensible stupor. This, however, seems evident, that in the disorders of the mind, the brain and its connexions are usually affected: and when, in some rare instances, we can discover no disease of these parts, we may conclude, either that it is seated in their very elementary particles, or has not been sought for with sufficient patience and attention."

To add to this uncertainty which attends our inquiries into the several specific states of the brain respectively productive of the several sorts of insanity, or other depravations, or defects, of the mental operations, it may be remarked, that there are instances upon record of a total destruction of that organ by disease, without any consequent injury to the faculties of the mind. These instances are indeed as rare, as they are unaccountable, and ought rather, perhaps, to be considered as anomalies which we cannot analyse, than as objections to the doctrine of the general agency of the brain in the production of sensation, of voluntary motion, and of the other perceptions and operations of the mind. Indeed, numberless clear, and decisive facts, forbid us to conclude with the late ingenious Dr. SIMSON— " that no bowel is more frequently mutilated, and even quite destroyed, with less injury to the economy,

·nomy, than the brain':"—or that " sense and
.motion are not" usually " derived from that organ":"—or that the objections arising from these
extraordinary phænomena against the utility of
the brain in the performance of these necessary
offices of animal life, and in the exercise of the
various faculties of the mind, are not equally valid,
or indeed much more so, against his singular
opinion, founded chiefly upon these objections,
that the sole use of the brain is to " keep stores
for the equal and ready supplies of nourishment
promiscuously to every part" of the body'.

Several instances of the defect, destruction,
and ossification of the brain, may be seen related
at length, and others referred to, in this ingenious physician's inquiry how far the vital and animal actions of the more perfect animals can be
accounted for independent of the brain". To
which may be added one given by BONETUS', and
extracted from PLATERUS, in which the brain was
converted into a thick white fluid pultaceous substance, or as he in another place describes it,
into a fluid substance of the colour, and con-

ᵗ Inquiry, p. 224.
ᵘ Ibid. p. 228.
ᵛ Ibid. p. 228.
ʷ Ibid. p. 224, 225, 226, and 259.
ˣ Sepulchret. lib. i. § 2. Obs. 54, tom. i. p. 123.

sistence

sistence of cream[y], which was perceived to fluctuate on taking off the upper part of the skull, and flowed out when the dura mater was cut through.

---

[y] Prax. Medic. lib. i. cap. ii. tom. i. p. 22.

END OF VOL. I.

Printed by B. M'Millan,
Bow Street, Covent Garden.

CPSIA information can be obtained
at www.ICGtesting.com
Printed in the USA
LVHW012157091219
639936LV00021B/735/P